Private Sponsorship of Refugees in Europe

Chiara Berneri

• HART •
OXFORD • LONDON • NEW YORK • NEW DELHI • SYDNEY

HART PUBLISHING

Bloomsbury Publishing Plc

Kemp House, Chawley Park, Cumnor Hill, Oxford, OX2 9PH, UK

1385 Broadway, New York, NY 10018, USA

29 Earlsfort Terrace, Dublin 2, Ireland

HART PUBLISHING, the Hart/Stag logo, BLOOMSBURY and the Diana logo are trademarks of Bloomsbury Publishing Plc

First published in Great Britain 2024

A catalogue record for this book is available from the British Library.

A catalogue record for this book is available from the Library of Congress.

Library of Congress Control Number: 2024940189

ISBN: HB: 978-1-50992-218-5
ePDF: 978-1-50992-220-8
ePub: 978-1-50992-219-2

Typeset by Compuscript Ltd, Shannon

Private Sponsorship of Refugees in Europe

Chiara Berneri

•HART•

OXFORD • LONDON • NEW YORK • NEW DELHI • SYDNEY

HART PUBLISHING

Bloomsbury Publishing Plc

Kemp House, Chawley Park, Cumnor Hill, Oxford, OX2 9PH, UK

1385 Broadway, New York, NY 10018, USA

29 Earlsfort Terrace, Dublin 2, Ireland

HART PUBLISHING, the Hart/Stag logo, BLOOMSBURY and the Diana logo are trademarks of Bloomsbury Publishing Plc

First published in Great Britain 2024

A catalogue record for this book is available from the British Library.

A catalogue record for this book is available from the Library of Congress.

Library of Congress Control Number: 2024940189

ISBN: HB: 978-1-50992-218-5
ePDF: 978-1-50992-220-8
ePub: 978-1-50992-219-2

Typeset by Compuscript Ltd, Shannon

ACKNOWLEDGEMENTS

This book is fruit of a long journey of personal reflection and conversations on the issue of private sponsorship of refugees. I owe a lot to many people who helped me and sustained me, both professionally and personally, along the way.

Firstly, I would like to express my sincere gratitude to Verity Stuart and Kate Whetter, who have been willing to patiently wait for this manuscript for a long time (throughout two maternity leave breaks and a pandemic). Thank you for not giving up on me! My sincere gratitude goes also to Joanne Choulerton, for all the help with the editing, and Linda Goss, for all the support during the proof phase.

I also would like to thank Professor Daniel Wilsher for the initial conversations on the topic, and Professors Elspeth Guild and Daria Davitti, for their support during the early phase of this project.

I am also very grateful to Professor Simon Lee, Doctor Brett Crumley, Doctor Gunjan Sondhi, Doctor Nelli Stavropoulou, Avvocato Sara Corradi and Avvocato Marco Cristiano Petrassi for some relevant questions that helped me to shape the direction of the project.

My sincere gratitude goes also to all the people that helped me to understand better how some private sponsorship of refugee schemes work in practice. I am deeply grateful to Professor Paolo Naso and Professor Daniela Pompei for sharing their insights on the humanitarian corridor schemes, to Theresa Schmidt and to the anonymous contributor of the Civil Society Contact Point for the NesT programme, to Doctor Giulia Muratori for the St Marino scheme, to Bárbara Oliveira and Clara Vaz for the Portuguese pilot programme, and to Carly Whyborn and Amina Khanom for UK Community Sponsorship. I also thank all the people who directly, by liaising with me, and indirectly, by their scholarly publications, helped me writing this book. All errors remain mine.

Finally, I owe a lot to my family. To my mum and dad, Carla Mazzocchi and Enrico Berneri, for allowing me to follow my passion, to my children Patrick, Raffaele, Mary and Joseph Larcom, for their love, laughs, hugs and smiles, to Felicia Lovin for looking after us all when I was busy writing and to my dear husband, Shaun Larcom, without whom this book would have never been written.

AMDG
Chiara Berneri
2024

CONTENTS

TABLE OF CASES

European Court of Justice

Human Rights Committee

TABLE OF LEGISLATION

International Legislation

EU Legislation

National Legislation

Andorra

Belgium

Canada

Italy

St Marino

Spain

Switzerland

Soft Law Instruments

European Union

Belgium

UK

Introduction

I decided to write a book on private sponsorship of refugees in the wake of the Syrian civil war and the following refugee crisis. The need to explore legal alternatives to perilous journeys to safe countries became apparent. Many called for a re-assessment of the challenges around migration, with a view to fostering a new approach to entry and integration of migrants.

In 2015, during his speech in Ireland at the meeting with resettled refugees from Afghanistan, Congo, Myanmar and Syria, the then UN Secretary General, Ban Ki-Moon, urged states to create 'additional safe and regular avenues for migration and access to protection'.[1] In the same year, in his speech on the state of the Union of 9 September 2015, the then President of the European Commission, Jean-Claude Junker, while proposing the relocation of 160,000 asylum seekers, urged EU Member States to act fast:

> But imagine for a second it were you, your child in your arms, the world you knew torn apart around you. There is no price you would not pay, there is no wall you would not climb, no sea you would not sail, no border you would not cross … So it is high time to act to manage the refugee crisis. There is no alternative to this.[2]

Religious leaders also engaged in the debate. In 2015 Pope Francis called for concrete help by appealing to parishes and religious communities in Europe to express the concreteness of the Gospel and welcome a family of refugees.[3] He reiterated the call in 2017, by reminding the faithful, society and states of the need to 'make space for a new social imagination' to build foundations for 'effective integration' and 'not to be afraid of experiencing new forms of relationships'.[4]

These calls were soon given legislative footing by some international instruments. In 2016, the New York Declaration for Refugees and Migrants[5] expressed

[1] Ban Ki Moon, 'Secretary-General's remarks at meeting with resettled refugees from Afghanistan, the Democratic Republic of the Congo, Myanmar and Syria [as prepared for delivery]' 25 May 2015, available at: www.un.org/sg/en/content/sg/statement/2015-05-25/secretary-generals-remarks-meeting-resettled-refugees-afghanistan.

[2] JC Junker, 'State of the Union 2015: Time for Honesty, Unity and Solidarity' 9 September 2015, available at: ec.europa.eu/commission/presscorner/detail/en/SPEECH_15_5614.

[3] Pope Francis, 'Angelus 6 September 2015', available at: www.vatican.va/content/francesco/en/angelus/2015/documents/papa-francesco_angelus_20150906.html.

[4] Pope Francis, 'Solemnity of the Nativity of the Lord Papal Mass, Homily of His Holiness Pope Francis' 24 December 2017, available at: www.vatican.va/content/francesco/en/homilies/2017/documents/papa-francesco_20171224_omelia-natale.html.

[5] Resolution adopted by the UN General Assembly on 19 September 2016, New York Declaration for Refugees and Migrants, available at: www.unhcr.org/media/new-york-declaration-refugees-and-migrants-0.

the will of countries to deal with the refugee matter on a global scale. States committed to 'expand the number and range of legal pathways available for refugees to be admitted to or resettled in third countries',[6] in particular,

> the expansion of existing humanitarian admission programmes, possible temporary evacuation programmes … flexible arrangements to assist family reunification, private sponsorship for individual refugees and opportunities for labour mobility for refugees, including through private sector partnerships, and for education, such as scholarships and student visas.[7]

Contextually, through the 2015 European Agenda on Migration, the EU Commission urged Member States, in addition to promoting state-led resettlement initiatives, to use 'other legal avenues available to persons in need of protection, including private/non-governmental sponsorships and humanitarian permits, and family reunification clauses'.[8]

Private sponsorship of refugees is one of the answers to these political and legislative calls. Its aim is to introduce further channels for vulnerable immigrants to enter and settle in a host country safely. Private sponsorships are born from the openness of governments and the goodwill, compassion and charity of civil society. Different models of private sponsorship of refugees have been introduced and currently run or trialled all around the world. While they are all characterised by slightly different features, as we shall see later in the book, at least as far as Europe is concerned, they all share the same objectives. These are: to broaden the capacity for entry of particularly vulnerable immigrants who, otherwise, would potentially resort to illegal ways of entry; to offer them better integration perspectives owing to the engagement of the civil society at the pre-departure and/or post-arrival point; and to enhance their involvement in the new society through the help of the hosting community.[9]

In this book a choice has been made to focus on the European experiences of private sponsorship of refugees. The reason underpinning this choice is twofold. Firstly, this choice was made to avoid repetitions in the academic arena. In 2020 the excellent book edited by Shauna Labman and Geoffrey Cameron, *Strangers to Neighbours: Refugee Sponsorship in Context*,[10] was published. Through the contributions of various leading experts in the field, this book extensively covers the nuances of the Canadian experience of private sponsorship of refugees and is a key bibliographic reference point on the topic. Moreover, in its comparative section, the book looks also at private sponsorship programmes in Australia and the United States.

[6] ibid, para 77.

[7] ibid, para 79.

[8] COM(2015) 240 final Agenda on Migration, available at: eur-lex.europa.eu/legal-content/EN/TXT/PDF/?uri=CELEX:52015DC0240, 5.

[9] Policy brief 'Private sponsorship per l'integrazione: verso il modello Europeo', available at: www.eurodiaconia.org/wordpress/wp-content/uploads/2021/01/Private_sponsorship_integration_verso_modello_europeo_WEB.pdf, 12.

[10] S Labman and G Cameron, *Strangers to Neighbours: Refugee Sponsorship in Context* (Montreal, McGill-Queens University Press, 2020).

The other reason that convinced me to focus on European experiences of private refugee initiatives is the gap of holistic discussion and analysis on what has been happening in Europe from a legal perspective. In the above-mentioned comparative section of Labman and Cameron's book, it is possible to find the contribution of Craig Damian Smith, 'A Model for the World: Policy Transfer Theory and the Challenges to "Exporting" Private Sponsorship to Europe'.[11] This extremely informative piece focuses on the knowledge exchange that occurred between Canada and some key European states interested in translating the Canadian experience to Europe. The author highlights how, despite European interest in the Canadian Private Sponsorship Scheme, this was not adopted in Europe due to costs and to the realisation that there are key historical and geographical differences between Canada and Europe.[12] The author then looks at how the incentives for having these schemes could be matched in the European context and what role the Canadian programme might have in this process.[13] Some other works look at policy transfer. One key piece of research on this point is 'Community Sponsorship in Europe: Taking Stock, Policy Transfer and What the Future might Hold',[14] by Nikolas Feith Tan. In this work the author focuses on definitions, key characteristics of the schemes and policy transfer. In the end, the author 'takes stock' of the European situation, by briefly mentioning the key programmes currently running in Europe. Literature is also increasingly looking at the private European schemes individually. Some recent pieces of research on the European schemes have been fundamental for my work on this book, particularly when I needed to collect information on how the different schemes work and to understand their strengths and weaknesses. However, to date, research seems to have tackled the topic from different angles or from the view of a specific jurisdiction, while this book tries to give a holistic, and as far as possible, a complete legal overview of what has happened and is happening in Europe.

Moreover, it is also worth pointing out at this stage that, while academic works on the European *private* experiences are now emerging, still many of the footnotes in Chapters three and four contain references to *government* websites, reports and policy papers. This is evidence of the fact that there is still a gap, in terms of legal academic analysis, in the European private sponsorship of refugees literature, which this book is aiming to make a contribution towards filling.

The approach proposed by this book is mainly doctrinal. Private sponsorships are initially historically contextualised within the context of asylum and

[11] CD Smith, 'A Model for the World? Policy Transfer Theory and the Challenges of "Exporting" Private Sponsorship to Europe' in S Labman and G Cameron (eds), *Strangers to Neighbours: Refugee Sponsorship in Context* (Montreal, McGill-Queens University Press, 2020) 286.

[12] ibid, 291.

[13] ibid, 295–99.

[14] NF Tan, 'Community Sponsorship in Europe: Taking Stock, Policy Transfer and What the Future might Hold' (2021) 3 *Frontiers in Human Dynamics:Refugees and Conflict*, available at: www.frontiersin.org/articles/10.3389/fhumd.2021.564084/full.

resettlement. The book then offers some definitions and a classification of the phenomenon. The different European models of private sponsorship are then analysed in turn, in a clear attempt to highlight their legislative foundations, key characteristics and the rights offered to the beneficiaries of the various programmes. The shortcomings and challenges pertaining to each programme are also included in the discussion. Finally, in the last chapter, the book provides a framework to look at private sponsorship in the light of state sovereignty, and how the programmes could be advanced without impinging on state sovereignty.

Following this path, the book is structured as follows. Chapter one contextualises private sponsorship within the background of asylum and resettlement. The chapter follows the development of the concept of asylum from its primordial conception of religious sanctuary to its modern, international law-based application. The chapter shows that, at the end of World War I, when dealing with refugees, the idea of resettlement was introduced into the international law debate, and how private sponsorships were originally born to complement this classic solution to refugee protection. Chapter two follows up and contextualises the private sponsorship of refugees experience further, by reference to Canada, the first country that trialled these solutions and that has become a role model for many other places turning to privatised schemes throughout the world. The chapter also offers some definitions of private sponsorship of refugees, which facilitate the classification of the various European programmes that are analysed in Chapters three and four. In particular, Chapter three focuses on the description and analysis of those European programmes categorised as tools for resettlement. Chapter four, instead, focuses on those programmes encompassed in the category of paths to other forms of entry. Both chapters conclude with a section proposing a holistic overview of the main strengths and challenges observed in the programmes belonging to the specific category. Chapter five, based on the evidence and considerations gathered in the previous chapters, highlights how naming (in the sense of identifying particular beneficiaries for sponsorship) and additionality (in that beneficiaries of the scheme are additional to existing state quotas for resettlement of refugees) are the two features that need to characterise private sponsorship schemes in Europe, for the schemes to be effective in protecting more vulnerable people. The chapter points out that this is difficult to achieve when states consider themselves sovereign in relation to immigration claims, and proposes an alternative approach to put the state 'at ease'. The chapter concludes by highlighting the practical limitations for the concrete application of this theory. Chapter six provides some conclusions.

Finally, a last remark. The title of this book refers to private sponsorship of refugees. The term is used hundreds of times throughout the book. The attentive reader will notice that the term community sponsorship is also utilised. Resorting to both terms can be sometimes misleading, as some consider community sponsorship as a sub-category of private sponsorship of refugees and the UNHCR sees them as two clearly distinguishable experiences, as it will be briefly seen in chapter two. However, the European Commission, in its Recommendation EU 2020/1364 indicates that while several countries have implemented community sponsorship schemes, in other countries equivalent programmes are called private sponsorship schemes.[15] Given the fluidity of the terminology in the mainstream European debate the book, while normally referring to 'private sponsorship of refugees', will utilise 'community sponsorship of refugees' as a synonym, unless specified otherwise.

[15] Commission Recommendation (EU) 2020/1364 L317/13, available at: eur-lex.europa.eu/legal-content/EN/TXT/PDF/?uri=CELEX:32020H1364&from=en, section 25 fn 13.

1

Putting Private Sponsorships of Refugees in Context: Refugee Protection from Sanctuary to Resettlement

I. Introduction

In 2015 I discovered a study entitled 'Welcoming Engagement: How Private Sponsorship Can Strengthen Refugee Resettlement in the European Union'.[1] I did not know exactly what private sponsorship of refugees was, but I was intrigued by the words 'private sponsorship', associated to the word 'refugees'. In my mind, anything related to refugees was something that only states could deal with. The idea that private sponsors could take charge sounded foreign to me. I became fascinated by these initiatives. Hence the decision to write this book. One of the key questions I became intrigued by was why is it that the state is the only entity to decide upon entry, residence and various other aspects of refugees' lives. Indeed, the experience of private sponsorship of refugees seemed to me to suggest something different; that is that refugees could also be helped and 'dealt with' by private entities, instead of, or in parallel, with states. While researching the subject in more depth I soon came to realise that the private sponsorship of refugees schemes currently functioning in the world, do not escape from the logic of state sovereignty. To put it in very simple terms, private sponsors cannot act beyond the boundaries that the state places on them. For example, ultimately sponsors cannot decide whether or not a refugee can enter their country, as it will be the state that makes that decision, following a positive outcome of the screening and vetting procedures. Nor can they decide how many refugees can be welcomed in their country, or for how long they will be able to provide help, etc. From this realisation, and quite honestly after facing the initial disillusion on the effectiveness of these schemes, I started wondering whether, historically, refugee protection had always been a prerogative of the state and how private sponsorship of refugees fits within this debate.

[1] J Kumin, 'Welcoming Engagement: How Private Sponsorship Can Strengthen Refugee Resettlement in the European Union' (2015), Brussels: Migration Policy Institute Europe, available at: www.migrationpolicy.org/research/welcoming-engagement-how-private-sponsorship-can-strengthen-refugee-resettlement-european.

In this chapter I explore this question through a chronological approach, starting from the origins of the concept of asylum, exploring the shift from the idea of 'sanctuary' to that of secular asylum, moving on to the twentieth century and the advent of international protection of refugees. The aim of this approach is twofold. On one side, this account helps us to better understand where private sponsorships can be placed against the broader legal background of refugee protection, both from a chronological and substantive point of view. On the other side, and even more importantly, this analysis helps us to set-up the framework for a debate that will be tackled in the last part of this book, on whether private sponsorship of refugees might stand a chance of piercing the veil of state sovereignty over immigration.

More specifically, in this first chapter, I will offer a concise outline of how the idea of granting protection to refugees was born and how it developed. This chapter will look at how the protection of asylees was originally a prerogative of the church, and how, slowly but steadily, and sometimes with conflict, it was taken over and embraced by the state. This chapter will also look at how, between the First and the Second World War, the protection of refugees became a topic of concern for international law. It will also look at the three classic solutions for the protection of refugees – local integration, voluntary repatriation and resettlement – how they developed and how recently, and ever more so over the last decade, the international community has been focusing on trying to enhance resettlement. In particular, it will be shown that there have been attempts to revive the idea of resettlement as a viable option, also by calling for increased participation of the civil society. The call to advance and promote resettlement has indeed triggered the interest and work of private citizens and organisations, who have developed, with the support of their countries, various projects that are now recognised by the international community and fall under the umbrella of complementary pathways. Private sponsorship of refugees schemes are one example of these pathways. Focusing on Europe in particular, the chapter will highlight how, following the experience of Canada and heeding the various calls from the UNHCR and European Union, some states have promptly and effectively engaged with these alternative models. The chapter will then conclude with some broader considerations on state sovereignty, highlighting how private sponsorships currently fit under the umbrella of state sovereignty.

II. The Origins of Asylum: The Institution of Sanctuary

The practice of asylum has deep and ancient roots in Western civilisation. The word asylum derives from ancient Greek and means 'inviolable'. Rabben beautifully recalls that in Greece the goddess Diana's sanctuary in Ephesos was famous for being a place of shelter and protection for refugees and fugitives. She also mentions several examples of how protection was granted to refugees in other ancient civilisations, from the Hebrew and Roman traditions, as well as from other places, such as Papua New Guinea, Egypt, Nigeria and America.[2]

The concept of asylum finds its origins in the institution of church sanctuary. The first reference to church sanctuary can be found in the Council of Serdia, as early as 343 AD.[3] At the Council of Serdia the rules for church sanctuary were laid down. These were later officially recognised by Theodosian Law Code of 392 and eventually confirmed by the Justinian Code in 565 AD.[4]

Those that were entitled to find protection by the church as asylees were people that had committed secular crimes. This differs from how we understand asylum today, as the protection is now granted to people that are persecuted. However, what the old and new asylees have in common is the fact that they both are seekers of refuge. How the idea of asylum has developed from protection granted to secular criminals to refuge accorded to persecuted people will soon be explored by this chapter in section III.

It is interesting to reflect upon the relationship between state and church, in order to better understand the rules that applied to those that committed secular crimes and sought sanctuary. The church exercised its full authority in regulating its sanctuaries, initially with little interference from the state. The church believed that the power to grant sanctuary derived from God, hence the state should not interfere. This came from the idea, promoted by St Thomas Aquinas, that in the division between secular and temporal matters, the church had priority in matters relating to the salvation of souls.[5] Although civil and religious concerns interfered with each other when dealing with sanctuary, Kings allowed the church to take priority over the matter, based on the presumption that the person entered the church premises to restore his relationship with God and not to avoid punishment.[6] Contextually, the church would put the retributive aims of the state at ease, by imposing whatever canonical punishment was deemed appropriate and necessary,[7] given the circumstances of the case.

[2] L Rabben, *Sanctuary and Asylum: A Social and Political History* (Seattle WA & London, University of Washington Press, 2016) 33–36.

[3] F Ricciardi Celsi, 'Asilo (diritto di)' in *Enciclopedia Giuridica Treccani* (Roma, Istitituto dell'Enciclopedia Italiana, 2010) 2.

[4] On this point see, in particular, JB Whisker and KR Spiker, *Asylum and Sanctuary in History and Law: A Social and Political Approach to Temporary Protections Around the World* (Irvine CA, Brown Walker Press, 2021) 49. See also Rabben, above n 2, 39. Church sanctuary is referred to in literature. Alessandro Manzoni, in *The Betrothed*, refers to the idea of sanctuary in the episode of Lodovico (who will become later Fra' Cristoforo), who murdered a noble man: 'All this has occurred near a Capuchin church, and, as everyone knows, such buildings were then places of refuge, out of bounds to the watch, and to the whole complex of men and institutions which was collectively known as the Law' (A Manzoni, *The Betrothed* (London, Penguin Classics, 1972) translation by B Penman).

[5] For a deep analysis of this matter see T Aquinas, *Scriptum super sententiis* (Aldershot, Avebury Publishing Company Limited, 1980).

[6] S Pope, 'Sanctuary: The Legal Institution in England' (1987) 10 *Seattle University Law Review* 677, 684.

[7] Council of Reims. See Rabben, above n 2, 40. In England that often meant a short period of sanctuary of 40 days and then exile. On this point see B Little, 'Claiming Sanctuary in a Medieval Church

However, as the state began to gain more control over the justice system, conflicts with the church increased. In particular, this happened when the church became willing to fight against the state to maintain the privilege of *libertas ecclesiae*.[8] In England, the end of church sanctuary was marked by the Reformation. When Henry VIII established the Church of England, he also made sure that the supremacy of the church was obliterated as far as its role of sanctuary for fugitives was concerned.[9] The end of sanctuary in England eventually occurred under the reign of James I, in 1624.[10]

The institution of sanctuary continued for longer in continental Europe, initially as a move to counter the Reformation. In the text of the Council of Trent, chapter XX, on 'The Immunities, Liberty, and other Rights of the Church are recommended to Secular Princes', the Council tried to regulate and reaffirm, although somewhat indirectly, the right of sanctuary by admonishing princes not to 'permit that their officers, or inferior magistrates, through any spirit of covetousness, or any heedlessness, violate that immunity of the church'.[11] In 1591 Pope Gregory XIV promulgated the Bull '*Cum Alias*'. The intent of the Bull was to clearly regulate the topic by translating the content of the Council of Trent on the matter. The Bull also highlighted some exceptions to the enjoyment of the right (public thieves, bandits of the streets, crop thieves, culprits of *lèse majesté* of the person of the prince, heretics, those that committed murders or mutilations in churches, those that committed highly specific murders such as treacherous murders, wife murders, father murders, murders of the landlord or of other family members, murders of guests or of children could not enjoy the protection granted by the sanctuary) but added that there could not be additional exceptions to those expressly stated.[12] The same Bull also provided that it was up to the bishop to assess the nature of the crime and the decision as to whether the culprit had to be handed to the civil authorities.[13] The sanction for those that violated the right of asylum was excommunication *latae sententiae* (automatic).[14]

Over this period, the crucial role of assessing disputes on asylum between civil and religious authorities was played by the Holy Congregation for Ecclesiastic Immunity (*Santa Congregazione dell'Immunità Ecclesiastica*), founded by Pope Urban VIII in 1626. The Congregation was authorised to adjudicate on the

Could Save Your life – But Lead to Exile', 18 April 2019 (updated on 19 September 2023) in *History*, available at: www.history.com/news/church-sanctuary-asylum-middle-ages.

[8] See Ricciardi Celsi, above n 3, 2.

[9] On this point see Rabben, above n 2, 50–52. The dispute on church sanctuaries – particularly in relation to the role of the church and state towards clergy that committed secular crimes, has older roots. See, in particular, the Becket controversy involving King Henry II, which culminated in the murder of the former.

[10] The reasons underlying the increasing detachment of England from the Catholic Church, hence from the sanctuary system, are well outlined in Pope, above n 6, 690–96

[11] Text of the Council of Trent (namely Trento, Northern Italy), available at: history.hanover.edu/texts/trent/trentall.html, 276.

[12] Ricciardi Celsi, above n 3, 3.

[13] ibid.

[14] ibid.

controversies concerning violations of the freedom and competence of the church committed by the civil authorities in matters concerning immunities, including asylum.[15]

However, the power of the church on the matter of asylum continued to decrease as the years went by. In 1725 Pope Benedict XIII, in his Constitution *Ex quo divina*, added more exceptions to the enjoyment of the right of asylum. The Constitution excluded this privilege also for those that committed murder with clear premeditated intention.[16] Furthermore, in 1734 Pope Clemens XII, in his Constitution *In supremo justitiae solio*, extended the exception to those who killed during a riot, unless the death was accidental or committed for self-defence.[17] Finally, all the above exceptions were extended to religious people, women and soldiers that could not benefit from military privileges, by Pope Benedict XIV in 1749 by the Bull *Officii Nostri*.[18] Progressively, from the eighteenth century, the sanctuary of immunity began to be officially abolished by state jurisdictions and, eventually, it did not extend beyond the geographical borders of the Papal States.[19] Eventually, in the first officially drafted Canon Code of 1917,[20] Canon 1179 stated that 'Churches enjoy the right of asylum such that pursued ones who take refuge in them shall not be removed, unless necessity urges, without the assent of the Ordinary or at least the Rector of the church'. This is a much more diluted version of the original right of sanctuary. The church right of asylum officially disappeared in the Canon Code of 1983, and by then the Church had finally renounced such a privilege.[21]

III. The Shift from Sanctuary to Secular Domestic Asylum

In the previous section we saw that, for many centuries, asylum was understood as a protected physical space, delimited by the church walls, where one could find refuge. However, at some point in history, asylum begun to be understood as the protection granted by a broader jurisdiction, namely a state and not a church

[15] ibid.

[16] ibid.

[17] ibid. See in particular *Bolla Officii Nostri* (1749), available at: www.vatican.va/content/benedictus-xiv/it/documents/bolla--i-officii-nostri--i---15-marzo-1749--poiche-sono-sorti-di.html.

[18] ibid.

[19] ibid. The right of asylum was abolished in France in 1789, in Germany in 1780 and in Italy by the Siccardi law no 1013 of 9 April 1850.

[20] This Canon Code was the first codified one. Codification process was strongly promoted and desired by Pope Benedict XV. This work encompasses The *Corpus Iuris Canonici* (which contained the Graziano decree 1140), The *Liber Extra* of Pope Gregory IX 1234, The *Liber Sextus* of Pope Boniface VIII 1298, The *Clementinae* of Clemens V 1317, *Extravagantes Communes* and norms from the Council of Trent (1545–1563).

[21] Scholars have been recently debating about the reintroduction and revitalisation of the institution of church sanctuaries for asylum seekers. In particular, see L Guardado, 'Sanctuary for Asylum Seekers: Revisiting the Religious Principle and Practice of Refuge in the Church' (2021) 82 *Theological Studies* 285.

building, to someone fleeing from another jurisdiction, normally another state,[22] and not necessarily a criminal. How did this shift occur? Liza Shuster, in her article 'Asylum and the Lessons from History',[23] offers an in-depth answer to this question. In her view, Macchiavelli's and Luther's philosophy (in the first half of the sixteenth century) indirectly helped to shape the new idea of asylum. Macchiavelli suggests that anything that serves the state should be maintained and anything that does not serve the state should be rejected. Luther argues that the church's competence does not exist, as the spiritual realm lies within every individual. Consequently, every issue falls within the remit of state power.[24] The synthesis of these two approaches, united in the birth of the modern state as we know it today, contributed to the development of an idea of secular asylum, detached and independent from the old idea of sanctuary.

As briefly seen above, Henry VIII successfully asserted the supremacy of the state over the church in England. This led to the birth of a 'truly independent sovereign state',[25] which in England came much earlier than many of its European counterparts. This also triggered, as already discussed, the initial suppression of the right of sanctuary, to which an end was finally put by James I in 1624. However, despite (or perhaps even owing to) the waning of religious asylum in England, by then 'the conditions necessary for territorial asylum were in place':[26] England was already a sovereign state, completely independent from any other spiritual or temporal power, and conscious that offering hospitality to some could bring long-term advantages to the country. Huguenots fleeing France were lucky enough to find these conditions in place in England.[27] Indeed, Huguenots were considered by England to be very advantageous to their economy, due to the skills and the various trades that they mastered and practised[28] and, consequently, found protection easily in the country.

In continental Europe, historically, it was the Peace of Westphalia[29] of 1648 that triggered the shift from religious to secular asylum. The Peace of Westphalia, which put an end to the Thirty- and Eighty-Years Wars, tackled three issues of particular importance: religious freedom, which was agreed and granted, the use

[22] Whisker and Spiker, above n 4, 8.

[23] L Shuster, 'Asylum and the Lessons of History' (2002) 44 *Race & Class* 40.

[24] ibid, 43–44.

[25] ibid, 44.

[26] ibid, 45.

[27] As early as 1562, under the reign of Elisabeth I, England gave refuge to the Huguenots communities. The Huguenots diaspora began in the sixteenth century when they fled from France to settle and form new communities in America, Africa and Europe. Huguenots were followers of the protestant theologian John Calvin.

[28] Shuster, above n 23, 44.

[29] For a more detailed historical background on the Peace of Westphalia and its consequences within the international community see S Patton, 'The Peace of Westphalia and it Affects (*sic*) on International Relations, Diplomacy and Foreign Policy' (2019) 10 *The Histories* 91 available at: digitalcommons.lasalle.edu/the_histories/vol10/iss1/5. The Peace of Westphalia and the creation of the nation state marked a broader process, which Torpey identifies as 'State monopolisation of legitimate means of movement'(See JC Torpey, *The invention of passport: surveillance, citizenship and the state* (Cambridge,

of diplomacy and negotiations as an alternative to war and a means to resolve conflicts and, crucially, state sovereignty. As far as the latter aspect is concerned, this meant, concretely, that the Holy Roman Empire saw its powers shrunk, while the powers of the various princes of its constituent territories increased. The new powers of the princes included the power of levying taxes, declaring war, ratifying peace treaties[30] and, crucially, recognising the territorial sovereignty of the member states of the Empire. Although the erosion of the Holy Roman Empire's powers in favour of its member states did not happen overnight, the Peace of Westphalia certainly paved the way to the 'development of the nation-state system'.[31] As Shuster puts it 'what emerged, slowly, was a system of absolutist states and the acceptance of the doctrine of *raison d'état*'.[32]

As far as asylum is concerned, the newly born independent states recurred to this practice when beneficial to their aims, and as a way to affirm their sovereignty.[33] For example, to help Prussia recover after the end of the Thirty Years War, Frederick William encouraged protestants from France to settle there to take advantage of their labour and skills.[34]

To the Peace of Westphalia goes the merit of having put in place some of the key elements that characterise asylum today. The power of the state to decide who could enter its territory, as well as the corollary principle that a state should not enter the territory of another state in pursuit of someone who had been granted protection by the latter, was universally accepted. Moreover, the decision to grant asylum would be legitimately taken, in light of the state's precise interests.[35] This is crucially important as it marks the moment in which a completely new conception of asylum was introduced: as a matter of fact, unlike the previous religious sanctuary, we now have an idea of asylum conceived from the point of view of the granter and not the receiver. As Rabben tells us, secular asylum 'came into formal existence as a universal right of states to grant, not of individuals to receive'.[36] The reality of this approach is evident if one looks at how states engaged with the pressures of various asylum seekers looking for refuge within their territories. For example, England, after having accepted various French citizens fleeing France from the Revolution, expelled them some years later for fear that they came to the country for the hostile purposes of exporting the Revolution there. Similar events occurred in Napoleonic France and in America.[37]

Cambridge University Press, 2010) ch 1). The author highlights how the birth of nation states triggered their monopolisation of immigration and their appropriation of the 'authority to restrict movement vis-à-vis other potential claimants, such as private economic or religious identities', at 5.

[30] See Patton, above n 29, 94–95.

[31] Shuster, above n 23, 45.

[32] ibid.

[33] ibid.

[34] ibid.

[35] ibid, 46.

[36] Rabben, above n 2, 57.

[37] The period following the French Revolution, up until the twentieth century, is characterised by a vicissitude of different phases and approaches, some favourable and some less so, to refugees and aliens

At this stage, it is important to note it was the flight from France of the Huguenots that marked the moment at which members of a persecuted religious group were, for the first time, officially called refugees and were given domestic protection in law.[38] Several German States accorded them protection through the use of Edicts, the Netherlands with the decree of 1709 and, in the same year, with an Act for Naturalising Foreign Protestants, England too granted them asylum.[39] A normative understanding, based on the fact that refugees were a unique category and had a right to exit their state, if persecuted, had indeed been established.[40]

The normative protection given to religious refugees was extended to political ones during the French Revolution. In this turbulent period concepts such as freedoms and liberties became the object of debate. The idea that a sovereign nation should grant its citizens such rights began to permeate society and slowly became accepted. Consequently, states felt that they had a duty to protect those fleeing from countries where such rights were impeded and not guaranteed and to grant them political asylum.[41] As well as for the Huguenots, domestic legislation played an important role in the protection of political refugees.[42] Particularly in the UK, France and US, domestic legislation was introduced to grant protection to political refugees and avoid their deportation back to their states of origin. In the UK, the initially controversial Aliens Act in 1793, which was challenged in Parliament because of the power given to the government to restrict the entry of immigrants, was followed by the Aliens Act in 1798, which included clear protection for French refugees.[43] France as well, after an initial hostility to foreigners following the end of the French Revolution, acknowledged and recognised the need to protect refugees via domestic legislation. The *Loi Relative aux Etrangers Refugies Qui Resideront en France*, of 1832, offered the first official codified protection to those foreigners who resided in France but were not under the protection

more generally. England passed the Aliens Bill (1793), which remained in force until 1826, to put an end to the influx of asylum seekers coming from France. Similar approaches to the potential perils brought by French revolutionaries were adopted by Austria and Prussia. France adopted Aliens Acts, at the beginning of the nineteenth century, and America did too in 1798, to deport anyone who could be a potential threat to national security. However, Britain went back to a more friendly approach towards refugees in 1827, when it opened its doors to myriads of Italian, Spanish, French, German and Polish immigrants. This once again, and as denounced by other European countries, was mainly dictated by the self-interest of replenishing its labour force, since many were leaving or had left England already, to seek new opportunities in the colonies in America. For a broader account of these matters, see Shuster, above n 23, from p 47, and Rabben, above n 2, from p 59.

[38] P Orchard, 'The Dawn of International Refugee Protection: States, Tacit Cooperation and Non-Extradition' (2017) 30 *Journal of Refugee Studies* 282, 285.

[39] ibid, 286.

[40] ibid, 285. According to Orchard, the origin of this normative shift was the Peace of Westphalia, which also introduced the principle of religious toleration and the right to emigrate and preserve the properties of persecuted groups for religious reasons. This idea also started to be shared and developed by early international law theorists, like Hugo Grotius.

[41] ibid, 287.

[42] ibid.

[43] ibid, 288–289. This was followed by the 1826 Registration of Aliens Act and the 1836 Aliens Registration Act, which abolished the power to deport foreigners.

of their own government.[44] Finally in the US, up until 1875,[45] people seeking asylum could find protection through the open American immigration policy, and through extradition law, which defended them against expulsion to their country of origin.[46]

IV. Asylum in the Twentieth Century: The Dawn of International Law Protection

Towards the end of the nineteenth century, a myriad of restrictions to entry began to be increasingly imposed by various countries, mainly for fear of the prospect of anarchy within their territories.[47] Indeed, it is likely that states shifted from their general laissez faire approach[48] on immigration, which characterised the first part of the nineteenth century, to a proper development of national norms that would regulate the entry of foreigners, owing to the extraordinary movements and upheavals occurring between the end of the nineteenth century and the beginning of the twentieth. Indeed, during this period, a remarkable proliferation of immigration laws was witnessed in Europe and internationally.[49]

This new and more restrictive approach on immigration had its effects on asylum. The British 1905 Aliens Act, despite containing a provision on the right of asylum to be granted to those fleeing religious and political persecution,[50] was effectively passed to exclude some undesirable migrants.[51] Moreover, in the US the

[44] ibid, 291.

[45] That was the year when immigration moved from being a matter of State competence to federal competence.

[46] Orchard, above n 38, 291–92. The idea underpinning this approach was that, in a world of open borders, asylum should be protected only by extradition law. On extradition see Orchard, 288. For the more detailed legislation and bilateral agreements on extradition see Orchard, 292–94.

[47] A Bashford and J McAdam, 'The Right to Asylum: Britain's 1950 Aliens Act and the Evolution of Refugee Law' (2014) 32 *Law and History Review* 309, 329.

[48] L Barnett, 'Global governance and the evolution of the international refugee regime' (2002) 14 *International Journal of Refugee Law* 238, 240.

[49] Some examples of these legislative measures are the Alien Act 1798 and the Chinese Exclusion Acts of 1882 in America, which eventually led to a nationalisation of the immigration issue with the Immigration Act 1891 and with the very restrictive Acts of 1920 and 1921. The latter introduced a quota system per country. In the UK, the Aliens Act of 1905 defined the notion of undesirable migrant. Contextually, also Germany, Italy and France introduced immigration measures, particularly focused in limiting emigration (Italy) and introducing identification and registration requirements for immigrants (France and Germany). For a detailed bibliography on the various immigration laws that were adopted internationally over this period see Bashford and McAdam, above n 47, fnn 1 and 2; Torpey, above n 29, 'Towards the crustacean type of nation' chapter; C Skran, *Refugees in Interwar Europe: the emergence of a regime* (Oxford, Oxford University Press, 1995) 22–23.

[50] For more details on the act and on the asylum provision see Bashford, McAdam, above n 47, 312–314.

[51] ibid, 310. See also Orchard, above n 38, 290. Indeed, up until then in England, the policy on asylum 'like all the best British freedoms … was maintained, not by law, by the absence of laws' in B Porter, *The Refugee Question in Mid Victorian Politics* (Cambridge, Cambridge University Press, 1979) 3.

refugee exemption disappeared with the introduction of the quota laws of 1920 and 1921.[52]

This new trend towards immigration and asylum was not, however, outside the remit of states' powers. As a matter of fact, as seen before, introduction of the concept of territorial sovereignty with the Peace of Westphalia inevitably crystallised the idea that the state is the ultimate judge in deciding who is entitled to access its borders.

The outbreak of the World Wars led to a drastic increase in numbers of displaced people. Kushner, quoting Auschwitz survivor Hugo Gryn, reminds us, in his book of 2006 *Remembering Refugees: Then and Now*, that the twentieth century was, more than any other era before, the century of the refugee,[53] with 'major population displacements' occurring since the beginning of the 1900.[54] In particular with the end of the First World War and its preliminaries (the Balkan Wars, the Greco-Turkish War, the Wars in the Caucasus, the Russian Revolution), the problem of refugees started to develop into even greater proportions and was perceived to be in much need of international attention and action.[55] Sovereign countries began to perceive the need to tackle the problem together, partly moved by the fear that they would not have been able to manage the mass influx individually. 'Political ideology, combined with a respect for territory and balance of power began to play an important role in bringing international recognition to the problem of refugees in the international system'.[56]

On 10 January 1920, with the Paris Peace Conference following the end of the First World War, the League of Nations was founded. The principal aim of this organisation was to maintain the world's peace. No interference in states' affairs or request of limitation of sovereignty was envisaged by the Covenant of the League, which was based on the firm belief that the role of the League was to help resolve international disputes among the states, whilst the internal ones could be better dealt by the states alone.[57] Probably for this reason, considering that asylum was a phenomenon that up until then was mainly dealt with domestically, the Covenant of the League of Nations did not include any specific provision concerning the international protection of refugees.[58] In spite of this, the League begun to involve itself in the matter on an ad hoc basis, by answering individual appeals. As an answer to the appeal from the International Committee of the

[52] Orchard, above n 38, 292.

[53] T Kushner, *Remembering Refugees: Then and Now* (Manchester, Manchester University Press, 2006) 15.

[54] Shuster, above n 23, 52.

[55] G Burgess, *The League of Nations and the Refugees from Nazi Germany* (London, Bloomsbury Academic, 2016) 7.

[56] Barnett, above n 48, 241.

[57] AWB Simpson, *Human Rights at the End of Empire: Britain and the Genesis of the European Convention* (Oxford, Oxford University Press, 2001) 121.

[58] LW Holborn, 'The League of Nations and the Refugee Problem' (1939) 203 *The ANNALS of the American Academy of Political and Social Science* 124, 124. On the period leading up to the Convention on the Protection of Refugees see G Jaeger, 'On the history of the international protection of refugees' (2001) 83 *International Review of the Red Cross* 727.

Red Cross, seeking help to find a solution for the exodus of Russian refugees from the Revolution, the League created a High Commission for Refugees, appointing Fridtjof Nansen as High Commissioner for Russian Refugees. This role was soon extended to other refugees in need, such as Turkish, Armenian, Assyrian and Assyro-Chaldean.[59] The strenuous, passionate and ingenious work of Nansen certainly shaped the way in which the High Commission for Refugees operated and set the path of the future for the involvement of international law in the issue of asylum and protection of refugees. For instance, he administered his work with refugees by recourse to practices that are now considered to be the classic ways of refugee protection, that is resettlement, voluntary repatriation and local integration.[60] Moreover, he devoted great attention to the international status of refugees.[61] His efforts led to the creation of the Nansen passport, adopted through the Arrangement with Regard to the Issue of Certificates of Identity to Russian Refugees, signed in Geneva on 5 July 1922.[62]

With the introduction of the Nansen passport and the signing of the Arrangement and similar subsequent legal instruments, the refugee debate became more evidently a topic of international concern and interest. From this moment, broader political dynamics within the international arena and consultations with state counterparts begun to be considered key factors determining the final decision, still taken domestically by the state, of whether or not to welcome refugees. In other words, the refugee problem ended up being no longer dealt with as simply a national issue,[63] but as a common concern to be tackled together under fair rules and taking into consideration international relations.

However, at this stage key legal instruments concerning asylum and refugees, such as the Arrangement relating to the Legal Status of Russian and Armenian Refugees, 1926, and the Arrangement concerning the Extension to Other Categories of Refugees of Certain Measures taken in favour of Russian and Armenian Refugees,[64] 1928, were still very much category oriented.[65] Along

[59] On these points see V Chetail, 'Fridtjof Nansen and the International Protection of Refugees: An Introduction' (2003) 22 *Refugee Survey Quarterly* 1, 4.

[60] ibid.

[61] ibid.

[62] ibid. This was officially the first international conference, whose outcome was signed by 52 states, that led to the adoption of the first effective legal instrument devoted to the protection of refugees. This 'unconventional proof of identity' enabled refugees to move and reside within other states. Although this type of passport is no longer issued, its legacy still exists today.

[63] Barnett, above n 48, 242.

[64] The states that signed these treaties were Germany, Austria, Belgium, Bulgaria, France, Poland, Latvia, Romania, Switzerland, Greece, Estonia and the Kingdom of Serbia, Slovakia and Slovenia.

[65] These two documents were later included in the Convention of 28 October 1933. The Convention dealt with the definition of refugees, administrative measures such as the issuing of the Nansen passports (Art 2), refoulment (Art 3), legal access (Art 6), labour conditions (Chapter 4), industrial accidents (Chapter 5), welfare and relief (Chapter 6), education (Chapter 7), the fiscal regime (Chapter 8), exemption from reciprocity (Chapter 9) and included the creation of committees for refugees (Chapter 10). The Convention was ratified by nine states, including France and the United Kingdom. See Jaeger, above n 58, 730. It is worth noting that the Convention of 1933 set up a model for the

the same lines, the advent of Nazism in Germany triggered the signing of other treaties – the Provisional Arrangement concerning the Status of Refugees coming from Germany, 1936, and the Convention concerning the Status of Refugees coming from Germany, 1938 – which were only directed at German refugees.[66] This is likely to have been because the problem of refugees was still seen as something temporary and, for this reason, the need for a universal definition of refugees was not yet perceived.[67]

The Second World War exacerbated the refugee problem.[68] In order to tackle the issue, the League of Nations was dissolved and its role was undertaken by the United Nations Relief and Rehabilitation Administration (UNRRA),[69] which in 1946 was replaced by the International Refugee Organisation (IRO). The IRO was created as a temporary, intergovernmental organisation within the umbrella of the United Nations. Its aim was the regularisation, repatriation and resettlement of persons displaced by the Second World War.[70] It was the IRO's Constitution that first used the term refugee, rather than displaced person, in an international legal context. Moreover, while the definition of refugee still referred to specific categories of European refugees, it included a broader provision that extended it to categories not expressly mentioned.[71]

1951 Convention Relating to the Status of Refugees. For a clear and detailed explanation of the 1933 Convention see also RY Jennings, 'Some International Law Aspects of the Refugee Question' (1939) 20 *The British Yearbook of International Law* 98.

[66] Burgess, above n 55, denounces how, despite the previous successes and the legacy of Nansen, the League initially refused to take responsibility for the refugees from the Nazi regime. According to the author, this choice was dictated by a mix of fear of alienating Germany from the other countries and being accused of interfering in German domestic affairs and sovereignty. A further confirmation of the general hostile indifference towards refugees coming from Germany and Austria was witnessed at the Evian Conference, where, with the exception of the Dominic Republic, no other country – including the US and the UK – agreed to accept more Jewish refugees.

[67] Barnett, above n 48, 242.

[68] It is calculated that '30 million people were left uprooted'. ibid, 243.

[69] UNRRA was established by agreement of 44 nations on 9 November 1943. It preceded the founding of the United Nations. It became part of it in 1945. Its operations terminated in 1947.The purpose of UNRRA was to 'plan, co-ordinate, administer or arrange for the administration of measures for the relief of victims of war in any area under the control of any of the United Nations through the provision of food, fuel, clothing, shelter and other basic necessities, medical and other essential services' (Agreement, Art 1(2)(a)). For more information see Britannica, The Editors of Encyclopaedia, 'United Nations Relief and Rehabilitation Administration' *Encyclopedia*, available at: www.britannica.com/topic/United-Nations-Relief-and-Rehabilitation-Administration. According to Barnett, its mandate terminated due to the tensions between the US and the Soviet Union. See Barnett, above n 48, 244.

[70] It is interesting to note that, due to the acrimony between the US and USSR, which already manifested itself at the time of UNRRA, the USSR decided not to support its activities. Barnett points out that USSR felt that IRO was mainly serving US policies (Barnett, above n 48, 244).

[71] In particular, see Constitution of the International Refugee Organization, Annex I, Part I, Section A (2): 'the term "refugee" also applies to a person, other than a displaced person as defined in section B below, who is outside of his country of nationality or former habitual residence, and who, as a result of events subsequent to the outbreak of the Second World War, is unable or unwilling to avail himself of the protection of the government of his country of nationality or former nationality', available at: treaties.un.org/pages/ViewDetails.aspx?src=IND&mtdsg_no=V-1&chapter=5&clang=_en.

By 1950, the international community was forced to recognise that the problem of refugees was not a temporary one and that it needed a permanent apparatus of support. On 1 January 1951, the United Nations High Commissioner for Refugees (from now on UNHCR) assumed office, taking over from the IRO. On 28 July of the same year, the Convention Relating to the Status of Refugees was adopted.[72]

V. A Universal Definition of Refugees: The 1951 Refugee Convention

The Convention relating to the Status of Refugees, whose application is supervised by the UNHCR, was, as Goodwin-Gill describes it, an 'evolutionary step in the development of treaty-based standards, substantially extending the scope of protection beyond the agreements concluded thus far'.[73] First of all, the initial reluctance to resort to the term refugees, witnessed in the constitution of UNRRA, which simply referred to displaced persons,[74] was overcome by the IRO Constitution and confirmed by the 1951 Convention and its Protocol. Moreover, unlike the previously signed intergovernmental agreements, characterised by a category-based approach, the Convention opted for a systematic general protection of refugees, although this protection was still qualified by the events occurring in Europe or elsewhere before 1 January 1951. This scope of application was removed on 4 October 1967, when the Protocol Relating to the Status of Refugees entered into force.[75] As a result of the Protocol, today, Convention refugees are identifiable by fulfilling the following cumulative elements:

- they are outside their country of nationality or of former habitual residence, not having the nationality of it;
- they are unable or unwilling to avail themselves of the protection of that country, or to return there;

[72] The Convention was adopted by the United Nations Conference on the Status of Refugees and Stateless Persons at Geneva, 28 July 1951. It entered into force on 22 April 1954.

[73] GS Goodwin-Gill, 'The International Protection of Refugees: What Future?' (2000) 12 *International Journal of Refugee Law* 1, 2.

[74] It is worth noting that displaced persons are not an official category protected by the 1951 Convention. Since the mid-seventies, one of the UNHCR's tasks has been to provide material assistance to displaced persons, which is normally approved via UN resolutions. This category is often referred to as internally displaced persons (IDPs). In line with the text of the Convention and the principle of state sovereignty, the national state is responsible for this category of people and not the international community. In 1998 the Guiding Principles on Internal Displacement were published. They sought to address the rights and guarantees relevant to protection for internally displaced people. These principles are not binding on the states, except to the extent that these principles mirror binding international treaties or customary law. See GS Goodwin-Gill and J McAdam, *The Refugee in International Law* (Oxford, Oxford University Press, 2021) 30–39.

[75] The UNHCR soon moved on from the post-World War II issues and began to be more involved with the Cold War problems of refugees fleeing from Communist countries. The expansion of the role if the UNHCR triggered the need for a truly universal and globalised definition of refugees, disentangled from temporal and geographical limits. This led to the introduction of the protocol which expanded the meaning of the term refugee. On this point see Barnett, above n 48, 248. Art 1(2) Protocol: 'For the

- the inability or unwillingness is linked to a well-founded fear of being persecuted; and
- the persecution feared is based on reasons of race, religion, nationality, membership of a particular social group, or political opinion.[76]

The Convention also covers their rights, the relevant procedures, the limitations to expulsion and the fundamental principle of *non-refoulment*.[77]

The historical trajectory of the development of asylum and refugee protection delineated so far suggests shifts from different sources of power. Indeed, it seems that after the church lost authority over asylum to the state, the latter willingly gave its power up, to comply with the expectations of the international community. However, this is not exactly true, if we consider the content of the Convention more closely. As far as procedures are concerned, and in particular in relation to the determination of the refugee status, the heritage of Westphalia on states' territorial sovereignty is evident. Indeed, while the 1951 Convention gives a clear definition of refugees and provides for certain rights and standards of treatment, it is still up to the states to choose how to implement these provisions and interpret them.[78] In other words, as Barnett underlines 'the individual refugee is subject to the right of the state to grant asylum – it is not the right of the individual to gain that status'.[79] Furthermore, in relation to enforcement, the correct functioning and application of the international legal regime of the 1951 Convention is supervised by the UNHCR. Indeed, its supervisory responsibility is established by paragraph 8 of the UNHCR Statute and Articles 35 and 36 of the 1951 Convention.[80] However, there are no procedures to implement the UNHCR findings, as the system lacks enforcement mechanisms.[81] This is indeed considered to be one of the most serious weaknesses of the Convention. Nevertheless, the lack of any enforcement mechanism should not surprise: the heritage of Westphalia is apparent in this context too, as states managed to create a hybrid protection system, caught

purpose of the present Protocol, the term "refugee" shall, except as regards the application of paragraph 3 of this article, mean any person within the definition of article 1 of the Convention as if the words "As a result of events occurring before 1 January 1951 …" "and the words" ".. a result of such events", in article 1 A (2) were omitted'.

[76] Art 1(A)(2) of the 1951 Convention, as amended by its 1967 Protocol. These are all elements of fact, apart from the 'well founded fear' of persecution, which is a legal standard that needs to be proved by objective evidence.

[77] See Art 33 Convention on Refugees. As far as non-refoulment is concerned, by the early eighties, the international community seemed to agree that the principle encompassed both non-expulsion of those being already within the state territory and non-rejection of those at the frontier. States have been often at pains in guaranteeing the correct application of this principle. Recently, the reception of migrants at sea has stirred the debate on the breach of the principle of non-refoulment by states.

[78] For clear examples of what this process entails, see Goodwin-Gill and McAdam, above n 74, 154–58.

[79] Barnett, above n 48, 258.

[80] However, broader acceptance of the UNHCR's role has been recognised, at EU level, for instance. On this point see V Turk, 'UNHCR's Supervisory Responsibility' working paper 67/2002 *New Issues in Refugee Research*, available at: www.refworld.org/pdfid/4fe405ef2.pdf, 1, 4–5.

[81] ibid, 5.

'between traditional notions of respect of territorial sovereignty and the need for international responsibility'.[82] The disjuncture between the content of the Convention and its application is strikingly evident when determining the application of the 1951 Convention's definition, in terms of rights to be granted and protection offered to refugees.[83] Indeed, the Convention does not go beyond stating who is entitled to seek refugee protection: it does not dictate the manner in which states should assess whether an individual fulfils the definition requirements, but rather leaves it to the state to determine it. This means that, naturally, there are differences in how states apply and interpret the Convention and the level of protection offered. As matter of fact, despite the remarkable steps towards international collaboration, the refugee issue still remains jealously included in the realm of state sovereignty.

VI. Contextualising the Introduction of Private Sponsorship of Refugees

In section IV we saw that, since the early twenties, the League of Nations began to respond to the problem of refugees by seeking ad hoc solutions to the mass exodus of many populations affected by wars and revolutions. To this aim, the League founded the High Commission for Refugees and appointed Nansen as High Commissioner. It was evidenced how Nansen, through his indomitable work, set the scene for the introduction of practices aiming to provide durable solutions for the protection of refugees. These practices have now become 'the basis of the past and present international regime for the protection of refugees'.[84]

The UNHCR refers to durable solutions as 'any means by which the situation of refugees can be satisfactorily and permanently resolved to enable them to live normal lives',[85] and it links the idea with residing permanently somewhere, 'whether in the host country, a third country or their country of origin'.[86] This classification delineates the distinction between local integration, voluntary repatriation and resettlement. In particular, local integration offers the refugee a durable right to reside in the host country and to participate to its life.[87] Voluntary

[82] Barnett, above n 48, 258.
[83] Goodwin-Gill and McAdam, above n 74, 51.
[84] Chetail, above n 59, 4.
[85] M Ineli-Ciger, 'Is Resettlement Still a Durable Solution? An Analysis in Light of the Proposal for a Regulation Establishing a Union Resettlement Framework' (2022) 24 *European Journal of Migration and Law* 27, 37 (see fn 49).
[86] ibid.
[87] On local integration see UNHCR executive committee meetings, 'Conclusion on Local Integration' No 104 (LVI)–2005, available at: www.unhcr.org/uk/excom/exconc/4357a91b2/conclusion-local-integration.html. The literature on local integration of refugees, with particular focus on case studies on how effectively integration happens within certain local communities, is vast. Among others see

repatriation is supposed to facilitate the return to the refugee's home country, when the conditions permit it and it is the refugee's wish.[88] Finally, resettlement is a solution that envisages refugees moving from the country in which they are hosted and have been granted temporary first asylum, to a third one, where they will reside permanently and start a new life.[89]

These solutions, particularly local integration and resettlement, imply a system of solidarity and burden sharing within the international community. However, this system is at the whim of states' goodwill because 'neither the Convention relating to the Status of Refugees nor any other international instrument explicitly obliges states to provide durable solutions'.[90] As a matter of fact, despite the work done by the League of Nations in the years before the signing of the Geneva Convention in relation to refugee protection and the development of durable solutions, these practices were not included in the text of the Convention. There is only one reference to the practice of resettlement, made in Article 30, about allowing the transfer of refugee assets to resettlement countries,[91] but this provision does not define what resettlement is or make it a compulsory path to be offered by states.[92] Express reference to these solutions is only made in the UNHCR's Statute of 1950[93] and in subsequent UN resolutions of the General Assembly, which are not legally binding in any case. The failure to mention durable solutions by the Convention confirms, once again, the Westphalian approach to refugee protection, which was envisaged as an area to remain diligently preserved within states' boundaries, despite increasing interest within the international arena.

S Sivis, 'Integrating Bottom-up into Top-down: The Role of Local Actors in Labour Market Integration of Syrian Refugees in Turkey' (2021) 59 *International Migration* 190.

[88] The Conclusion on Local Integration 2005, adopted by the UNHCR Executive Committee, reiterated that 'voluntary repatriation, in safety and dignity, where and when feasible, remains the most preferred solution in the majority of refugee situations'. The problem of promotion and consent in voluntary repatriations has been analysed by M Gerver, 'Refugee repatriation and the problem of consent' (2018) 48 *British Journal of Political Science* 855; F Webber, 'How voluntary are voluntary returns?' (2011) 52 *Race & Class* 98; S Zimmermann, 'Understanding repatriation: refugee perspectives on the importance of safety, reintegration and hope' (2012) 18 *Population, Space and Place* 45.

[89] Resettlement is a process that requires the collaboration between the UNHCR and the states and is constituted of different phases. The UNHCR, based on the data of the Projected Global Resettlement Needs, figures out how many refugees can be resettled in a specific year and identifies those refugees that could be entitled, based on the specific selection criteria. Refugees can ask to be resettled but cannot choose the destination. It is then the state, once received the files from the UNHCR, that will decide whether the individual can be resettled there, after having undertaken all the necessary screening checks. For more details on resettlement see UNHCR, 'What is resettlement?' available at www.unhcr.org/5fe06e8b4.

[90] Ineli-Ciger, above n 85, 28.

[91] Art 30(1) states 'A Contracting State shall, in conformity with its laws and regulations, permit refugees to transfer assets which they have brought into its territory, to another country where they have been admitted for the purposes of resettlement'.

[92] Ineli-Ciger, above n 85, 31.

[93] Express reference to these measures can be found in the Statute at Chapter 1, para 1; Chapter 2, paras 8(c) and 9.

From a historical and practical perspective, refugee protection has gone through different waves, depending on which durable path of protection the international arena preferred at any point in time. In particular, resettlement and repatriation have been mostly explored and alternatively promoted,[94] while local integration has not encountered great popularity.[95] The 40 years between 1945 and 1985 were characterised by an insistence on the resettlement solution. While recognising the importance of the freedom of choice between resettlement and repatriation,[96] and formally supporting repatriation as the ideal solution,[97] the latter was not seen immediately as a viable option, particularly in relation to certain refugees.[98] There seem to be two reasons behind the strong claim for resettlement, to the detriment of repatriations. On one side, the issue of refugees became a contentious topic during the Cold War period, and the hostilities between the West and Russia turned repatriation, at least of those refugees coming from a country belonging to the Soviet Union, into a politically difficult option.[99] On the other side, after the initial recovery years following the Second World War, many western states experienced a period of economic prosperity. This economic success was in part facilitated by the presence of resettled refugees, who contributed to the replacement of labour lost during the war.[100]

The years after 1985, however, saw a change in approach and a switch towards the durable solution of repatriation. It has been suggested that the change was driven by economic needs: since extra labour was not needed anymore, the approach to refugee protection had to be adjusted. Moreover, the end of the Cold War might have triggered a new vision of refugee protection too.[101] In 1985, the Executive Committee of UNHCR adopted a conclusion,[102] which stressed voluntary repatriation as the most appropriate solution.[103] Repatriation was promoted as a viable solution to resettlement in the follow up of the War in the Balkans, and has continued to be so up until today.[104]

[94] On how these phases developed and alternated see BS Chimni, 'From Resettlement to Involuntary Repatriation: Towards a Critical History of Durable Solutions to Refugee Problems' (2004) 23 *Refugee Survey Quarterly* 55.

[95] It was often labelled as the 'forgotten option'. See Goodwin-Gill and McAdam, above n 74, 547.

[96] Chimni, above n 94, 57.

[97] ibid.

[98] ibid, 56.

[99] ibid.

[100] ibid, 57.

[101] ibid, 58–59.

[102] UNHCR, Voluntary Repatriation No. 40 (XXXVI) – 1985 available at www.unhcr.org/publications/voluntary-repatriation. For more details see Goodwin-Gill, McAdam, above n 74, 550.

[103] ibid. At the same time, the conclusions stressed the importance of arranging mechanisms to make sure that voluntariness in the refugees' decision to go home was properly developed, such as preventive visits to the country of origins and adequate collection of information.

[104] Despite currently being considered the best option, the international community seems to have suggested a rereading of the Geneva convention, particularly on the idea of safe return. This is because this idea is based on an objective assessment, rather than on the preference of the refugee, who after many years spent in a country, legitimately might be averse to the idea of restarting again in their home country. On the point see Goodwin-Gill and McAdam, above n 74, 553.

Despite the consolidated preference of the international community for repatriation, the UNHCR has never stopped working on resettlement and has tirelessly continued the promotion of this option to member states. Indeed, with the dramatic increase of the refugee population in the early nineteen nineties and the decrease of refugee spaces – moving from a ratio of one resettled refugee in every twenty to one resettled refugee in every four hundred, ie from 5 per cent to 0.25 per cent[105] – the UNHCR introduced annual consultations with governments on resettlement, called The Annual Tripartite Consultations on Resettlement (ATCR), developed resettlement policies and procedures and worked on capacity building of states.[106] The work of UNHCR has had significant impact, moving from only 10 resettlement states participating in the first ATCR in 1995, to a much bigger community of resettlement states over the years.[107]

In spite of the work of UNHCR, the reluctance of the international community to pursue resettlement on a big scale has not allowed the latter to achieve its full potential.[108] To respond to the many cases where neither repatriation nor resettlement are pursued, since the mid-two-thousands the UNHCR has begun to table alternative ideas. Initially, the UNHCR suggested migration mobility as a potential fourth available durable solution,[109] for those in need of protection but not officially qualified as refugees and stuck in a limbo because of not being able to access local integration, repatriation or resettlement. This idea was initially welcomed by some African states[110] and has found new impetus more recently in a series of projects such as Canada's Economic Mobility Pathways Pilot, the Australian Skilled Refugee Labour Agreement Programme and the UK Displaced Talent Mobility Pilot.

However, it was the Syrian refugee crisis of 2012 and 2013 that eventually triggered a widespread interest in exploring other viable alternatives to resettlement. The UN came to a recognition of the alternative routes to resettlement in 2019, and described them as 'safe and regulated avenues for refugees that complement resettlement by providing lawful stay in a third country where their international protection needs are met'.[111] Concretely, these alternative pathways include schemes aimed at the selection and safe transfer from a third country

[105] UNHCR 'The History of Resettlement: Celebrating 25 Years of the ATCR', available at: www.unhcr.org/5d1633657.pdf, 9.

[106] ibid, 11.

[107] ibid, 14.

[108] On the issue of resettlement gaps see B Solf and K Rehberg, 'The Resettlement Gap: a Record Number of Global Refugees, but Few are Resettled' (2021), available at: www.migrationpolicy.org/article/refugee-resettlement-gap.

[109] UNHCR, 'Refugee Protection and Mixed Migration: A 10 Point Plan of Action' (2007), available at: www.unhcr.org/sites/default/files/legacy-pdf/4742a30b4.pdf, point 7.

[110] K Long and J Crisp, 'Migration, mobility and solutions: an evolving perspective' (2010) 35 *Forced Migration Review* 56, 57. For further bibliography see Goodwin-Gill and McAdam, above n 74, at fn 149, part 3, ch 10.

[111] UNHCR, 'Complementary Pathways for Admission of Refugees to Third Countries: Key Considerations' (2019), available at: www.refworld.org/docid/5cebf3fc4.html, 5.

in which the beneficiaries of the programme live as refugees, recognised or not by the UNHCR, to another host country. Among these alternative solutions, the UN officially included not only labour mobility, previously mentioned, but also other routes, such as humanitarian visas, education opportunities and, crucially, community sponsorship of refugees.[112]

The years immediately following the Syrian crisis saw the states as protagonists and architects of a myriad of different solutions, particularly in Europe, to offer help to more than one million Syrian refugees. Indeed, states started to act early and independently, before any official call from the UNHCR or of the European Union. This led to the creation and introduction of several different schemes. As a result, these solutions began to be seen as a 'politically palatable alternative to traditional solutions for refugees and as a way of demonstrating to their constituencies that arrivals can be managed'.[113]

Various projects were adopted by several states in Europe, some more successful than others. Given the lack of a holistic humanitarian visa discipline at EU level,[114] some states decided to resort to humanitarian admissions. These admissions, unlike resettlement, are characterised by the temporariness of the length of stay. Quite a few humanitarian admissions projects were successfully adopted in Europe since 2013.[115] Moreover, as far as educational opportunities are concerned, some European countries established forms of student scholarships for refugees. For example, in 2015 the Czech Republic introduced a government grant programme to sponsor Syrian students for six years. France adopted a similar programme, although mainly directed at masters level students, for Syrians coming from Lebanon in 2015, and Germany employed its DAAD programme, funded by the federal government, to support Syrian students to enrol at university in Germany, allowing also family members to join.[116]

Among these early initiatives, states also began experimenting with private sponsorships of refugees. We will engage with a more precise definition of what this phenomenon entails in the next chapter. For the moment, it suffices to know

[112] ibid.

[113] J Van Selm, 'Complementary Pathways to Protection: Promoting the Integration and Inclusion of Refugees in Europe?' (2020) 690 *The ANNALS of the American Academy of Political and Social Science* 136, 143.

[114] Despite the proposal of the European Parliament to amend the EU Visa Code, the Court of Justice of the European Union, in case C-638/16, *X and X v État Belge* ECLI:EU:C:2017:173, ruled that the Member States are not obliged to grant humanitarian visas to persons seeking asylum but they can decide in accordance to their sovereignty and legislation. After this case and following opposition from the Commission and the Council, the Parliament withdrew its proposal.

[115] For more details on the humanitarian admission schemes see ERN scoping paper 'Humanitarian Admission Programmes in Europe: expanding complementary pathways of admission for persons in need of international protection' (2018), available at: www.iom.int/sites/g/files/tmzbdl486/files/documents/ERN%2Bscoping-paper-Humanitarian-Admission-Programmes-in-Europe.pdf, 10–18. Some of the humanitarian admission schemes included by this paper will be analysed in this book, since they also include private sponsorship elements.

[116] For more details on these programmes see ERN scoping paper 'Student Scholarships for Refugees: Expanding complementary pathways of admission to Europe' (2017), available at: www.iom.int/sites/g/files/tmzbdl486/files/documents/ERN%2Bscoping-paper-Student-Scholarships-for-Refugees.pdf.

that these are arrangements that allow private individuals or organisations, to support the entry, residence and integration of refugees from an emotional, social and financial point of view. As early as 2013, Germany established its regional schemes,[117] now closed, with private sponsorship of refugees and family reunification components. Italy introduced the pilot humanitarian corridor programme in 2015,[118] followed by France in 2017. The UK established its own sponsorship programme in 2016[119] and other countries such as Ireland and Switzerland adopted some temporary sponsorship programmes, which targeted Syrian refugees, as early as 2013 and 2014 respectively.[120]

In this section a journey was outlined, that took us from the international community's application of resettlement and of the other durable solutions to refugee protection, to the creation of alternative paths to admission of vulnerable migrants, to which private sponsorship of refugees belongs The next section will further contextualise this phenomenon, with particular focus on Europe. It will address the reasons for the success of these alternative paths and highlight how these initiatives soon received the endorsement of international actors like the EU and UNHCR. It will conclude by showing how support within the international arena does not imply any obligation on the states to include these schemes within their jurisdiction, since resettlement, and more broadly, immigration, are still considered to be matters covered by state sovereignty.

VII. Private Sponsorship in Europe: Academic Interest and International Actors' Endorsement

The recent sudden proliferation of private sponsorship schemes for refugees in Europe is not a random event. Indeed, this phenomenon is something that brewed, although over a reasonably short period of time, through conversations and encounters of various stakeholders on this side and on the other side of the Atlantic.

To Canada goes the credit for initiating the discussion. As will be better explained in the next chapter, Canada was the country that first introduced private sponsorship of refugees. Indeed, these schemes were implemented in an informal fashion by the government, in collaboration with some religious organisations, during the years following the two world wars. They were eventually crystallised into statute by the Immigration Act of 1976. In the years following the Syrian refugee crisis, some senior bureaucrats and academics of the University of Ottawa, supported by the UNHCR and the Open Society Initiative, initiated informal

[117] Chapter 4 of this book will look at this experience in detail.
[118] Chapter 3 of this book will explore this programme in detail.
[119] Chapter 3 of this book will explore this programme in detail.
[120] These programmes, however, only last for a few months. They will be discussed in Chapter 3 of this book.

discussions on how to offer help to refugees escaping from the Syrian civil war. These actors agreed that one feasible way to provide concrete help was to promote the implementation of the Canadian model of private sponsorship of refugees in other countries, particularly in South America and Europe.[121] This idea took shape in the Global Refugee Sponsorship Initiative (from now on GRSI), which was announced in 2016 at the New York Declaration for Refugees and Migrants, under the auspices of the Trudeau government.[122] Following the announcement, various European delegations of state representatives and various stakeholders were invited to Canada to learn more about the schemes, talk to sponsors and experts and ask questions. Some workshops took place in Europe too, such as the EASO-GRSI (European Asylum Support Office – Global Refugee Sponsorship Initiative) workshop, which took place in Malta on 19–20 April 2018, where 10 European Member States interested in implementing these schemes participated.[123]

The aim of GRSI was not achieved in the way that Canada initially envisaged. Indeed, the initiative had to scale down from the initial aim of exporting the Canadian model to Europe, to Canada being asked to simply share its best practices.[124] This is because many European delegations believed that the geographical and historical differences between Canada and Europe, on top of the 'high political costs and significant changes in the immigration regimes',[125] would have made the transplant of the scheme infeasible. However, these encounters led to a fruitful exchange of ideas and knowledge that turned something that was a foreign practice into reality in Europe.

Already in 2015, quite a few sponsorship schemes had been trialled by some European states, as Judith Kumin highlights in her report entitled 'Welcoming Engagement: How Private Sponsorship Can Strengthen Refugee Resettlement in The European Union'.[126] At this point, the pressing interest of academics and policy-makers became more evident, as the scientific research output on the topic, focusing on Europe, began to increase. The paper by Kumin is the first[127]

[121] Canada is the first country that allowed and promoted private sponsorships of refugees, which date back to 1976. This topic will be further explored in Chapter 2 of this book.

[122] The New York Declaration for Refugees and Migrants was adopted unanimously by the United Nations General Assembly on 19 September 2016. Among the many commitments, Member States 'agreed to work towards the adoption of a global compact on refugees and a global compact for safe, orderly and regular migration'. For further information see UNHCR, 'New York Declaration for Refugees and Migrants', available at: www.unhcr.org/uk/new-york-declaration-for-refugees-and-migrants.html.

[123] NF Tan, 'Community Sponsorship in Europe: Taking Stock, Policy Transfer and What the Future might Hold' (2021) 3 *Frontiers in Human Dynamics: Refugees and Conflict*, available at: www.frontiersin.org/articles/10.3389/fhumd.2021.564084/full.

[124] CD Smith, 'A Model for the World? Policy Transfer Theory and the Challenges of "Exporting" Private Sponsorship to Europe' in S Labman and G Cameron (eds), *Strangers to Neighbours: Refugee-Sponsorship in Context* (Montreal, McGill-Queens University Press, 2000) 286–87.

[125] ibid, 291.

[126] Kumin, above n 1.

[127] In 2013 the European Parliament published a report on best integration practices for refugees, but it did not mention private sponsorships of refugees (ibid, 4).

European study that attempts to assess the feasibility of the private refugee scheme as a safe and legal route to access safe states. In this paper the author makes the case that private sponsorship programmes can serve as safe pathways for refugees in Europe. After describing what private sponsorships of refugees are and the key issues that a state should consider before embarking on the promotion of such schemes,[128] the report focuses on the gains that the European Union could achieve if it decided to embrace these practices. Among other points, the author stresses that private sponsorship of refugees schemes should be implemented because of their capacity to expand the classic resettlement route at reduced cost to government, while enhancing integration.[129]

Susan Fratzke, writing for MPI some years after, took stock of some of these early European experiences and reiterated the importance of private sponsorship of refugees for Europe, praising the various and multifaced initiatives, highlighting their potential and suggesting how to design successful schemes and how to integrate them fully into refugee resettlement and reception in Europe.[130] Along the same lines, the European Resettlement Network (ERN), in a project co-funded by the European Commission, published first a scoping paper (2017),[131] then a feasibility study on suggested models for private sponsorship of refugees in France (2018)[132] and finally a strategic assessment and recommendation paper (2018) on the development of private sponsorship schemes in Europe.[133] In the strategic assessment paper, recommendations on how to expand the schemes were included, paying particular attention to the need to find alternative funding mechanisms, relying also on the EU and engaging several actors in society.

It is perhaps owing to this early academic and policy work, when often the participation of the EU was tabled, that eventually the European Commission joined the debate. In May 2015, in the European Agenda on Migration the Commission encouraged the Member States to adopt some of these models, expressly, although briefly, referring to 'private/non-governmental sponsorships and humanitarian permits, and family reunification clauses'.[134] This brief reference was properly considered by a feasibility study, published by the Commission

[128] ibid, 6–14.
[129] ibid, 15–21.
[130] S Fratzke, 'Engaging Communities in Refugee Protection: the Potential of Private Sponsorship in Europe' (2017) Brussels, Migration Policy Institute Europe, available at: www.migrationpolicy.org/research/engaging-communities-refugee-protection-potential-private-sponsorship-europe.
[131] ERN scoping paper 'Private Sponsorship in Europe: expanding complementary pathways for refugee resettlement' (2017) available at: www.iom.int/sites/g/files/tmzbdl486/files/documents/ERN%2Bscoping-paper-Private-Sponsorship-in-Europe.pdf.
[132] ERN feasibility study 'Towards a Private Sponsorship Model in France' (2018), available at: www.iom.int/sites/g/files/tmzbdl486/files/documents/ERN%2Bfeasibility-study-Towards-a-Private-Sponsorship-Model-in-France.pdf.
[133] ERN strategic assessment 'Expanding Solutions for Refugees: Complementary Pathways of Admission to Europe' (2018), available at: www.iom.int/sites/g/files/tmzbdl486/files/documents/ERN%2BFinal-Study-A-strategic-assessment-of-expanding-complementary-pathways-of-admission-to-Europe.pdf.
[134] COM(2015) 240 final, Agenda on Migration, available at: eur-lex.europa.eu/legal-content/EN/TXT/PDF/?uri=CELEX:52015DC0240, 5.

in 2018.[135] In this study the Commission, after consulting with relevant stakeholders, identified four options through which the EU could be involved in the introduction of private sponsorship of refugees within Member States. The first option is identified as the status quo, and consists of allowing the Member States to decide whether or not to introduce these schemes. The second one, known as soft measures, consists of allowing the EU to get partially involved by sustaining the programmes through training, capacity-building and peer-learning activities. The third option refers to funding opportunities, whereby the EU would support the sponsorship schemes using specific funding instruments. Finally, legislative action is the most intrusive solution as it aims to harmonise the sponsorship schemes of refugees throughout the EU.[136] The paper showed that stakeholders wanted a light touch EU intervention, through soft measures and funding, and the study also showed the lack of an expressed need or desire to achieve a harmonised legislative system of European refugee sponsorship.[137] In line with these findings, in the 2020 New Pact on Migration and Asylum,[138] the Commission confirmed that the EU involvement in private sponsorships would amount to 'funding, capacity building and knowledge-sharing, in cooperation with civil society, with the aim of developing a European model of community sponsorship, which can lead to better integration outcomes in the longer term'.[139] Concretely, these aims took shape in the European Asylum Support Office (EASO) Pilot Project Network,[140] which aims to promote and share best practices on resettlement and alternative pathways, including private sponsorships, and with the Asylum, Migration, and Integration Fund (AMIF), which provided several funding options to support resettlement and integration within Member States.[141] The AMIF 2021–27 programme has now explicitly provided direct funding for private sponsorship of refugees schemes, which will be directly implemented by DG Home.[142]

Concomitantly to the publication of the Commission feasibility study, the Global Compact on Refugees was signed in New York in December 2018, under

[135] European Commission, 'Study on the feasibility and added value of sponsorship schemes as possible pathway to safe channels for admission to the EU, including resettlement' final report (2018), available at: op.europa.eu/en/publication-detail/-/publication/1dbb0873-d349-11e8-9424-01aa75ed71a1.

[136] ibid, from page 86 section 5.

[137] ibid, 118–21.

[138] COM (2020) 609 final, Communication from the Commission on a New Pact on Migration and Asylum available at: eur-lex.europa.eu/legal-content/EN/TXT/HTML/?uri=CELEX:52020DC0609&from=EN.

[139] ibid, section 6.6.

[140] CO de Andrés, 'EASO and the European Commission:2020 first meeting and of its Resettlement and Humanitarian Admission Network' 28 January 2020, available at: www.europeancommunicationstrategies.com/EASO-and-the-European-Commission-2020-first-meeting-of-its-Resettlement-and-Humanitarian-Admission-Network_a109.html.

[141] Sponsorship activities were not specifically listed in the AMIF funding calls. That proved to be difficult for Member States, which were not aware of this financial opportunity. See S Fraztke and H Beirens, 'Three things the European Union can do to support private sponsorship for refugees' (2018) Migration Policy Institute, available at: www.migrationpolicy.org/news/three-things-european-union-can-do-support-private-sponsorship-refugees.

[142] C (2021) 8458 final, Commission implementing decision on the financing of components of the Thematic Facility under the Asylum, Migration and Integration Fund and adoption of the Work

the supervision of the UNHCR. The Compact is not binding under international law. Nevertheless, it is important because it expresses intergovernmental willingness to equitably share responsibility for issues related to refugees.[143] In order to achieve the ambitious aims of the Compact, the UN also inaugurated the Global Refugee Forum, which facilitates the meeting of stakeholders, states and other actors, roughly every four years, to share good practices and contribute with financial or other kinds of support to the achievement of the aims of the Compact.[144] The first Global Refugee Forum took place in 2019 and the second one in December 2023. Whether the Global Compact on Refugees and the Global Refugee Forum can be considered successful is yet to be seen. Certainly, they have contributed to spreading awareness of the need to consolidate alternative paths to resettlement, including private sponsorships of refugees.

It is owing to these initiatives that today we are witnessing the flourishing of many examples of private sponsorship of refugees in Europe. However, neither the interest in private sponsorship of refugees expressed by the international arena, nor the willingness to promote it as much as possible, can cancel out the fact that resettlement (and immigration more broadly) is a matter still at the full discretion of the state. There is no obligation on states to include the schemes within their jurisdiction and, as the feasibility paper published by the European Commission highlights, this possibility has been excluded in the near future in Europe, since stakeholders have rejected the idea of having a common European system of private sponsorship of refugees. This also concretely means that, despite the use of the adjective 'private', sponsorships are very much led by the state even when it comes to the sponsor's tasks. Indeed, in several current European models of sponsorship, there is little space left to the discretion of the sponsor in terms of who they want to support, how and how many.

VIII. Conclusion: Some Considerations on Refugee Protection, State Sovereignty and Private Sponsorship

The aim of this chapter was to offer an account of how refugee protection developed historically, in order to contextualise the phenomenon of private sponsorship of refugees. At the same time, this chapter has tried to highlight how refugee protection, despite the influence of international law, is still a matter that, ultimately, is grounded within the remit of state sovereignty.

Programme for 2021 and 2022, available at: ec.europa.eu/home-affairs/system/files/2021-12/AMIF%20-%20Thematic%20Facility%20Work%20Programme%202021-2022_en.pdf, 7.

[143] See UNHCR, 'Global Compact on Refugees', available at: www.unhcr.org/about-unhcr/who-we-are/global-compact-refugees.

[144] UNHCR, 'Global Refugee Forum' available at globalcompactrefugees.org/global-refugee-forum.

Throughout the chapter, it has been seen that refugee protection – or protection of asylees, if we consider the historical context in which the practice originated – was originally provided by church sanctuaries. Asylum was granted in a physical place – within the walls of a church – where the person that committed a crime could find refuge and protection against the secular authorities. The asylee, commonly, did not have to cross state or city borders, as the sanctuary where they would seek refuge was often geographically located in the same city from whose authorities they were escaping from. However, eventually asylum began to be understood as the sort of protection granted by the secular authority – namely, the state – to someone fleeing from another jurisdiction, normally another state, and that has not necessarily committed a crime. It is at this point that the idea of sovereignty of the state over its territory, also conceived as protection of that territory from *personae non grate*, began to take root. In a few centuries, the state became the one to decide who could cross its borders and whether they could do it.[145] Asylum too turned into a practice at the whim of the sovereign state. Indeed, with the advent of the sovereign state, the protection of asylees shifted perspective: it was no longer a form of protection to which individuals were entitled, but something that states could decide to grant, or not.

The interest that international law showed in the refugee issue during the interwar period and aftermath of the Second World War, culminating with the drafting of the Geneva Convention, did not manage to fully change the primacy of state sovereignty over refugee protection. As seen above, the Convention lacks a proper enforcement mechanism and, despite the clear definition of refugees, it is up to the individual states when and how to grant them protection. This is not surprising, as it is fully in line with the broader 'take' that international law has endorsed on migration between sovereign states. Referring to the right to emigrate from the state of origin, recognised by the Universal Declaration of Human Rights,[146] by the International Covenant on Civil and Political Rights (ICCPR)[147] and, at European level, by Article 2 of Protocol n 4 to the European Convention of Human Rights,[148] Fauchille says that

> the rights of man are no more absolute than the rights of the state … This being so, it is impossible to recognise absolute liberty of emigration, but one may admit a liberty regulated to the extent demanded by the security of the state.[149]

[145] This is a process that took some time to come to fruition. As Torpey put it: 'The process took place unevenly, in different places, following the line where modern states replaced non-territorial forms of political organisations and free wage labour replaced various forms of servitude … Ultimately, the authority to regulate movement came to be primarily a property of the international system as a whole – that is, of nation states acting in concert to enforce their interests in controlling who comes and goes'. JC Torpey, above n 29, 11.

[146] Art 13.

[147] Art 12.

[148] Art 2 of Protocol no 4 replicates Art 12 ICCPR.

[149] 'Paul Fauchille on the Rights of Emigration and Immigration' (2005) 31 *Population and Development Review* 765, 767–68.

In other words, it is the state that ultimately has the final say on the right to emigrate and, a fortiori, also to the right to immigrate.

Where can we place the phenomenon of private sponsorship of refugees within the state-centred approach to immigration and refugee protection? It has already been mentioned, but it will be better explored in the next chapter, that these schemes involve strong participation by the private sector, often in the form of charities, religious or secular organisations, or groups of individuals. This strong private involvement may suggest that these organisations have achieved a certain power over immigration decision-making. This seems to be reinforced by the fact that some sponsorship of refugees schemes – historically, the Canadian one and currently some others in Europe, to a more limited extent – have endorsed 'naming' as one of their key characteristics. This feature, as will be soon explored, allows the sponsor, rather than the state, to select who they would like to enter their state territory.

The naming feature, endorsed by some private sponsorship schemes, seems to be able to alter the classic sovereignty approach, leaving the choice and freedom of who to welcome, to the sponsor. Consequentially, private sponsorship of refugees schemes – those that allow naming – could be seen as the Trojan Horse sent into the state sovereignty arena, as they seem to be capable of relying on the self-determination of the sponsor, trumping the self-preservation claims of the recipient state.

As much as this view of private sponsorship of refugees can sound captivating, in reality this might just have been true during the initial experience of private sponsorships, in Canada. Indeed, as it will be highlighted in the next chapter, the Canadian experience of refugee sponsorship, up until the Immigration Act of 1976, was characterised by a lack of formalities between private sponsors and state institutions. The programme would run based on a mutual relationship of trust between the private stakeholders and the officers of the Immigration Office. These informal relationships allowed the schemes to prosper and flourish. Despite some of the conflicts that occurred between private stakeholders and the state, which led also to a cessation of the schemes for some time, the lobbying power of the various churches involved shaped the schemes in terms of their functioning and characteristics. The various churches that acted as private sponsors in Canada advocated and lobbied for schemes that would allow the naming of the sponsored refugees and they succeeded in their intent, notwithstanding the objections of the Immigration Office. Not only that, but they also managed to secure additionality, meaning that Canadian citizens would be allowed to sponsor whoever they wanted, without strict limitations on numbers. However, the codification of the private sponsorship of refugees by the 1976 Immigration Act meant that while the Canadian scheme gained in legal certainty, clarity and predictability, at the same time, intentionally or not, it became officially curtailed within the realm of state sovereignty. At that point, it was the Canadian state that, in its magnanimity, allowed the private sector to be involved in resettling refugees, provided that the conditions set out by the law were fulfilled. Moreover, should the state decide that private resettlement of refugees was no longer a priority, it could simply amend the legislation to cast it away.

Unlike post-1976 Canada, some of the European experiences of sponsorship of refugees do not find their basis in a statute.[150] The humanitarian corridors that take place in Italy, France, Belgium, Andorra and St Marino, where the sponsors are allowed to select the beneficiaries (although through a diluted version of the Canadian naming, as will be seen), for instance, find their roots in some memoranda of understanding between the various states and the religious organisations involved in the projects. This level of informality could suggest that private stakeholders in Europe have enough room for manoeuvre to shape immigration policies, as the schemes are not crystallised in the law. However, despite the lack of official codification of the schemes, governments are still very much involved in curtailing the action of private sponsors. In the case of humanitarian corridors, for example, the memoranda of understanding detail the number of beneficiaries allowed to enter the country, the conditions under which they are entitled to benefit from the schemes, and the security checks that need to be carried out by the state authorities. Furthermore, crucially, these agreements normally last for only two years, with the possibility of them being renewed at the discretion of the government.

In conclusion, it seems that the European sponsorship programmes for refugees are far from being able to pierce the veil of state sovereignty on immigration and, on the contrary, are part of its realm. Hence, going back to the initial question of where to place private sponsorship within the current state-centred approach to immigration, the answer seems to be that they can be placed right under its umbrella, and in full compliance with it. Indeed, despite apparently evocating freedom from the state, private sponsorships of refugees are immersed within state power dynamics. In the end, it is the state that has the last say on how the schemes should be framed and operated, and eventually whether they should be continued or stopped. Whether private sponsorship of refugees schemes stand a chance of piercing the veil of state sovereignty on refugee protection is a matter that will be tackled in the final chapter of this book.

[150] The exception seems to be the German NesT programme, which finds its grounds in the admission order issued under s 23(4) of the Residence Act (available at: www.gesetze-im-internet.de/aufenthg_2004/__23.html). According to this provision 'The Federal Ministry of the Interior, Building and Community may, in consultation with the supreme Land authorities, order that the Federal Office for Migration and Refugees grant acceptance to certain persons seeking protection (resettlement refugees) selected for resettlement within the framework of the resettlement of persons seeking protection.'

2

Defining and Classifying Private Sponsorship of Refugees

I. Introduction

The previous chapter provided a brief history of asylum and how refugee protection evolved with the advent of the Westphalian state and international law. This overview was aimed at enabling a better understanding of where private sponsorship of refugees sits, in terms of refugee protection and state sovereignty. Analysis of the relationship between private sponsorship of refugees and state sovereignty will be continued in the final part of this book.

One aspect that has only been touched upon so far is the definition and classification of private sponsorship of refugees. While at this point one might have a rough idea of what private sponsorship schemes amount to, on the basis on what has already been said, it is now time to engage in a more specific analysis. This will help the reader to identify the key characteristics of the schemes and should also provide a better conceptual understanding of the various European sponsorship experiences.

In order to delve deeper into this analysis, it is important to recall something that was mentioned in the previous chapter. Chapter one outlined the debate over the introduction of private sponsorship programmes in Europe. The reader might remember that the discourse was initiated with the help of the international community, via the Global Refugee Initiative, with the support of the European Union and the independent work of several European states. With reference to the international community and the Global Refugee Initiative, it was noted that a key crucial player was Canada. Indeed Canada, the country with the longest experience in the field, took the initiative in trying to export its sponsorship of refugees model to Europe.[1] The role-model status of Canada in the field of private

[1] Outside of Europe and Canada, there are other countries that have experimented with private sponsorship of refugee schemes.

- The US has led a community sponsorship of refugees programme for several years. The programme is not officially recognised in a specific legal provision and can be better described as a co-sponsorship. The Immigration and Nationality Act of 1985 gives discretion to the President to set the annual target of refugee quotas for resettlement. The Office of Refugee Resettlement, established by the aforementioned act, funds and enforces the US resettlement programme. In particular, the Office can spend money and sign contracts with other

sponsorship of refugees is recognised. Considering also the influence of Canada in the development of the schemes in Europe, it seems important to first look at

stakeholders to make sure that resettlement is effectively developed. To do so, the Office works with nine official resettlement agencies. These agencies make sure that the needs of the refugees, such as food, housing, integration, etc are effectively met. Within this loose framework, certain agencies have decided to further delegate their activities to local affiliates. These local affiliates often look for the partnership of sponsors from local communities (See J Bond and A Kwadrans 'Resettling Refugees through Community Sponsorship: a Revolutionary Operational Approach Built on Traditional Legal Infrastructure' (2019) 35 *Refuge: Canada's Journal on Refugees* 87, 95). At the 2023 Global Refugee Forum the US pledged to expand the community sponsorship programme. To this aim, the government intends to continue funding Refugee Welcome Collective, a consortium that enhances capacity-building and strengthens resources aimed at the expansion of community sponsorships (see Reliefweb, 'United States Announces New Pledges at the 2023 Global Refugee Forum' 16 December 2023, available at: reliefweb.int/report/world/united-states-announces-new-pledges-2023-global-refugee-forum). In January 2023 the US government launched a new private sponsorship programme called Welcome Corps. At the Global Refugee Forum of 2023 the US committed to expanding the programme to welcome 10,000 refugees within the 2024 fiscal year (see Reliefweb, above).

- In 2016, New Zealand decided to pilot a community sponsorship of refugees programme. The pilot was implemented through the Operational Manual, a Department of Immigration document, which complements New Zealand's 1987 Immigration Act. The manual sets out the requirements that have to be fulfilled for a sponsor and a refugee to become part of the programme. To be sponsored, the refugee has to be recognised by the UNHCR, have knowledge of basic English, a minimum of three years' work experience and has to be between 18 and 45 years old. Sponsors, for their part, have to be recognised legal entities, have experience in working with refugees, have financial resources to support the refugees, and be willing to enter into an agreement with the Immigration Office (see Bond and Kwadrans, above, 92). The Community Organisation Refugee Sponsorship Category (CORS visa) was piloted in 2018. The pilot was extended for a further three years in July 2021. This has enabled 150 refugees to be sponsored between 1 July 2021 and 30 June 2024 (see UNHCR, 'Resettlement Country: New Zealand', available at: www.unhcr.org/resettlement-handbook/wp-content/uploads/sites/153/2023/04/Country-Chapter-New-Zealand-2023.pdf, 2).
- In Argentina, the sponsorship of refugees scheme was introduced owing to the 2004 Migration Law. This law does not explicitly refer to private sponsorship of refugees, but it provides the legal grounds for permission to stay in Argentina on humanitarian grounds. In October 2014 Argentina's National Directorate for Migration passed an administrative provision (First Syria Programme Provision), which established the country's private sponsorship scheme. This programme enabled Argentinian relatives of Syrian and Palestinian refugees to sponsor their family members to be resettled in the country. The programme was renewed in 2016 when the requirement of family ties between sponsor and resettled refugee were removed and the broader UNHCR referral mechanism became available (see Bond and Kwadrans, above, 93–94).
- Australia too has had a long experience of private sponsorship of refugees. Community sponsorship was used to support the resettlement of refugees through the Community Refugee Settlement Scheme, which ran from 1979 to 1997. This scheme tailored a mechanism that allowed refugees to be moved under the care and supervision of Australian communities that would provide housing and more general assistance, effectively bypassing the government-run migrant centres. The programme stopped in 1997. However, in 2012, the Australian government expressed its interest in exploring the idea of a private sponsorship of refugee pilot. The pilot was formally announced in 2013. Sponsors could be individuals, businesses or communities. It was open to refugees outside their home country that experienced gross violations of their human rights. The programme was not additional but counted towards state quotas. In 2017 Australia finally launched the Community Sponsorship Programme, which mirrors the design of the previous pilot scheme.(for more information see AL Hirsh, K Hoang and A Vogl, 'Australia's private refugee sponsorship programme: creating complementary pathways or privatising humanitarianism' (2019) 35 *Refuge: Canada's Journal on Refugees* 110, 110–15).

the Canadian sponsorship experience more closely. In particular, reporting the Canadian experience in detail will allow the reader to understand a key element of the history of private sponsorship of refugees. Furthermore, discussing the Canadian experience is crucially important because it helps to understand some of the key features that identify a programme as a private sponsorship scheme.

To this end, the next section will be dedicated to an overview of the historical development and analysis of the Canadian private sponsorship of refugees. Once completed, the chapter will move on to look at definitions and propose a classification for the schemes currently available in Europe. Following the proposed classification, the various European schemes will be briefly referred to at the end of the chapter, while their deeper individual analysis will be the subject of Chapters three and four.

II. The Canadian Experience of Private Sponsorship of Refugees[2]

The Canadian experience of private sponsorship of refugees found its roots in the informal assistance and support granted by religious organisations in the aftermath of World War I. In this period, the Mennonite Central Committee and the Jewish Immigrant Aid Services of Canada were funded and became particularly engaged in trying to assist refugees fleeing Europe.[3] In an Order in Council of

At the Global Refugee Forum 2023, the Refugee Council of Australia pledged to support 'the expansion of community sponsorship and advocating for the successful introduction of an improved named sponsorship pathway informed by learnings from the Community Refugee Integration and Settlement Pilot, the Community Support Program and similar programs in other countries' (see Refugee Council of Australia, 'Global Refugee Forum pledge on resettlement and complementary pathways' 20 December 2023, available at: www.refugeecouncil.org.au/global-refugee-forum-pledge-on-resettlement-and-complementary-pathways/).

- Finally, Brazil pledged to explore the feasibility of introducing a pilot private sponsorship scheme in December 2019, at the first Global Refugee Forum. The plan is to make sponsors responsible for refugees already chosen for resettlement though the UNHCR lists (see UNHCR report, 'Brazil', available at: reporting.unhcr.org/sites/default/files/Brazil%20Factsheet_August%202021.pdf, 5).

[2] For an extended bibliography on the topic see J Hyndman, W Payne and S Jimenez, 'Private Sponsorship of Refugees in Canada' (2017) 54 *Forced Migration Review* 56; A Macklin, K Berber, L Goldring, J Hyndman, A Korteweg, S Labman and J Zyfi, 'A preliminary investigation into Private Refugee Sponsors' (2018) 50 *Canadian Ethnic Studies* 35; S Labman, 'Private Sponsorship: Complementary of Conflicting Interests?' (2016) 32 *Refuge: Canada's Journal on Refugees* 67; A Chapman, 'Private Sponsorship and Public Policy: Political Barriers to Church-Connected resettlement in Canada' (2014) report prepared for Citizens for Public Justice, available at: cpj.ca/wp-content/uploads/PrivateSponsorshipandPublicPolicyReport-1.pdf; B Treviranus and M Casasola, 'Canada's Private Sponsorship of Refugees Program: A practitioner's Perspective of its past and future'(2003) 4 *Journal of International Migration and Integration* 177; S Labman and M Pearlman, 'Blending, Bargaining and Burden Sharing: Canada's Resettlement Programs' (2018) 19 *Journal of International Migration and Integration* 439; T Denton, 'Understanding private refugee sponsorship in Manitoba' (2003) 4 *Journal of International Migration and Integration* 257.

[3] S Labman, *Crossing Law's Border: Canada's Refugee Resettlement Programme* (Vancouver/Toronto, UBC Press, 2020) 83.

1922, it is reported that Canada agreed that Mennonites fleeing from the Soviet Union could be admitted to the country as long as the Mennonite community provided for them, to avoid them becoming a burden on the state.[4]

Private support to refugees continued and strengthened in the aftermath of the Second World War. The War left Europe with around 30 million displaced people. This became an international issue that needed to find a solution. Canada took the lead in this matter by starting early negotiations and discussions at governmental level on how to provide a durable and sustainable solutions. Two main reasons underpinned the Canadian decision to resettle displaced people and refugees from Europe. On one side, the Department of External Affairs supported the admission of refugees from Europe to show Canadian leadership in the rebuilding of a post-war order.[5] However, the most convincing argument, which eventually triggered the capitulation of the original strict position of the Immigration Branch of the Department of Mines and Resources on accepting refugees from Europe, originated from the talks that the latter undertook with the Departments of Labour, Health and External Affairs. In particular, they agreed on the fact that Canada needed more people in order to build the country and 'Europe's refugees were identified as primary means for meeting this goal'.[6] European camps hosting refugees and displaced people were suddenly seen as the potential source of labour.[7] This approach is summarised by the highly quoted speech of the Canadian Prime Minister WL MacKenzie King who, in 1947, stated that

> the government will seek … to ensure the careful selection and permanent settlement of such numbers of immigrants that can advantageously be absorbed in our national economy … It is not a 'fundamental human right' of any alien to enter Canada. It is a privilege. It is a matter of domestic policy.[8]

The first approved programmes that helped to resettle refugees were the 'close relatives' and 'bulk labour' schemes in 1946 and 1947 respectively.[9] Private sponsorship of refugees developed from the close relatives programme. The reason underpinning this development is partially grounded in the fact that the close relatives scheme excluded ethnically German family members,[10] who were considered

[4] ibid.

[5] See G Cameron, 'Reluctant Partnership: A Political History of Private Sponsorship in Canada (1947–1980)' in S Labman and G Cameron (eds), *Strangers to Neighbours: Refugee- Sponsorship in Context* (Montreal, McGill-Queens University Press, 2000), 21.

[6] ibid.

[7] ibid. CD Howe, a member of the Mackenzie King cabinet, was adamantly convinced that displaced people were 'the simplest, cheapest and quickest way to find labour'.

[8] N Kelley and M Trebilcock, *The Making of the Mosaic: A History of Canadian Immigration Policy* (Toronto, University of Toronto Press, 2010), 312 quoting Prime Minister WL Mackenzie King, in Canadian House of Commons debates, 1 May 1947, 2644-7, available at: https://www.lipad.ca/full/permalink/1466185/.

[9] Cameron, above n 5, 21.

[10] For more details on this matter see J Panagiotidis, '"Not the Concern of the Organisation?" The IRO and Overseas Resettlement of Ethnic Germans from Eastern Europe After World War II' (2020) 45 *Historical Social Research* 173.

to be enemies under Canadian law.[11] As a reaction to this, private sponsorship schemes were modelled in such a way to circumvent the exclusion of certain categories of people from the IRO mandate.[12]

In the late nineteen forties the Canadian National Committee for Refugees (CNCR) called for improvements in the Canadian approach to welcoming European displaced people.[13] Some religious organisations, including the Canadian Mennonite Board of Colonisation, Canadian Lutheran World relief, the German Baptist Union and the Catholic Immigration Aid Society, joined the efforts and took the matter into their own hands. Together with the Canadian Government and the transportation companies, they founded the Canadian Christian Council for the resettlement of Refugees (CCCRR) and managed to successfully lobby the Immigration Branch to resettle European displaced family members, even those that were outside the IRO mandate.[14] The CCCRR's task was to find and select refugees abroad and to resettle them in Canada. CCCRR representatives would travel to Europe to identify the refugees to resettle and present them to the Canadian immigration authorities, which would proceed with the screening.[15]

Following the CCCRR's steps, other religious congregations, like the Canadian Jewish Congress, asked and obtained permission to resettle displaced people from Europe. Eventually, once the family reunification calls began to decrease, the CCCRR sought and obtained leave from the Immigration Branch, to successfully promote and initiate a programme through which Canadians could also sponsor non-family members.[16] In 1949 the Canadian Council of Churches (CCC), following the CCCRR's experience, started its own sponsorship project too,[17] followed by other religious congregations.

The resettlement of refugees in Canada ended with the conclusion of the IRO mandate in 1951. However, the church sponsorship remained open, as the number of displaced people in Europe was still high.[18] Indeed, for a couple of years the

[11] Cameron, above n 5, 21.

[12] Annex I of the IRO Constitution specifies the organisation's mandate. Crucially, Part II 4 states that 'Persons of German ethnic origin (whether German nationals or members of German minorities in other countries) who:(*a*) Have been or may be transferred to Germany from other countries; (*b*) Have been evacuated from Germany to other countries during the Second World War; (*c*) Have fled from, or into, Germany, or from their places of residence into countries other than Germany in order to avoid falling into the hands of Allied Armies' are excluded from the scope of the Constitution.

[13] Kelley, Trebilcock, above n 8, 337.

[14] The lobbying power of the Mennonite community was particularly influential in the entire process. See Panagiotidis, above n 10, 192. On the influence of the Mennonite community see also W Janzen, 'The 1979 MCC Canada Master Agreement for the Sponsorship of Refugees in Historical Perspective' (2006) 24 *Journal of Mennonite Studies* 211.

[15] C McKinlay, 'Welcoming the Stranger: the Canadian Church and the Private Sponsorship of Refugees Programme' (2008) Toronto Metropolitan University thesis, available at: rshare.library.torontomu.ca/articles/thesis/Welcoming_the_Stranger_The_Canadian_Church_and_the_Private_Sponsorship_of_Refugees_Program/14647872, 35.

[16] Cameron, above n 5, 22.

[17] ibid, 23.

[18] ibid, 24.

various sponsorship schemes, promoted by different religious organisations and approved by the Immigration Branch continued.

However, the first signs of the need of the government to crystallise the various programmes into a standardised form began to appear. Due to the sheer number of different programmes that were spontaneously born, the government found the need to rationalise the number of initiatives under the umbrella of a New Approved Church Programme.[19] This programme, which was particularly favourable as it allowed the entry of displaced people from Europe without having to show proof of a Canadian contract of work or accommodation,[20] nevertheless exacerbated the conflict between religious groups and the immigration department. The clash occurred, in particular, over the type of immigrants to be resettled in Canada. The religious groups preferred the vulnerable and those most in need, while the Department of Citizenship and Immigration preferred able workers. In other words, while the former were keen to promote private resettlement based on humanitarian grounds, the latter's intentions were driven by Canadian labour needs.[21]

The tension between church organisations and the government became very evident during the Hungarian refugee crisis of 1956. The Canadian government's original proposition not to resettle refugees from Hungary changed when the Minister of Citizenship and Immigration, Jack Pickersgill, announced the intention to resettle eligible Hungarians, and that they would be prioritised over all other immigrants.[22] This announcement was highly criticised, mostly because Hungarians were put at the top of the waiting list but were only allowed to be admitted if they fulfilled all immigration requirements. As result, there were insistent requests from church groups and private citizens to put pressure on the government to admit greater numbers of refugees from Hungary. Eventually, Canadian immigration officials recommended that the Canadian government expand the existing private sponsorship programme.[23] Since Austria was overwhelmed with refugees, and Canada could not admit them all at once, Canada convinced the UK and the Netherlands to temporarily welcome Hungarian refugees, who would eventually be moved to Canada.[24]

The formal end to the Approved Church Programme occurred in 1958, after 37,565 Hungarians were resettled in Canada.[25] However, soon after, in 1960, owing to the pressure for Canada to play a role in World Refugee Year,[26] another scheme

[19] ibid, 25.

[20] ibid.

[21] Kelley and Trebilcock, above n 8, 338–339: 'Canada was clearly selecting the most healthy candidates. It was not interested in accepting "hard core" cases of injured, sick and old displaced persons. John Holmes, an External Affairs officer, claimed that Canada selected refugees like "good beef cattle"'.

[22] ibid, 340.

[23] Cameron, above n 5, 27.

[24] Kelley and Trebilcock, above n 8, 340.

[25] Cameron, above n 5, 27–28.

[26] Cameron, above n 5, 28. See also Kelley and Trebilcock, above n 8, 342. To mark the World Refugee Year Canada agreed to take displaced European persons affected by tuberculosis, as an exception to the usual good health and character screening requirements, and their family members (refugees were already exempted from age and occupational criteria).

was adopted and several hundred refugees still waiting in camps in Europe were relocated and resettled in Canada. This scheme, while preserving some of the key features of the previous Church programme, allowed the sponsoring of people that would normally not be approved for immigration to Canada, as long as the sponsor agreed to finance their first year in Canada. This new feature was a source of discontent for religious groups, because not allowing sponsored refugees to access welfare benefits during the first year of resettlement was considered an unfair shift of responsibility from the government to private actors. However, the government wanted the religious groups to be less involved in the selection process and to make sure that if the refugees had to be chosen by the sponsors, then at least the first year of financial responsibility had to fall on the latter, to avoid newcomers drawing on the state's finances straight away.[27]

The relationship between church organisations and the government continued, although the terms of the debate became more and more 'adversarial'.[28] Church organisations continued to argue that beneficiaries of the scheme should be freely chosen and selected by their sponsors, regardless of their capacity to contribute to the Canadian economy, while still being able to rely on the Canadian welfare support from the very beginning of their sponsorship.[29] The Canadian government, however, continued to see the role of the private sponsors as conducive to integration and reception, but not involved in selection.[30] Little by little, from a position of mutual cooperation, the relationship deteriorated into lack of communication in the decade spanning between 1960 and 1970.[31] The programme went through years of stalemate and was nearly abandoned by church organisations, which dramatically reduced the numbers of sponsored refugees and which disappeared from public discourse.

Church engagement in private sponsorship reignited in the 1970s, to support the Chilean refugee crisis, following the coup of Salvador Allende.[32] By 1973 ties between church organisations and immigration officials were re-established and the sponsorship programme was ready to be revitalised.[33] As Cameron puts it, the churches' 'adversarial, "outsider" advocacy tactics, generated sufficient pressure to provoke a policy change, leading to the resettlement of thousands of Chilean refugees, many of them with church sponsorship'.[34]

[27] Cameron, above n 5, 28.
[28] ibid, 29.
[29] ibid.
[30] ibid.
[31] ibid.
[32] Kelley, Trebilcock, above n 8, 365–66. Church organisations put pressure on the Canadian government to take action in order to grant more exiles and asylum seekers refugee status. The Canadian Council of Churches heavily criticised the Canadian government for its slow response to the Chilean crisis, particularly in relation to the very slow response to processing refugee requests.
[33] Cameron, above n 5, 30–31.
[34] ibid, 30.

The private sponsorship of refugees programme was, for the first time, crystallised into law by the Immigration Act of 1976, which entered into force in 1978.[35] The need to codify into statute of something that had been good practice up until then perhaps found its roots in the difficulties experienced between private actors and the government in the previous 10 years. The provision on private sponsorship was included not to create something new but with the aim to recognise a phenomenon that had established itself as a practice in Canada over the previous years and, little by little, had become a reality.[36]

However, it is fair to say that the Immigration Act significantly changed Canadian refugee policy, as it formalised in law 'what had previously been an *ad hoc* approach to refugee determination and selection'.[37] The provision on private sponsorship was broad and not specific, to allow future elaboration.[38] The programme was properly tested when the Indochinese refugee crisis struck. After the Communist party took control of Vietnam in 1975, a great mass of Vietnamese people, fearing persecution, began to flee from the country. Canada's initial resistance to answer the to the call of these Vietnamese migrants was soon replaced by a striking engagement, owing also to the pressure of public opinion. Owing to the Mennonite Central Committee of Canada organisation (MCC Canada), a proper policy to put the flesh on the legislative bones of the private sponsorship programme was finally developed.[39] Master Agreements (between private sponsors and government) were created. Master Agreements allowed the introduction of national corporate bodies/organisations, in addition to groups of five people, that would take on the liability for sponsored refugees.[40] Master Agreements also curtailed the state's vetting responsibility on the individual sponsoring groups, shifting this responsibility to the agreement holders.[41] By June 1979, the Canadian government increased its intake of Vietnamese refugees to 12,000, 4,000 of whom were financed by Canadian private sponsors.[42]

Following the advances in private sponsorship triggered by the Indochinese crisis, the legal basis was organised around two main streams, as far as sponsors were concerned: sponsors could be organised groups joining an organisation holding a Master Agreement with the government, or groups of five or more individuals.[43]

[35] Moreover, in 2001 the Immigration and Refugee Protection Act was published, which specifies the sponsorship formats.

[36] Cameron, above n 5, 31. The author, quoting Janzen, above n 14, recalls that 'officials who worked in the Immigration Department at that time said they had not known what to expect from the private sponsorship provision. They had just felt that it would be good to have [in] the Act, to be used if necessary' (at 216–17).

[37] Kelley and Trebilcock, above n 8, 404.

[38] Cameron, above n 5, 31.

[39] ibid, 33.

[40] ibid. This allowed smaller groups that were not capable of taking on the full liability to come forward as sponsors, since the full liability would be borne by the Master Agreement holder. On this point see Labman, above n 3, 84.

[41] Labman, above n 3, 84.

[42] Kelley and Trebilcock, above n 8, 407.

[43] Cameron, above n 5, 33.

It is also noteworthy that the 1976 Act gave the power to the Cabinet to create designated classes of 'displaced and persecuted people' that could be granted refugee status outside the normal selection criteria. The Indochinese special class was introduced on 21 January 1979.[44] Designating the Indochinese as a class greatly helped in reducing the waiting times for their resettlement, as the need for protection and refugee status was taken for granted.[45] An individual could then apply to a Canadian mission abroad as a UN refugee or as a member of one of the classes. Back in Canada, the individual could be sponsored either by the government or under the private sponsorship programme for refugees.[46]

The full implications of private sponsorship of refugees in Canada were only fully grasped at the end of the Indochinese emergency. The Indochinese crisis strengthened the private sponsorship schemes. Moreover, it provided the opportunity to reinvigorate the relationship between private parties and the state. Interestingly, the private sponsorship programme was so successful that the Immigration Department began to plan for privately sponsored refugees in its refugee resettlement numbers.[47] Indeed, owing also to the private schemes, Canada was able to move from a position of looking at refugees 'as an ad hoc affair, into an enduring framework for refugee admissions and resettlement'.[48]

III. The Canadian Alternatives to State-Led Resettlement

A. The Classic Private Sponsorship of Refugees Scheme

The Immigration Act 1976 saw the establishment of the Government Assisted Resettlement Scheme (GAR)[49] and the Private Sponsorship of Refugees (PSR) scheme. The PSR scheme, with the implementation policy that followed, already contained the key features of what still today characterises the programmes for private sponsorship of refugees in Canada.

[44] Kelley and Trebilcock, above n 8, 406. The other two classes were Latin American Political Prisoners and Oppressed Persons and the Eastern European Self-Exiled Persons.

[45] Labman, above n 3, 90. See also S Lehr and B Dick, '"Naming" refugees in the Canadian Private Sponsorship of Refugees Program: Diverse Intentions and Consequences' in S Labman and G Cameron (eds), *Strangers to Neighbours: Refugee Sponsorship in Context* (Montreal, McGill-Queens University Press, 2000) 42, 45.

[46] Kelley and Trebilcock, above n 8, 404–5.

[47] Cameron, above n 5, 34.

[48] MJ Molloy and L Madokoro, 'Effecting Change: Civil Servants and Refugee Policy in 1970s Canada' (2017) 33 *Refuge: Canada's Journal on Refugees* 52, 60.

[49] Through the GAR programme, refugees in need of resettlement are identified by UNHCR. They receive government support for one year, according to the family's needs, or even less than one year, if the refugee becomes independent quickly. See Government of Canada, 'Financial support for Government-Assisted Refugees', available at: www.cic.gc.ca/english/helpcentre/results-by-topic.asp?st=11.2 (under 'How long does the support for government-assisted refugees last?').

As for today, the PSR scheme has its legal grounds in section 13(1) of the Immigration and Refugee Protection Act (IRPA) 2002,[50] which states that:

> A Canadian citizen or permanent resident, or a group of Canadian citizens or permanent residents, a corporation incorporated under a law of Canada or of a province or an unincorporated organization or association under federal or provincial law – or any combination of them – may sponsor a foreign national, subject to the regulations.[51]

The PSR scheme currently allows three types of sponsors. First, Sponsorship Agreement Holders (SAH) are allowed to sponsor refugees. These are recognised organisations that sign Agreements with the government of Canada to help and support refugees and have developed from the Master Agreements, which were mentioned earlier. Currently there are more than 120 SAHs in Canada, excluding Quebec.[52] An organisation can become a SAH by submitting an application to Immigration, Refugees and Citizenship Canada and by fulfilling some financial and criminal clearance checks.[53] Within this category, constituent groups can also sponsor a refugee but have to do so with the connection and under the responsibility of an SAH. What characterises the SAH sponsorship is the fact that the organisation does not have to sign an agreement for every sponsorship it would like to issue, but rather the umbrella agreement is capable of being used for multiple sponsorships.

Secondly, sponsors can be groups of five or more individuals – Canadian citizens or permanent residents – who decide to sponsor refugees to integrate within their communities. Finally, Community Sponsors, such like organisations, associations or corporations based in the location where refugees are expected to settle, without a formal Sponsorship Agreement with the government, can also sponsor refugees.

Under the PSR sponsor-referred scheme, the sponsors can support a specific refugee or a refugee family. This is called naming, as the sponsor has the facility to name the person/persons they want to help.[54] As seen before, this is a key feature of the Canadian sponsorship system, which was a characteristic well before the

[50] Immigration and Refugee Protection Act, S.C. 2001, c. 27, available at: laws.justice.gc.ca/eng/acts/i-2.5/FullText.html.

[51] Immigration and Refugee Protection Regulations SOR/2002-227, available at: laws-lois.justice.gc.ca/eng/regulations/sor-2002-227/FullText.html.

[52] The province of Quebec has its own jurisdiction over private sponsorship of refugees. Sponsors can be a group of people or individual legal persons. The financial responsibilities are very similar to those under the federal scheme.

[53] For more information see Government of Canada, 'Sponsor a refugee', available at: www.canada.ca/en/immigration-refugees-citizenship/services/refugees/help-outside-canada/private-sponsorship-program.html.

[54] Historically, refugees that are privately sponsored could be 'sponsor-referred' (naming), or 'visa office-referred'. The difference between the two is based on the fact that sponsor-referred refugees are chosen by the sponsor before their eligibility is finally assessed by Immigration, Refugees and Citizenship Canada, while the visa office-referred refugees have been chosen directly by Immigration, Refugees and Citizenship Canada; hence their eligibility has already been attested. The available data show that the majority of private sponsorships are sponsor-referred. On this point see Labman, above n 3, 85–86.

introduction of private sponsorship within the Immigration Act. The ability of the sponsor to name and choose the potential beneficiaries of the programme gives great flexibility and openness to the scheme. Indeed, 'sponsors may draw their referrals from anywhere in the world … as Canada's resettlement classes reach beyond the refugee definition to a broader consideration of individuals in need of protection'.[55] Concretely,

> the sponsoring group submits the name of a refugee or refugee family it is interested in sponsoring. The group may have obtained the referral from an overseas contact, a friend, community member, relative of a member of the organization, or elsewhere.[56]

The sponsorship application is submitted to the Resettlement Operation Centre in Ottawa (ROC-O).

The PSR programme has also inherited elements of additionality as its key feature, meaning that private sponsorship numbers are additional to the government-led resettlement programme. Indeed, as is highlighted in the government Guide to the Private Sponsorship of Refugees Program, the Canadian private sponsorship scheme aims to complement the government-assisted programme.[57] Historically, private sponsorship schemes were 'conceived as being limited only by the generosity and willingness of private Canadians'.[58] This traditional view, based on the belief that refugee numbers were impossible to plan in advance, given the unpredictability of refugee crises, was superseded by the 1976 Immigration Act, which required, on a yearly basis, a large governmental consultation on immigration intake and an advance announcement of the numbers to be admitted.[59] Practically speaking, the immigration minister decides on annual targets, after having consulted provincial governments, NGOs and UNHCR.[60] Ranges and targets are set both for government-led resettlement and privately sponsored refugees.[61] However, the current arrangement allows the possibility to request additional places.[62]

As far as additionality is concerned, more stringent directives were introduced in 2012. Indeed, since 2012 the PSR programme, when an SAH is the sponsor, has a global cap on the number of sponsorships that can be undertaken every year.[63] The

[55] ibid, 94.

[56] See Government of Canada, '2. Private Sponsorship of Refugees program' (2022), available at: www.canada.ca/en/immigration-refugees-citizenship/corporate/publications-manuals/guide-private-sponsorship-refugees-program/section-2.html, 2.10 1).

[57] Government of Canada, 'Guide to the Private Sponsorship of Refugees program, introduction', available at: www.canada.ca/en/immigration-refugees-citizenship/corporate/publications-manuals/guide-private-sponsorship-refugees-program/section-1.html.

[58] Labman, above n 3, 92.

[59] Molloy and Madokoro, above n 48, 58.

[60] Labman, above n 3, 56.

[61] UNCHR Resettlement Handbook, 'Country chapter: Canada', available at: www.unhcr.org/protection/resettlement/3c5e55594/unhcr-resettlement-handbook-country-chapter-canada.html, p 6, section 4.3.

[62] Labman, above n 3, 57.

[63] In 2011 the cap was on the number of refugees that could be sponsored from the missions of Nairobi, followed, for 2012, by the missions of Pretoria, Islamabad and Cairo. See Canadian Council for

Canadian government argued that this reform was necessary due to the backlog of unprocessed applications, caused by the fact that sponsors submitted more requests than the immigration officials were able to process.[64] Currently, the cap is reviewed on a yearly basis. In 2021, SAHs outside Quebec were given a cap of 12,500 global refugees, on top of the unused spaces from 2020.[65] No caps have been introduced for 'Groups of five' and 'Community sponsors', although changes in the law limited their ability to select who to sponsor. As a matter of fact, since 2011, Groups of five and Community sponsors can only sponsor recognised UNHCR refugees or state-recognised refugees. Following this change, SAH sponsorship increased while numbers of Group-of-five and Community sponsorship decreased.[66]

Designated classes are another key feature of the PSR programme. As seen above, these were introduced for the first time via Regulations under the Immigration Act of 1976 in 1979, to cope with a wave of Southeast Asian refugees and Cold War issues.[67] Originally, the classes were classified as Self-Exiled Persons, Indochinese, and Political Prisoners. In 2002 these three groups were incorporated into the broader class of 'Humanitarian Protected Persons Abroad Class', which also contained the Country of Asylum Class, of people that do not fall within the definition of refugee, and the Source of Country Class, of people that did not seek refuge in a third country, were nationals of specific countries included in the schedule of the Regulations[68] and were affected by civil war and armed conflict, or had been detained or imprisoned for expressing their rights, or fulfilled the refugee definition, aside from not residing in a third country.[69] Until 2011, these were the recognised classes, in addition to the Convention Refugee Abroad Class, composed of those who fulfil the Geneva Convention's refugee definition.[70] The Source of Country Class was repealed from the Regulations in 2011.[71] Despite the criticism,[72] the government justified repealing the Source of Country Class on the grounds that it would allow Canada to better allocate resources and to focus

Refugees, 'Important changes in Canada's Private Sponsorship of Refugees Program' (2013), available at: ccrweb.ca/en/changes-private-sponsorship-refugees.

[64] IV Haren, 'Canada's Private Sponsorship Model Represents and Complementary Pathway for refugee Resettlement'(2021) Migration Policy Institute, available at: www.migrationpolicy.org/article/canada-private-sponsorship-model-refugee-resettlement under 'Caps on new sponsorships'.

[65] Government of Canada, 'Global cap for sponsorship agreement holders' (2021), available at: www.canada.ca/en/immigration-refugees-citizenship/corporate/mandate/policies-operational-instructions-agreements/timely-protection-privately-sponsored-refugees.html.

[66] Labman, above n 3, 76.

[67] Lehr and Dick, above n 45, 45.

[68] Immigration and Refugee Protection Regulations, above n 51. In 2011, when the source of country was removed, the countries included in the schedule were Colombia, the Democratic Republic of Congo, El Salvador, Guatemala, Sierra Leone and Sudan.

[69] Labman, above n 3, 60.

[70] The Convention Relating to the Status of Refugees of 28 July 1951 (Geneva).

[71] Immigration and Refugee Protection Act, Regulations Amending the Immigration and Refugee Protection Regulations, PC 2011-1162 (2011), available at: gazette.gc.ca/rp-pr/p2/2011/2011-10-26/html/sor-dors222-eng.html.

[72] Canadian Council for Refugees, above n 63.

on priority refugee situations.[73] Despite abandoning the Source of Country Class, it seems that the Country of Asylum Class has still been capable of broadening the number of people that can be sponsored, outside the UNHCR definition of refugee.[74]

As far as the financial responsibility is concerned, the sponsor is financially responsible for one year (or less, if the beneficiaries of the programme become independent before 12 months). In some cases, responsibility can be extended to more than one year but to no more than three years.[75] In terms of finances, the sponsor should at least match the rates of the Resettlement Assistance Programme.[76] which broadly covers the costs of settling in Canada (Start Up Allowance), monthly income support and the costs of transportation.[77] Put in very simple terms, sponsors take on the responsibility to cover what the state would otherwise cover as social welfare.[78] Indeed, over the period of sponsorship, privately sponsored refugees cannot claim federal or provincial government assistance.[79] At the end of the sponsorship period, in case the individual or family are not yet capable of providing for themselves, the beneficiaries of the scheme can rely on the provincial government (income support for low income families). Privately sponsored refugees, as well as those sponsored by the government, are responsible for paying for their medical tests and travel to Canada, and they normally borrow the money from the federal government.[80]

As far as residence rights are concerned, once in Canada, privately sponsored refugees immediately receive permanent residence status – via a permanent residence visa, according to section 139(1) Immigration and Refugee Protection Regulations.

In case of sponsorship breakdown, Immigration, Refugees and Citizenship Canada (IRCC) will try to negotiate a solution between the sponsor and the resettled refugees to work out responsibilities. If the sponsorship group is found to be at fault, they will still be required to fulfil their duties, including the financial ones, until the end of the 12 months. On the other hand, if the sponsoring group is found blameless, it is absolved of any further responsibility. IRCC will have to issue a formal notice of sponsorship breakdown, which cancels the sponsorship

[73] Immigration and Refugee Protection Act, above n 71, under 'objectives'. The government also pointed out that 'As a discretionary measure, the Minister may also choose to offer admission to Canada to vulnerable persons who do not qualify for the refugee classes by using subsection 25(1), 25.1(1) or 25.2(1) of the Immigration and Refugee Protection Act'.

[74] Lehr and Dick, above n 45, 45.

[75] Immigration and Refugee Protection Regulations, above n 51, Regulation 154(1)(a), 154(2) and 154(3).

[76] See Refugee Sponsorship Training Program, 'Overview of Sponsorship Responsibilities', available at: www.rstp.ca/en/sponsorship-responsibilities/responsibilities/.

[77] See Refugee Sponsorship Training Program, 'RAP (Resettlement Assistance Program) Rates', available at: www.rstp.ca/en/bvor/rap-rates/.

[78] Labman, above n 3, 82.

[79] ibid, 86.

[80] ibid.

agreement, to allow the sponsored refugees to get municipal or provincial funding and benefits.[81] An example of an ad hoc safety net that is provided is that of the city of Winnipeg, in the province of Manitoba, which established an 'assurance scheme' in case of sponsorship breakdown due to a sponsor's financial difficulties.[82]

B. A Brief Overview of the Blended Visa Office-Referred and the Joint Assistance Sponsorship Programmes

In 2013 Canada introduced another scheme, called the Blended Visa Office-Referred Program (BVOR). This programme allows sponsoring groups to sponsor refugees identified by the UNHCR. In return for not allowing naming, the government offers more funding. The programme builds upon previous pilot blended programmes that targeted specific groups of refugees since 1994.[83] Once the UNHCR has identified the refugees that would be entitled to resettlement, and the screening is completed by the Canadian authorities, including security and medical checks, the BVOR programme puts the refugees in contact with the potential sponsors. Just as for the PSR scheme, sponsors can be SAHs, Group-of-five or Community sponsors. Sponsors have a choice on the BVOR list to decide which nationality to sponsor.[84] The sponsor is financially responsible for six months, on top of start-up costs, and for one year for broader emotional support. The government provides up to six months of financial support after the refugees arrive in Canada.[85] BVOR was originally established to replace GAR;[86] hence additionality was not envisaged. To date, it is yet to be seen whether the programme can develop further and become more sustainable.[87]

[81] See Welcome to Ontario, 'What Happens When a Sponsorship Breaks Down?', available at: welcome-ontario.ca/en/articles/what-happens-when-a-sponsorship-breaks-down#:~:text=Breakdown%20process&text=They%20should%20contact%20the%20Resettlement,to%20fix%20the%20issue%20independently.

[82] J Kumin, 'Welcoming Engagement: How Private Sponsorship Can Strengthen Refugee Resettlement in the European Union' (2015) Brussels: Migration Policy Institute Europe, available at: www.migrationpolicy.org/research/welcoming-engagement-how-private-sponsorship-can-strengthen-refugee-resettlement-european, 10, fn 38.

[83] See R McNally, 'Blended Visa Office-Referred Program: Perspectives and Experiences from Rural Nova Scotia' in S Labman and G Cameron (eds), *Strangers to Neighbours: Refugee Sponsorship in Context* (Montreal, McGill-Queens University Press, 2000) 135. See also Labman, above n 3, 98–104.

[84] ibid, 137.

[85] Labman, above n 3, 86.

[86] Canadian Council for Refugees, 'Blended Visa Office-Referred (BVOR) Program CCR Positions' (2018), available at: ccrweb.ca/sites/ccrweb.ca/files/bvor-feb-2018-positions.pdf, 2.

[87] The programme started as a small resettlement scheme but soon developed in response to the Syrian migration crisis, reaching its apex between 2015 and 2018. However, as for today, the programme seems to struggle to involve sponsors and to remain a sustainable scheme of resettlement. For example, many sponsors in Canada are motivated by family links and value highly the opportunity of being able to select and name the people they are going to sponsor, and the lack of this feature is considered a limitation in the scheme. On this point see McNally, above n 83, 135 and 142.

Canada currently also hosts the Joint Assistance Sponsorship (JAS) programme. This is available only to SAHs and their constituent groups and targets refugees with special needs.[88] Sponsors work with IRCC and the Canadian government to provide emotional support for up to 24 months to the resettled individuals. All of the financial costs are covered by the government.[89] Labman specifies that, in terms of numbers, JAS cases are considered to fall within the GAR programme.[90] Indeed, the support given by the sponsors is non-financial and refugees are identified and referred by visa officers, rather than by the sponsors themselves.[91]

C. Some Considerations on the Canadian Privatised Protection of Refugees: The 'Public–Private Pull'

The previous sections have explained how private sponsorship of refugees was initiated and developed in Canada over the years, up until today. The programme, while remaining fundamentally faithful to its origins, has undergone some notable changes. The suppression of the Source of Country Class; caps on SAH sponsorship; the addition of the legal requirement of being a Convention or state-recognised refugee to be potentially eligible for Group-of-five or Community sponsorship; and the introduction of the BVOR scheme are some of the most notable ones.

These changes suggest that the Canadian approach has been slowly but steadily more and more influenced by governmental actions. In her book, *Crossing the Law's Borders*, Labman describes the evolution of the Canadian sponsorship programme as a 'Public–Private Pull'.[92] When, in 1990, a review of the private sponsorship programme began, the government found that a key challenging aspect of the programme, in need of change, was 'maintaining the focus on refugee protection in the drive for family reunification through sponsorship'.[93] As a matter of fact, the Canadian scheme has always been characterised by an extension of the protection to categories that go beyond the Convention Refugee Abroad Class. The sponsors have always negotiated with the government, over the years, for the possibility to influence the eligibility and admissibility criteria. The current privatised protection of refugees in Canada – including the naming element and the introduction and development of the humanitarian class – are the fruit of the strenuous work

[88] Special needs may be 'trauma from violence or torture, medical disabilities, the effects of systemic discrimination, or a large number of family members': https //www.canada.ca/en/immigration-refugees-citizenship/services/refugees/help-outside-canada/private-sponsorship-program/joint-assistance-program.html.

[89] Refugee Sponsorship Training Programme, 'The Joint Assistance Sponsorship (JAS) Program' (2023), available at: www.rstp.ca/en/jas/joint-assistance-sponsorships/#:~:text=Joint%20Assistance%20Sponsorship%20(JAS)%20refers,in%20Canada%20than%20other%20refugees.

[90] Labman, above n 3, 85.

[91] ibid.

[92] ibid, 87.

[93] ibid, 93.

of the private sector in trying to increase the scope of the programme beyond the Convention's limits. The flexibility of the private Canadian scheme inevitably made the programme suitable also for family reunification purposes. Indeed, those who do not find it easy to enter the country by relying on the classic family reunification categories can attempt the route of private sponsorship. While wanting to reunite with families is a perfectly natural desire, and family reunification is the most expedited path to integration, the concern is that, in this way, the resettlement places are allocated to people that do not need them the most. The Canadian government, conscious of this concern, initially decided to tackle it drastically, often refusing sponsor-referred names between 1998 and 2007.[94] Eventually, government action became less draconian and more balanced, allowing the introduction of a series of reforms such as BVOR and caps on SAH against no caps on programmes supported by other sponsors, as long as the beneficiaries can claim refugee status. These reforms show that the 'Public–Private Pull' seems now have found a compromise between the governmental concern to keep the private programme truly open to those most in need and the drive of the private stakeholders to maintain their privilege to select the beneficiaries with no regard to strict legal categories.

IV. Private Sponsorship: Definitions, Characteristics and Classification

To date, we do not have a common, standardised definition of private sponsorship of refugees. This is partly because the available models are so variegated and differentiated that it is difficult to come to a general definition that is approved and accepted by all. However, the rich Canadian experience of private sponsorship, including its blended form and JAS experience, is a helpful yardstick that can aid the identification of some key features of this phenomenon.

In the previous chapter it was shown that key policy reports by Kumin, Fratzke and the ERN try to identify the common characteristics that characterise private sponsorship of refugees. Kumin suggests that private sponsorship arrangements should be characterised by two core elements: the individual, group or organisation takes the responsibility of providing financial, emotional and social support for a period of time, and sponsors have the option of naming the refugee they want to support.[95] Interestingly, Kumin does not seem to include the element of additionality as a central and identifying feature of private sponsorship of refugees. This is not surprising. The Canadian experience shows indeed that additionality is not always envisaged – like in the Canadian JAS scheme – and in some European examples that will be later analysed. Fratzke, on the other hand, provides a description that refers

[94] Labman, above n 2, 69.
[95] Kumin, above n 82, 3.

to the element of additionality. She highlights how some sponsorships do not count towards any government quotas, as they are additional to the numbers pledged by governments for their state-led sponsorship programmes. This is currently how the Canadian PSR scheme works. However, indirectly confirming Kumin, Fratzke also adds that naming, additionality and the level of sponsors' responsibility are not necessarily cumulative requirements, and that sponsorship can involve 'all – or some combination – of these core elements'.[96] The ERN seems to draw from the lines traced by Fratzke, by confirming the three core features suggested in her report and recognising that, in any case, not all programmes would conform to all these elements.[97]

More recently, the European Commission too decided to engage with this topic. Its feasibility report of 2018, while not attempting to offer a precise definition or classification, highlights a very important element that marks all schemes for private sponsorship of refugees and expands the scope of what can be classified as one – that is, the fact that private schemes require a shift in responsibilities from the state to private parties.[98] As a matter of fact, the responsibility shift can occur at different phases of the programme, depending on how it has been arranged and agreed by the state and private actors. In practice, the responsibility transfer from the state to the private sponsor may simply affect the integration process. This is typical, for example, of the Canadian JAS programme, briefly referred to before, where the sponsors are required to offer emotional support, while the costs are covered by the government. However, the shift could also, and more frequently it does, involve finances, and may do so in different ways, such as pre-departure costs, rent costs, utility bills, food, language courses, medical expenses, etc.

Probably the most inclusive description is the one used by the UNHCR, presented in 'Complementary Pathways for Admission of Refugees to Third Countries: Key Considerations'.[99] This is a follow-up document on what was agreed by the Global Compact on Refugees back in 2018. In this document the UNHCR describes sponsorship of refugees (or, as it is referred to in the document, community sponsorship of refugees) as follows:

> Community sponsorship of refugees allows individuals, groups of individuals or organizations to come together to provide financial, emotional and practical support for the reception and integration of refugees admitted to third countries. A clear distinction can

[96] S Fratzke, 'Engaging Communities in Refugee Protection: the Potential of Private Sponsorship in Europe' (2017) Brussels Migration Policy Institute Europe, available at: www.migrationpolicy.org/research/engaging-communities-refugee-protection-potential-private-sponsorship-europe, 1.

[97] ERN scoping paper 'Private Sponsorship in Europe: expanding complementary pathways for refugee resettlement' (2017), available at: www.iom.int/sites/g/files/tmzbdl486/files/documents/ERN%2Bscoping-paper-Private-Sponsorship-in-Europe.pdf, 11.

[98] European Commission, 'Study on the feasibility and added value of sponsorship schemes as possible pathway to safe channels for admission to the EU, including resettlement' final report (2018), available at: op.europa.eu/en/publication-detail/-/publication/1dbb0873-d349-11e8-9424-01aa75ed71a1, 4.

[99] UN High Commissioner for Refugees (UNHCR) 'Complementary Pathways for Admission of Refugees to Third Countries: Key Considerations' (2019), available at: www.refworld.org/docid/5cebf3fc4.html, 8.

> be made between community sponsorship as a complementary pathway for admission and community sponsorship as a tool to support refugees admitted through other pathways. As a pathway for admission, community sponsorship programmes allow sponsors to support the entry and stay of nominated refugees in third countries. Conversely as a tool, community sponsorship can be used as a mechanism to engage individuals and communities in the reception and integration of refugees arriving through resettlement programmes, or other pathways, such as educational pathways or humanitarian visas. Community sponsorship programmes that offer a pathway for admission in complement to resettlement and that are protection-sensitive can serve to expand the number of refugees who have access to protection and solutions and contribute to enhanced responsibility-sharing.

As can be noted, the UNHCR too prefers to describe the phenomenon, rather than to offer a synthetic definition of it. Unpacking this description will help highlight the key characteristics of private sponsorship schemes. In order to do so, the description above is broken down as follows:

1) 'Community sponsorship of refugees allows individuals, groups of individuals or organizations …'. The UNHCR uses the term community sponsorship to refer to schemes funded by private stakeholders and schemes funded by non-state organisations. Often, in the literature, the terms community sponsorship and private sponsorship are used interchangeably, as they both refer to the private nature of the funding bestowed by the sponsors, be they individuals or communities. This is the approach that is adopted in this book, although not by the UNHCR, as it will be evidenced below.[100]
2) '… to provide financial, emotional and practical support for the reception and integration of refugees admitted to third countries'. Like the reports discussed above, the UNHCR recognises that that the shift of responsibility from the state to the sponsor implies some financial, emotional and practical support to be offered to the beneficiaries of the programme.
3) 'A clear distinction can be made between community sponsorship as a complementary pathway for admission and community sponsorship as a tool to support refugees admitted through other pathways'. The UNHRC, unlike the previous accounts, specifies that the definition of community sponsorship of refugees covers two types of modalities, which are the base of the distinction between private sponsorship and community sponsorship, that the UNHCR has been proposing.[101]
4) 'As a pathway for admission, community sponsorship programmes allow sponsors to support the entry and stay of nominated refugees in third countries'. These schemes have been more recently described by the UNHCR as private sponsorship.[102] The UNHCR specifies that the beneficiaries of these schemes are nominated (naming).

[100] On this point see the Introduction to this book.
[101] UNHCR, 'Community Sponsorship' available at: www.unhcr.org/what-we-do/build-better-futures/long-term-solutions/local-integration/community-sponsorship.
[102] ibid.

5) 'Community sponsorship programmes that offer a pathway for admission in complement to resettlement and that are protection-sensitive can serve to expand the number of refugees who have access to protection and solutions'. The UNHCR subtly refers to the concept of additionality, as a key characteristic of what they now refer to as private sponsorship of refugees by saying that it 'can serve to expand the number of refugees'. The UNHCR recognises that additionality may be optional.
6) 'Conversely as a tool, community sponsorship can be used as a mechanism to engage individuals and communities in the reception and integration of refugees arriving through resettlement programmes, or other pathways …'. This is now referred to as community sponsorship by the UNHCR, in clear distinction with private sponsorship.[103] Unlike private sponsorship of refugees, community sponsorship accompany government-led resettlement schemes or other forms of entry and engage the sponsors, at different levels, in the phase of reception and integration. This is the case for the JAS programme in Canada, where the cases are counted within the GAR programme, while still relying on private sponsors to help in the integration phase of the beneficiaries.

The UNHCR's approach has proposed a broad description, which is capable of encompassing various forms of expression of the phenomenon of refugee sponsorship. The categorisation offered by this book is based on the holistic nature of the programmes, that is whether they are, intuitively, more similar to resettlement in the way the operate, or whether they amount to forms of admission that are different from resettlement. In this sense, it differs from the UNHCR description. Indeed, rather than distinguishing the various experiences of sponsorship between sponsored resettlement or sponsored entry through other pathways (community sponsorship), and pathways to admission (private sponsorship)[104], it applies a more general approach, in order to group together experiences that are, overall, similar. This is done to better highlight their differences and common traits. While most of the European experiences fall within the first category (programmes similar to resettlement), there are also some notable examples, that can be included in the second one (programmes that are different from resettlement).[105]

[103] ibid.

[104] See NF Tan, 'A study for the potential of introducing a community sponsorship program for refugees in Sweden', scoping report prepared for UNHCR's Representation for the Nordic and Baltic countries (2020), available at: www.unhcr.org/neu/wp-content/uploads/sites/15/2020/12/UNHCR-Study-on-Community-Sponsorship-Program-in-Sweden.pdf, 7.

[105] See Chapters 3 and 4 of this book. It is also worth noting that, at the time of writing, the opportunity for the introduction of community sponsorship pilots is being debated in Sweden and Finland. On the Swedish debate see Tan, above n 104. On Finland see K Turtiainen, H Sapir, 'Feasibility study on the potential of community-based sponsorship in Finland' Publications of the Ministry of Economic Affairs and Employment 2021:37, available at julkaisut.valtioneuvosto.fi/bitstream/handle/10024/163177/TEM_2021_37.pdf. It is also worth noting that at the 2019 first Global Refugee Forum Malta too discussed the introduction of pilot refugee programmes. As far as Malta is concerned, a feasibility study on the opportunity to introduce private sponsorship of refugees is expected (see Global Compact on Refugees, 'Pledges and contributions' reference GRF-00646, available at globalcompactrefugees.org/pledges-contributions).

However, it should also be noted that reality, in all its complexity, goes often beyond descriptions and classifications. This is particularly the case for private sponsorship schemes, which are proving to be very malleable and flexible tools and are currently trialled in different forms and shapes. For this reason, it is worth reminding the reader that, at times, some schemes might look as they do not neatly fit within one group or the other. As a matter of fact, this classification is useful to the narrative of this book to describe the various programmes in a systematic manner and it is also relevant in the final analysis proposed in Chapter five. However, this does not imply that this is the only or best way to look at the various private sponsorship schemes, as other descriptions or key characteristics of the programmes could be used as discriminants to propose an alternative conceptualisation and analysis of the phenomenon.[106]

Following the distinction proposed by this book, the next two chapters will look at the following, respectively:

Chapter three: Under the umbrella of sponsorship of refugees that operatively resemble resettlement, this chapter will include the experience of the humanitarian corridors in Italy, France, Belgium and Andorra. These schemes are characterised by a substantive shift in responsibility from the state to the sponsor, both in terms of emotional and financial support. These schemes are not defined by a strict naming element, in comparison to Canada. However, within the European context, humanitarian corridors are the approved schemes that grant wide freedom to the sponsors in choosing the potential beneficiaries. Indeed, as it will be seen in the next chapter, the selection criteria are broader than those included in the Geneva Convention. Furthermore, it is effectively the task of the sponsor's partners, acting in loco, to interview and choose those that they think would benefit the most from the programme. Finally, these schemes are additional, although subject to a quota agreed with the relevant government.

Similarly, the now expired programmes in Poland, Slovakia and Czech Republic are included in this category. These schemes allowed entry to small groups of Christians from Syria via religious organisations. These schemes were also characterised by naming and additionality.

Moreover, the very recent Portuguese Community Sponsorship pilot is also examined within Chapter three. While initially neither naming nor additionality were envisaged, in late 2023 a naming stream was opened, with the government also committing to looking into reserving specific quotas for private sponsorship, as and when the pilot is eventually judged successful and confirmed.

[106] For example, some scholars have proposed another distinction that departs from a simple comparison of features that characterise the individual schemes, trying to develop a classification based on how the elements of the various private sponsorships could be affected by their national cultural context. Within this frame, the authors have proposed a classification based on sponsor-related design choices – whether based on sponsoring entities, legal residence of the sponsors or time of sponsor's commitment –, and beneficiary-related design choices, mainly based on the status of the beneficiaries of the programme upon arrival. For more information about this classification see D Bertram, A Maleki and N Karsten, 'Factoring in Societal Culture in Policy Transfer Design: the Proliferation of Private Sponsorship of Refugees' (2020) 21 *Journal of International Migration & Integration* 253.

Some other schemes are included in Chapter three. These are the UK experience of Community Sponsorship and the German programme, NesT. The difference between these schemes and the previous ones is that, while additionality is envisaged in these programmes too, naming is not allowed. The UK programme was originally conceived as part of fulfilling the government resettlement quotas. Since 2021 however, the UK has embraced additionality. Naming is not allowed, and the beneficiaries are chosen by strictly applying the criteria of the UK Resettlement Scheme – a government-led programme. Likewise, the German NesT programme is additional and naming is not allowed.

Finally, Chapter three will also include the Community Sponsorship Ireland scheme, the Auzolana II programme of the Basque Country and the Belgian Community Sponsorship programme. These are schemes where neither additionality to state quotas nor naming are allowed.

Chapter four: Under the category of sponsorship as admissions different from resettlement, the expired Irish, Swiss and German family reunification schemes will be analysed. These temporary schemes, while tailored around family reunification rules and categorised by some as humanitarian admission schemes, had a strong private sponsorship component, particularly in relation to the various responsibilities borne by the sponsor.

Moreover, the UK Homes for Ukraine scheme is also included in this analysis. The scheme consists of a temporary humanitarian admission of three years. Despite being generously funded by the British government, the role of the sponsor in providing the beneficiaries with accommodation is crucial.

Likewise, also the St Marino humanitarian corridor, the Portuguese private relocation scheme and the Vatican humanitarian corridors will be considered, as they effectively amount to private ancillary initiatives to aid the intra-EU relocation system. As a matter of fact, the beneficiaries of the programmes are selected from within the European Union and relocated within its borders, and the private sponsors support this process.

V. Conclusion

The first part of this chapter looked at the Canadian experience of private sponsorship of refugees. The reason behind this choice is twofold. First of all, it was important to review the Canadian experience in order to clarify how the phenomenon of private sponsorship of refugees originated. Furthermore, the Canadian experience helps us to better understand the nuances that characterise the structure and the application of the models of private sponsorship in Europe. This approach has allowed us to enter the second part of the chapter with a better appreciation of what private sponsorship of refugees is, and to propose a logical classification of the different European schemes, which is going to be used for the development of the two following chapters of this book, as outlined above.

Importantly, in this chapter the theme of private versus state relationships has started to emerge. The example of the 'Public–Private Pull' on the shift of the private Canadian sponsorship scheme from resettlement to family reunification, and the subsequent legislative changes to the programme, is emblematic of the fact that the state, after all, considered the programme to be a concession, and not a relinquishment of sovereignty. As Labman, quoting Hathaway reports, 'the government agreed to permit Canadian organisations and groups of individuals to privately sponsor the admission of Convention refugees and designated class members from abroad'.[107]

[107] Labman, above n 3, 89 – quote from J Hathaway, 'Selective Concern: An Overview of Refugee Law in Canada' (1987–88) 33 *McGill Law Journal* 676, 685.

3

Private Sponsorship of Refugees as a Resettlement Tool

I. Introduction

This chapter will focus on private sponsorship of refugees that are linked to or resemble resettlement. The European experiences of this kind of private sponsorship, to date, include programmes that provide protection that is similar to state resettlement (eg they target vulnerable people and they provide a durable solution).

As far as the analysis proposed by this chapter is concerned, sections II, III and IV will be dedicated to those European schemes that support state-led resettlement programmes and that more resemble the original Canadian model. These are programmes that include the features of naming and additionality. In this group are the European humanitarian corridors of Italy, France, Belgium and Andorra. Furthermore, this part of the chapter also covers the now expired smaller projects hosted by Poland, Slovakia and Czech Republic, that particularly targeted Christian refugees during the Syrian crisis, and the Portuguese Community Sponsorship pilot.

Sections V and VI of the chapter will then focus on schemes that are slightly more distant from the classic PSR Canadian model, since they maintain the additionality element, but lack the naming. Within this group, the chapter will refer to the Community Sponsorship programme in the UK and to the German NesT programme.

Finally, sections VII, VIII and IX of the chapter will look at Community Sponsorship Ireland, the Spanish Auzolana II programme, and at the Community Sponsorship programme in Belgium, as examples of private sponsorship schemes that lack both the elements of additionality and naming.

Finally, section X of this chapter will provide some conclusions. The section will identify the advantages and shortcomings of this category of private sponsorship, in order to identify broader key issues. This rationalisation will be particularly useful in view of the analysis contained in Chapter five.

II. Humanitarian Corridors

Humanitarian corridors aim to assist the most vulnerable people who find themselves in third countries. After the selection process and security checks have been carried out, the sponsored individuals are allowed to travel to the safe hosting country, where they will be allowed to apply for asylum. The sponsored individuals or families are normally relocated in the area where members of the sponsoring organisation are based, in order to receive better support and more chance of integration. There are several humanitarian corridors currently operating in Europe. This chapter will look at them in turn.

A. The Italian Humanitarian Corridors

Italy has run a state-led resettlement programme since 2015.[1] The programme normally works on a two-year cycle.[2] It provides assistance to a limited number of refugees, according to the numbers pledged by Italy on biennial basis. The Italian humanitarian corridor projects operate in parallel with the state-led resettlement scheme, adding to the overall number of refugees entitled to protection.[3]

The humanitarian corridor initiative originates from Italy. The first pilot humanitarian corridor programme was established through a memorandum of understanding, signed by the Italian Minister of the Interior and the Italian Minister of Foreign Affairs, with the Catholic Community of St Egidio, the Federation of Evangelical Churches and the Waldensian Board.[4]

On 3 October 2013, a boat carrying 500 migrants from Libya to Italy sank off the coast of the island of Lampedusa. In the incident, 155 people were rescued, while more than 360 died.[5] The shock caused by this episode triggered intense political debate. The Italian government initially decided to fund the 'Mare Nostrum' operation, whose scope was to rescue boat immigrants coming from north Africa.

[1] The willingness to commit to such an important task came following the positive experience of the pilot project run from the Al Tanf camp in Syria in 2009.

[2] For more information on the Italian state-led scheme see UNHCR Resettlement Handbook, 'Country chapter: Italy', available at: www.unhcr.org/uk/media/unhcr-resettlement-handbook-country-chapter-italy.

[3] In addition to state-led resettlement and humanitarian corridors, Italy also introduced a higher education pathway, called UNICORE, in 2022. This is organised by the UNHCR, the Italian Ministry of Foreign Affairs and International Cooperation, Caritas Italiana, Diaconia Valdese, Centro Astalli and the Ghandi Charity. Through this scheme students receive scholarships and are housed in university halls. For more information see Share Network, 'Resettlement and Community Sponsorship across Europe', available at: www.share-network.eu/articles-and-resources/sponsorship.

[4] The idea of a private sponsor had already been experimented with in Italy by the Turco-Napolitano law (law n 40/1998) which, at Art 21, allowed Italian citizens to sponsor foreign workers in order to facilitate their integration in the Italian labour market. This provision has now been repealed.

[5] See Rai news, 'Migranti. Strage 3 ottobre 2013, Lampedusa ricorda le 368 vittime', 3 October 2021, available at: www.rainews.it/archivio-rainews/articoli/migranti-strage-3-ottobre-lampedusa-ricordo-vittime-0ac90280-80d6-4748-b903-483781d5502e.html.

The operation closed in 2014. On 18 April 2015, another tragedy at sea occurred. This time 675 Eritrean citizens died and only 28 survived.[6] This further tragic incident prompted various Christian communities to think about concrete ways to prevent the reoccurrence of these tragedies, as it became evident that the state could not act alone. Following the tragedy, the ecclesiastical leaders of St Egidio Community, the Federation of the Evangelical Churches and the Waldensian Board created a working group of experts to discuss viable ways to reduce deaths at sea. The group soon agreed that limiting the scope of their work to proposing rescue operations was not enough. Indeed, what came out of the discussion between the experts was the necessity of opening new legal channels for regular migration.

The working group of experts tried to develop a solution that allowed the opening of new legal channels. This task did not prove easy. Indeed, the targeted people were almost entirely immigrants in vulnerable situations, who could only be legally admitted in Italy as refugees. However, to apply for asylum and to become a refugee, the candidate necessarily has to make the request within the state's borders. How to bring immigrants safely to Italy was a conundrum almost insuperable. Initially, the group of experts suggested the option of lobbying Parliament to change the current Italian immigration law,[7] in order to allow asylum applications from abroad. However, this option was soon found to be unfeasible, particularly because the issue was pressing, and the law would have taken too long to be amended. The working group then proposed a more effective legislative alternative. Indeed, they suggested relying on Article 25 of the EU Visa Code.[8] This article allows EU Member States to issue a visa with limited territorial validity under certain conditions, and also when 'the Member State concerned considers it necessary on humanitarian grounds … to derogate from the principle that the entry conditions laid down in Article 5(1)(a), (c), (d) and (e) of the Schengen Border Code must be fulfilled'. The words 'humanitarian grounds' are not clearly defined but practice has shown that states normally issue these visas, on a small scale, for health and protection reasons.[9] Relying on Article 25 of the EU Visa Code seemed the perfect solution to allow the successful implementation

[6] See BBC news, 'Mediterranean migrants: Hundreds feared dead after boat capsizes', 19 April 2015, available at: www.bbc.com/news/world-europe-32371348.

[7] Immigration is regulated in Italy by Law 189/2002, better known as Legge Bossi-Fini, from the names of the two politicians that promoted it (Legge 30 Luglio 2002 n 189 Modifica alla normativa in materia di immigrazione e di asilo, available at: www.normattiva.it/uri-res/N2Ls?urn:nir:stato:legge:2002;189).

[8] Regulation (EC) No 810/2009 of the European Parliament and of the Council of 13 July 2009 establishing a Community Code on Visas (Visa Code) OJ L 243, 15.9.2009, 1–58, 14.

[9] See K Bianchini, 'Humanitarian Admission to Italy through Humanitarian Visas and Corridors' in MC Foblets and L Leboeuf (eds), *Humanitarian Admission to Europe* (Baden-Baden, Nomos/Hart Publishing, 2020) 157, 162.

of the humanitarian corridor programmes. Indeed, this provision would have allowed the sponsored candidates to receive Art 25 temporary EU visas in the third country and to gain safe passage to Italy. Once in the Italian territory, the candidate could have immediately applied for asylum at the Territorial Commission for Immigration.[10]

This potential solution was proposed to the Italian Ministry of the Interior and to the Italian Ministry of Foreign Affairs. Initially, the proposal struggled to gain traction due to some bureaucratic difficulties, mainly linked to the lack of previous initiatives of this kind to use as benchmark. However, eventually, the Italian government began to look at this initiative favourably. One of the underlying reasons for this shift may be connected to the fact that Italy, at the time, was struggling to gain credibility in Europe in relation to how the government had managed to deal with immigration. Italy was under pressure to show that it was moving in the right direction, and embracing the humanitarian corridor initiative might have looked like a way forward.[11]

The legal mechanism that was chosen to carry out this project was a memorandum of understanding (in Italian '*protocollo*'). This is a non-legally binding document, aimed at reaching a 'common goal'.[12] The first memorandum was signed on 15 December 2015, by the Minister of the Interior, the Minister of International Affairs and of International Cooperation, the Community of St Egidio, The Italian Federation of Evangelical Churches and the Waldensian Board. This first protocol aimed to resettle 1,000 people between 2016 and 2017. The recipient country of this first humanitarian corridor was Lebanon.[13] By the end of 2017, 1,000 people, mainly of Syrian nationality, were resettled from Lebanon to Italy. The memorandum was renewed on 7 November 2017 for an additional 1,000 people, to be resettled between 2018 and 2019.[14] The agreement was renewed again on

[10] It should be noted that relying on Art 25 of the Visa Code is currently at the discretion of the Member States. Following Case C-638/16, *X and X v État Belge* EU:C:2017:173, the idea of relying on Art 25 for a general EU endorsement of the humanitarian corridors scheme has been ruled out. However, it has been argued that humanitarian corridors could be applied and embraced by the EU by relying on a broader interpretation of the principle of *non refoulment*. On this point see C Ricci, 'The Necessity for Alternative Legal Pathways: The Best Practice of Humanitarian Corridors Opened by Private Sponsors in Italy' (2020) 21 *German Law Journal* 265, 271, 277–78. Furthermore, for a detailed explanation of the background on the issue of EU humanitarian visas see C Siccardi, 'Quali Vie di Ingresso Legale per i Richiedenti Protezione in Europa? Contesto Europeo e Costituzionale' (2022) 2 *Diritto, Immigrazione e Cittadinanza* 75, 87.

[11] Information gathered from the conversation with Professor Paolo Naso, political scientist at Università La Sapienza (Rome), member of the 'working group of experts to discuss viable ways to reduce deaths at sea', on 9 February 2022.

[12] Bianchini, above n 9, 163.

[13] Originally, the first *protocollo* aimed to target Lebanon and Morocco. Lebanon and Morocco were chosen because of their status of being transit countries and for the links that some of the faith-based organisations already had in loco. However, the Moroccan scheme was not implemented, due to a step back from the Moroccan government. Bianchini, above n 9, 165.

[14] E Cappello, 'Corridoi umanitari: accoglienza, integrazione e contagio', 2018/2019 tesi del corso di laurea in scienze internazionali, dello sviluppo e della cooperazione, University of Turin, under the

5 August 2021, with the target of 1,000 people to be resettled within the following two years.[15]

The second memorandum of understanding was signed by the Minister of Interior, the Minister of International Affairs and of International Cooperation, the Italian Episcopal Conference – through Caritas and the Migrantes Foundation – and the Community of St Egidio, on 12 January 2017. This humanitarian corridor aimed to resettle 500 people from Ethiopia.[16] This memorandum was renewed in May 2019, for other 24 months or, in case of necessity, even 36 months, for other 600 people from Ethiopia, Niger, Jordan and, potentially, other transit countries.[17]

A specific memorandum of understanding for the introduction of humanitarian corridors from Libya was signed by the same stakeholders for the entry of 500 people from Libya on 23 April 2021.[18] This corridor has been renewed in December 2023 for the entry of another 1500 people from Libya.[19]

Furthermore, on 4 November 2021, in answer to the Afghan crisis, the Minister of the Interior, the Minister of International Affairs and of International Cooperation, the Community of St Egidio, the Italian Federation of Evangelical Churches and the Waldensian Board, ARCI (Italian Recreative and Cultural Association), INMP (National Institute for the promotion of the health of migrants), IOM (International Organisation for Migration) and UNHCR signed another memorandum of understanding, which targeted Afghan refugees in Iran, Pakistan, Qatar and bordering countries. The protocol aims to resettle 1,200 refugees

supervision of Professor R Ricucci, available at: inmigration.caritas.it/sites/default/files/docs/2021-09/Emanuele%20Cappello%20Tesi%20triennale%20SISCO%20Corridoi%20umanitari.pdf, 40.

[15] See St Egidio, 'Corridoi umanitari: firmato un nuovo protocollo per mille arrivi di profughi dal Libano' 5 August 2021, available at: www.santegidio.org/pageID/30284/langID/it/itemID/43657/Corridoi-umanitari-firmato-un-nuovo-protocollo-per-mille-arrivi-di-profughi-dal-Libano.html.

[16] Cappello, above n 14, 40.

[17] Bianchini, above n 9, 164–65. Effectively, the scheme was extended to Ethiopia only with the second memorandum in 2017. The second memorandum broadened further in 2019, to include Niger and Jordan. Bianchini reports that, although not indicated in the text of the Protocol, the reason for the extension to Niger was due to providing durable solutions to refugees that were evacuated from immigration centres in Libya (p 166). The 2019 memorandum also introduced the family reunification route. This viable route was opened to the family members of those refugees that had already been resettled in Italy through the programme. On this point see B Panchetti and I Schnyder von Wartensee, 'L' esperienza dei corridoi umanitari' (10 March 2020) HLR 1 report, available at: humanlines.org/media/publications/HLR1_ITA_VERSION.pdf, 14. Moreover, the 2019 memorandum also introduced the role of the 'cultural mediator'. A cultural mediator has now to be assigned to every family that is resettled through the scheme in order to avoid misunderstandings due to language or cultural barriers. For more information on the role of the cultural mediator see Panchetti and Schnyder von Wartensee, ibid, 13.

[18] See Agenzia stampa della federazione delle chiese evangeliche in Italia, 'La buona pratica dei corridoi umanitari. L'annuncio del protocollo per la Libia', 17 June 2021, available at: www.nev.it/nev/2021/06/17/governare-le-migrazioni-la-buona-pratica-dei-corridoi-umanitari-2/.

[19] Onu Italia.com, Il giornale italiano della Nazioni Unite, 'Corridoi umanitari: con nuovo protocollo speranza in Italia per 1500 rifugiati dalla Libia' 20 December 2023, available at; www.onuitalia.com/2023/12/20/corridoi-umanitari-con-nuovo-protocollo-speranza-in-italia-per-1500-rifugiati-dalla-libia/.

in Italy within the next two years, with the possibility of extending the project for a further 12 months.[20]

In 2023, the target for welcoming people through humanitarian corridors was set at 850 people.[21]

Unfortunately, the texts of the protocols are not available to the public. We know that the texts of the protocols are quite brief and that the key content relates to selection criteria, parties' obligations, recipient countries and timings, and evaluation of the programme itself. Professor Ricci, who was granted access to the texts of the Italian memoranda reported how the first memorandum, at Article 3, targeted two different groups of beneficiaries, besides those fulfilling the standard definition of refugee. The first one concerns people for whom 'there are reasonable grounds to believe that, in case of return to their countries of origin, they would suffer significant damage also as a consequence of a situation of armed conflict, endemic violence or systemic violation of human rights'. The second group relates to individuals that are not necessarily included in the previous category but that, nevertheless,

> 'lie in a situation of particular vulnerability for their personal situation, age or health conditions', including *inter alia* 'single women with children, women victims of human trafficking, unaccompanied minors, elderly people,' disabled or traumatized persons, and people with serious medical needs.[22]

The author also noted that the text of Article 3 of the second and third protocols granted a further extension of the beneficiary group compared to the first agreement, by generically referring to those individuals in conditions of serious 'vulnerability determined by their personal situation, age or state of health', and by not specifying the causes upon which these conditions of vulnerability could be grounded.[23] Finally, complementing the previously listed criteria, other factors are normally taken into account by the sponsoring organisations, in order to optimise the success of the project and limit potential voluntary secondary movements to other states. These are: people that can benefit from the support of private individuals, churches or associations in Italy for an initial period; and people that already have a family or social network in Italy and, for this reason, have shown the desire to establish themselves and integrate in the country.[24] As a matter of fact, it is important to note that going beyond the UNHCR selection criteria is of crucial importance, as it allows flexibility, reducing the risk for migrants getting stuck at procedural hurdles. For instance, in 2014 Lebanon, overwhelmed by the influx of

[20] Vatican news, 'Afghanistan, al via per 1200 profughi un corridoio umanitario verso l'Italia' 4 November 2021, available at: www.vaticannews.va/it/mondo/news/2021-11/afghanistan-profughi-italia-protocollo-corridoi-umanitari-egidio.html.
[21] Share Network, above n 3.
[22] Ricci, above n 10, 272, Art 3(b) and Art 3(c).
[23] ibid.
[24] ibid.

Syrian refugees, asked UNHCR to deregister Syrians as refugees if they arrived after 5 January 2015 and to suspend new registrations. Since government resettlement programmes do not normally prescind from UNHCR registration, many Syrian refugees, still in a serious situation of vulnerability and fragility, found themselves excluded from resettlement protection due to a mere procedural issue. The fact that the humanitarian corridors go beyond the strict legal UNHCR classification and consider the actual vulnerability of the person, makes them broader and more far-reaching instruments.[25]

In terms of how the selection of the beneficiaries works, the sponsors – the various churches and associations involved in the agreement with the Italian government – work with their referral contacts in each of the corridor partnership countries. The referral contacts are normally members of parishes or NGOs, linked to the sponsor association,[26] or representatives of the sponsoring organisation itself. They provide concrete assistance in identifying and naming the persons that could potentially benefit from resettlement. However, referrals can also be made by organisations such as *Medecins Sans Frontieres* and the UNHCR itself.[27] Once the referrals are made, it is still up to the organisation to engage with the potential beneficiaries and decide whether to propose them for the programme or not.

The role of the referral contacts is of crucial importance. They directly engage with the potential recipients of the project. At their first meetings they explain the terms and conditions of the programme to the potential beneficiaries and undertake an initial screening of the candidates. The initial screening is important to ascertain whether the individual is truly in a vulnerable situation, hence in need of resettlement, and, crucially, if the individual wants to be resettled in Italy.[28] Normally three interviews take place. In the first interview the local representatives of Caritas, the Community of St Egidio or other local operators that work in close collaboration with the sponsor organisations, get to know the potential

[25] P Morozzo della Rocca, 'I due protocolli d'intesa sui "corridoi umanitari" tra alcuni enti di ispirazione religiosa ed il governo ed il loro possibile impatto sulle politiche di asilo e immigrazione' (2017) 1 *Diritto, Immigrazione e Cittadinanza* 1, 12–13.

[26] ERN scoping paper 'Private Sponsorship in Europe: expanding complementary pathways for refugee resettlement' (2017), available at: www.iom.int/sites/g/files/tmzbdl486/files/documents/ERN%2Bscoping-paper-Private-Sponsorship-in-Europe.pdf, 19. In particular, as far as Ethiopia is concerned, Caritas and St Egidio Community work in close collaboration with the UNHCR, the Government of Ethiopia Agency for the Protection of Refugees and the Ghandi Charity. The Ghandi Charity was founded in 2003 and works in Sudan and Ethiopia to help Eritreans that flee their country. For more information see also Panchetti and Schnyder von Wartensee, above n 17, 6. As far as Lebanon is concerned, the faith-based organisations rely on the local associations of Mediterranean Hope and Operazione Colomba. For more information on these local organisations see Bianchini, above n 9, 166.

[27] Bianchini, above n 9, 167.

[28] Naso, above n 11. From the conversation it came to my attention that in some cases people, despite their vulnerability, do not want to be resettled out of reluctance to leave their family behind or because they do not agree with the principles of the scheme. For example, once a family decided not to be resettled because the scheme strongly encourages women to look for a job in Italy and the family was not willing to compromise on this point.

beneficiaries and begin to understand their personal situation. During the second interview, the beneficiaries' personal documents are checked and more information on the programme is shared with them. During the third interview, the operators finally explain the requirements of the programme in detail.

After having compiled a dossier for each sponsored candidate, the representatives of the organisations hand the list over to the local governmental refugee agencies to obtain exit permits. After approval has been granted, the list is handed to the Italian embassies in loco, which proceed with the official screening and security checks for each candidate. The embassies will then send the candidate's files for a second vetting by the Italian Minister of the Interior.[29] Other follow-up screenings are processed by the Territorial Commission for Immigration after the sponsored individuals enter Italy.[30]

The religious organisations acting as private sponsors take on a series of commitments. As mentioned before, they are responsible for the identification of the beneficiaries and the creation of their dossiers, in accordance with the relevant privacy criteria. Moreover, they also take on the financial costs of the trip from the designated country to Italy. Finally, they are financially responsible for housing costs, food, utilities and extra expenses that refugees cannot immediately afford. On this point, it is interesting to note that, unlike other European examples, the organisations acting as private sponsors had initially to commit for one year, which was extended eventually to two years and can now be extended further if needed.[31] This aspect of the scheme has been criticised because of the lack of clarity on 'how long sponsors will provide settlement support, and to what extent public social assistance will be available to sponsored persons when the sponsorship period comes to an end'.[32] In reality, normally, the individuals are successfully integrated after 12/18 months and can successfully and fully provide for themselves. If this does not happen after 18 months, the situation is reassessed. If appropriate, the organisation may decide to reduce the benefits, but disengaging completely from the beneficiaries of the programme is not contemplated as an option.[33] The

[29] Bianchini has reported that some issues have been encountered in Lebanon, when some requests were denied by the Ministry of the Interior. The exact reasons for the denials are unknown but it is believed that they could be due to the origins of the potential beneficiary – from countries where terrorist groups are operating – or for diplomatic issues with other countries of potential first asylum (Bianchini, above n 9, 167–68).

[30] Once the beneficiaries of the scheme land at the Rome-Fiumicino airport, they have to apply for asylum immediately at the border police. After a few days, they have to complete the application at the 'Questura' of the place in which they will be resettled. At the end of this procedure, the beneficiaries of the programme receive a form, called form C 3, that grants legal stay in Italy until they are heard by the local Territorial Commission that will assess their asylum claims. For more information on the point see Panchetti and Schnyder von Wartensee, above n 17, 7.

[31] Bianchini, above n 9, 177.

[32] ERN scoping paper, above n 26, 20.

[33] Please note that, regardless of the level of disengagement of the sponsored individuals in the project, the beneficiaries are never evicted from the home provided by the organisation. In some circumstances the project fails because the sponsored refugees decide to be supported by other units, most commonly family members already residing in Italy, or to emigrate to other EU states (Naso, above n 11).

organisations grant financial, social and emotional support during the integration phase – eg support in learning the Italian language, looking for a job etc, and they also provide legal assistance during the refugee application process.[34]

As far as the refugee application process is concerned, as has been mentioned, the Ministry of Foreign Affairs, through its embassies in the relevant countries, will issue visas with limited territorial validity to the sponsored individuals to allow their legal entry onto Italian soil. Moreover, the Ministry of the Interior also makes sure that the circumstances of each sponsored individual are brought to the attention of the Territorial Commission for Immigration that will examine their applications, stressing particularly the identification criteria used during the selection process. Following the approval of the Commission, the Ministry of the Interior will issue the resident permit as a refugee or as a beneficiary of international protection.[35]

It is worth noting that the memoranda not only cover the sponsor's duties but also the beneficiary's responsibilities. Indeed, the beneficiaries have to sign an agreement where their duties are spelled out. These consist of collaborating cooperatively, participating in the activities as proposed by the sponsor (recreation, training, learning of the language, etc) and searching for a job and accommodation.[36]

In relation to the rights granted to the beneficiaries, once refugee status or the status of beneficiary of international protection has been obtained, the individual can claim a series of rights such as legal access to work, family reunification, access to the public health system, access to public schools and welfare assistance[37] (although this last aspect is normally covered by the sponsoring organisations).

As far as the financial responsibility is concerned, the sponsoring organisations rely on the money gathered through the '8 per mille' (0.8 per cent) charitable donations that are a compulsory element in Italian tax revenue. Moreover, some organisations rely on the financial support of parishes and various solidarity

[34] Panchetti and Schnyder von Wartensee, above n 17, 10. It is also worth noting that the organisations are involved in quite a few pre-arrival welcoming activities such as hosting meetings with the local communities where the beneficiaries of the scheme will be resettled, preparation of the volunteers and mentor families, liaising with the schools that the children will be attending, engaging with the cultural mediator, and preparing for physical and psychological health care. For more information see B Panchetti and I Schnyder von Wartensee, 'Humanitarian Corridors and Reception: Pre-Arrival Preparation and Challenges' (2020) HLR 2 report, available at: humanlines.org/media/publications/HLR2_ENG.pdf, from 10.

[35] Bianchini, above n 9, 174–75.

[36] Panchetti, Schnyder von Wartensee, above n 17, 10.

[37] Bianchini, above n 9, 175: 'the Italian government provides … if the beneficiaries cannot integrate in the labour market, the support of welfare benefits'. See also Naso, above n 11. From the conversation with Professor Naso, it came to my attention that, effectively, the organisations continue providing financial assistance until integration is achieved, since the support of the state is quite minimal anyway. This is not surprising, since, as Bianchini points out at 176 'in Italy, public institutions have set up minimal interventions to facilitate integration into society and as a result refugee treatment has resembled that of economic migrants: social networks are crucial for finding employment and civil society organisations are the reference point for many needs'.

networks. For example, it is often through these networks that donations of goods and money are collected, and inexpensive or even free accommodations are made available to support the sponsorship programmes.

The approach adopted by the Italian humanitarian corridors has been defined as '*accoglienza accompagnata e diffusa*' (accompanied and widespread hospitality).[38] It is accompanied hospitality, because the members of the sponsors are fully involved, economically and emotionally, in the integration process of the hosted refugees. It is widespread hospitality because the sponsoring organisations prefer to resettle the refugees in smaller local communities – which often provide a 'soft landing' for the refugees[39] – throughout Italy. Normally only one or two families are hosted in the same local setting.[40] It is interesting to note that, unlike the UK experience of Community Sponsorship, where local authorities can refuse to resettle the refugees within their territory, the Italian local authorities do not have any veto power. This is most likely because the local authority is not required to bear any of the direct costs of the resettlement, which are instead covered by the sponsoring organisations. However, the sponsor organisations liaise with the relevant local councils to explain the project and present the family that will be resettled, and often find support and help.[41]

Finally, the memoranda contain a provision according to which all the parties to the agreement are expected to work together in order to coordinate, evaluate and monitor the success of each project.[42]

While the humanitarian corridor agreements that have been signed have limited duration (normally two years), they have been renewed several times. Over the years, both the Italian government and the religious and other organisations involved have started to refer to the humanitarian corridors experience as 'best practice'. This is an important achievement for the project, as it is growing towards being accepted as a national policy.[43] As a matter of fact these projects have achieved broad-based political consensus, having been supported by different governments under different political coalitions.

Research has highlighted several successful aspects of the Italian experience of humanitarian corridors. For instance, it has been argued that this initiative

[38] Morozzo della Rocca, above n 25, 26.

[39] ERN scoping paper, above n 26, 20. This was also confirmed by Professor Paolo Naso (Naso, above n 11).

[40] M Ambrosini and I Schnyder von Wartensee, 'Actions speak louder than claims: humanitarian corridors, civil society and asylum policies' (2022) 48 *Journal of Ethnic and Migration Studies* 3965, 3971.

[41] Naso, above n 11. The local authorities would technically be responsible for providing financial assistance to the resettled refugees, in case of sponsorship breakdown. This eventuality, however, does not seem to be of particular concern to local authorities or to the Italian state in terms of welfare, since the programme, in its flexibility, puts the main financial responsibility on the sponsoring organisations.

[42] Naso, above n 11.

[43] ibid.

'counteracts the current trends of securitisation and externalisation of asylum',[44] as it allows vulnerable people to reach Italy in a safe manner and apply for international protection within the country, with near full certainty that the request will be accepted. Moreover, owing to the way the schemes have been framed, people that would not otherwise be entitled to resettlement are allowed to seek protection and reach the Italy safely.[45] Also, this programme has already proved itself to be of little financial burden to the state, due to the fact that the work is done by volunteers, accommodation is often offered by people or religious communities for free,[46] and the financial costs of the sponsorship, as seen above, are mainly covered by the sponsors of the project, who are also willing to continue their assistance beyond the agreed standard period, if necessary.

However, the success of the Italian humanitarian corridors experience, proved by its capillary expansion to other European countries, does come with some shortcomings. Interviews with some operators working locally on the selection phase of the programme show that volunteers seem to have developed 'an operational definition of "vulnerability" … allowing an assessment based on a more nuanced understanding of the beneficiaries' experience and eligibility for the programme according to the specificity of the situations they face.'[47] While this could indicate a desirable level of openness and flexibility, it has been suggested that this approach could end up leading to arbitrary categorisation refugees in more or less worthy categories of protection, far from relying on objective standards.[48] In a recent study on the 2017–19 humanitarian corridor from Ethiopia, the authors have shown how there are still some difficulties in matching the refugees' understandable desire for autonomy and the resources available to allow them to achieve this aim.[49] For instance, in some particularly vulnerable cases, the volunteers associated with the religious organisation are not capable of supporting the needs of the refugees for lack of expertise and skills. This requires, in certain cases, the reaching of a balance between volunteer support and professional aid, such as increased involvement of a social worker, psychological support and in some cases, psychiatric help. Another aspect relates to social isolation, due to resettlement in some cases being provided in provincial or remote areas. Indeed, resettlement in provincial settings often leads to a lack of employment opportunities, which are fundamental to allowing the beneficiaries of the programme to achieve integration and independence.[50]

[44] S Trotta, 'Safe and Legal Passages to Europe: A Case Study of Faith-Based Humanitarian Corridors to Italy' (2017) 5 UCL migration research unit, available at: www.ucl.ac.uk/geography/sites/geography_redesign/files/mru_wp_susanna_trotta_2017_5.pdf, 34.

[45] ibid. On the point see also Morozzo della Rocca, above n 25, 13.

[46] Morozzo della Rocca, above n 25, 27.

[47] Bianchini, above n 9, 171.

[48] ibid.

[49] Ambrosini and Schnyder von Wartensee, above n 40, 3980.

[50] ibid.

B. Humanitarian Corridors in France

France has been involved in ad hoc resettlement since 1957, when it started to resettle refugees from Hungary and then from Vietnam and Kosovo. However, the country fully developed a state-led resettlement programme only in 2008, when it signed an agreement with the UNHCR.[51] The agreement is renewed automatically every year with a target of roughly 100 refugees per year, but additional places can be decided by the government. In addition to mainstream state-led resettlement, in 2014/2015 France also signed ad hoc agreements with UNHCR for humanitarian admissions for Syrians from Lebanon, Jordan, Egypt and Turkey.[52] Moreover, France also allows humanitarian visa applications. Applicants in need of international protection can apply for humanitarian visas at the French consulates in their country or in a third host country.[53]

France also introduced humanitarian corridor schemes, which are run by private sponsors. Inspired by the Italian experience,[54] the first memorandum of understanding was signed in March 2017, by a coalition of five religious organisations – Secours Catholique, Community of St Egidio, Conférence des Évêques de France, Fédération d'Entraide Protestante, Fédération Protestante de France – with the Ministry of the Interior and the Ministry of Foreign Affairs.[55] This first memorandum of understanding aimed to resettle 500 people of Syrian and Iraqi nationality residing in Lebanon.[56] The agreement was renewed in 2021 for other two years, under the same conditions, for the safe passage and entry into France of another 300 refugees residing in Lebanon.[57] The agreement has been further renewed and

[51] Ten years later, the Asylum and Migration Law of 10 September 2018 (Law number n° 2018-778) finally gave a legal basis to resettlement in France.

[52] UNCHR Resettlement Handbook, 'Country chapter: France', available at: www.unhcr.org/media/unhcr-resettlement-handbook-country-chapter-france, 3.

[53] ibid, 4. In addition to state-led resettlement and the humanitarian corridor initiative, France also introduced a higher education pathway. Through this pathway, organised by UNHCR, Agence Universtaire de la Francophonie (AUF) and Réseau MenS (migrants in higher education network), 21 students received scholarships for university studies in France in 2022. For more details see Share Network, above n 3.

[54] A feasibility study on the opportunity to open a humanitarian corridor in France was published in April 2018. See ERN feasibility study 'Towards a Private Sponsorship Model in France' (2018), available at: www.iom.int/sites/g/files/tmzbdl486/files/documents/ERN%2Bfeasibility-study-Towards-a-Private-Sponsorship-Model-in-France.pdf.

[55] A representive of the French Council for the Muslim Faith was invited to take part in the negotiations but, in the end, they did not take part in the project. See M Ngombe, 'Les Couloirs Humanitaires: un régime d'exception pour gérer des réfugiés « désirables»'(2020) 1 *Revue internationale des études du développement* 65, 75.

[56] C Paravati and A Ricci (eds), 'Sponsoring Integration: Impact assessment of Humanitarian Corridors Program primary achievements in Italy and France' (2020), available at: www.eurodiaconia.org/wordpress/wp-content/uploads/2020/08/AMIF-PPI-Impact-Assessment-Report-FINAL-27072020.pdf, 84.

[57] St Egidio, 'Humanitarian Corridors in France: a new agreement for the entry of 300 refugees' 13 April 2021, available at: www.santegidio.org/pageID/30284/langID/en/itemID/41621/Humanitarian-Corridors-in-France-a-new-agreement-for-the-entry-of-300-refugees.html.

the current third protocol sets a quota of 300 visas to be granted to Syrians or Iraqis in Lebanon between 2023 and 2026.[58] As for the Italian schemes, the French humanitarian corridors are also additional to the numbers pledged by the state for resettlement.[59]

The texts of the French memoranda are not publicly shared; hence the following analysis is based on the few pieces of research that are currently available. As far as selection is concerned, the French corridor very much resembles the Italian one. The potential beneficiaries are identified by the representatives of the religious associations in Lebanon, according to vulnerability criteria similar to those in the Italian protocol. Moreover, potential beneficiaries are also required to have a particular link to France.[60] The representatives of the sponsoring organisations collect the relevant information during two to four interviews, and direct the potential beneficiaries to the French route only if they consider that they fulfil the criteria and that they are likely to be successful in obtaining the temporary visa from the French consulate.[61] If the conditions are met, and after having carried out the first security checks and a final interview with its officials, the consulate will issue a long-stay visa that will allow the sponsored refugees to enter into France and apply for asylum.

Before leaving Lebanon, the beneficiaries of the French programme are expected to attend some training, to prepare them for their new life in France and set their expectations.[62] Moreover, the beneficiaries are also expected to sign a declaration in which they state their intention to start a new life in France and not to return to Lebanon.[63] At that point the Lebanese authorities will issue an exit permit.[64]

After their arrival in France, the sponsored refugees have 15 days to register at the prefecture to obtain a permit to stay and to enable them to apply for asylum. The beneficiaries will lodge their asylum claims with the French Office for the Protection of Refugees and Stateless Persons (OFPRA), which will provide a decision within three months.[65] This accelerated time-frame is granted to the beneficiaries of the humanitarian corridors only. Indeed, humanitarian corridors seem to have established themselves as a privileged path to asylum, compared to

[58] Share Network, above n 3.

[59] UNCHR Resettlement Handbook, above n 52, 4.

[60] Paravati, Ricci, above n 56, 84.

[61] ibid.

[62] ibid. The Lebanese organisation that provides the training is called Metanoia. Metanoia is a mental health centre in Lebanon that works with adults and children who suffer from a variety of psychological and behavioural difficulties.

[63] ibid.

[64] ERN scoping paper, above 26, 23.

[65] ibid. Specific data on the OFPRA timeframes for answering asylum applications from humanitarian corridors beneficiaries can be found in Paravati and Ricci, above n 56, 99–101.

the classic route.[66] After having obtained refugee status, the resettled sponsored refugees are entitled to work.[67]

Unlike the Italian programme, the French state is more involved in relation to providing social benefits. For example, as discussed above, most of the expenses are covered by the religious organisations involved in the Italian humanitarian corridor. On the other hand, in France, the state provides a regular allowance and services to which all the refugees are entitled, apart from covering the costs of housing. The beneficiaries are invited to become independent from the programme as soon as possible by relying, in the first instance, on the *Allocation pour Demandeur d'Asile* while still asylum seekers and, once granted refugee status or subsidiary protection, on other benefits guaranteed by the French state to refugees.[68] Moreover, as far as housing is concerned, the involvement of the local authorities is more prominent in the French case. For instance, while in Italy it is up to the sponsoring organisation to find suitable accommodation, generally owned by private landlords, in France a portion of the accommodation offered to refugees consist of apartments rented by the local authority and provided to the volunteers from one of the associations.[69] Participants are requested ultimately to become independent from the accommodation provided, initially by relying on state benefits. Indeed, once the beneficiaries can recover the costs of rent via benefits, and hopefully eventually by wages, they should leave the accommodation that was initially provided.[70]

There are also other key similarities and differences between schemes. For instance, like in the Italian programme the volunteers, known as CC (*Collectifs Citoyens*), provide accommodation, support integration, pay for French language courses and offer administrative assistance. Moreover, like the Italian corridor, resettlement is spread throughout France. Sponsors seem to prefer resettling sponsored refugees in small municipalities, due to the lower living costs.[71] However, unlike the Italian programme, volunteers from the different religious associations are more supported by social workers.[72] The social workers are experienced professionals who have previously worked in associations and programmes dealing with refugees. They play a crucial role as mediators in the relationship between

[66] This is due to the strong connections that have been established between the interested ministries and the five religious organisations involved in the initiative in France. In addition to the accelerated procedure, the fruits of these strong connections are privileged meetings between politicians and the representatives of the religious organisations, and also the existence of an informal 'helpline', by which the association agents can obtain up-to-date information on their applications by telephone or by e-mail. See Ngombe, above n 55, 76.

[67] ERN scoping paper, above 26, 23.

[68] Paravati and Ricci, above n 56, 101. 'Once participants secure the status of refugee or the "protection subsidiaire," they can claim … [two] social benefits, [called] RSA (Inclusion Income support) and APL (Personalised Housing Allowance). They are then considered financially independent'.

[69] ERN scoping paper, above 26, 23.

[70] Paravati and Ricci, above n 56, 104.

[71] ERN scoping paper, above 26, 23.

[72] ibid.

the sponsoring religious organisations and the sponsored refugees. Furthermore, the French programme is more structured. Indeed, there are five regional divisions, each one managed by one of the five religious organisations, with a social worker in charge of the humanitarian corridor programme for the refugees resettled in that area. The practices of each division vary. A central platform, run by the Fédération d'Entraide Protestante in Paris, works as the national and international coordinator. This central platform is also responsible for a sixth division called Hors-Pôle, representing the remaining regions.[73]

The French experience of humanitarian corridors has been highly praised and welcomed by civil society. Initial research findings have shown that most of the beneficiaries of the programme have judged it very positively.[74] However, initial surveys have also highlighted some difficulties in each of the different phases of the programme. Obstacles have been particularly evident in the integration phase, where it has become evident that it is not at all easy for refugees to find a job and independent accommodation within a short period of time. This is often due to the difficulty in learning the language.[75] Another factor, which is a common criticism in other humanitarian corridor experiences, is the lack of homogenous integration achieved geographically, with a higher integration rates in rural areas than in urban ones.[76]

Academics have also been highly critical of humanitarian corridors in France. Ngombe has highlighted how these programmes have led to an arbitrary situation. In particular, she denounces the fact that the discretionary power to choose the beneficiaries of the programme has been delegated to private actors, with only the final decision of whether the person is entitled to enter left to the state. This, she recalls, confirms the concern already expressed by Wihtol de Wenden, who evoked the development of a 'grey zone' around asylum policies, in which there is, increasingly, room for discretion.[77] The arbitrariness issue is denounced in the selection criteria of the French humanitarian corridors programme, due to the coupling of the vulnerability requirement with the idea of resilience, which effectively translates into an assessment, done by the organisations and the consulates themselves, of whether the potential beneficiaries can effectively and successfully integrate in the host country. The pairing of these criteria, Ngombe highlights, becomes effectively a limitation, because age, disability, and illiteracy, despite being primary signs of vulnerability, constitute a disadvantage, due to the assumption that the person will struggle more to integrate into French society.[78] Moreover, despite the aspiration of the programme to promote openness and fraternity, the scheme has

[73] Paravati and Ricci, above n 56, 86.
[74] ibid, 128.
[75] ibid, 129.
[76] ibid, 130.
[77] Ngombe, above n 55, 79. The author refers to C Wihtol de Wenden, 'La crise de l'asile' (2002) 1238 *Hommes & Migrations* 6.
[78] ibid, 81.

been criticised for exacerbating procedural arbitrariness. As a matter of fact, if one fails the screening in the host country through the embassy, there is no appeal against the decision, which simply has to be accepted by the applicant, unlike those who manage to apply for refugee protection in France, who have access to the Court of Appeal that can reconsider their request.[79] This seems to have made the programme 'ambiguous', caught between humanitarian aims and security concerns.[80] The contradictions that characterise the French programme, according to research, can cause fragmentation of the international humanitarian sector operating in France, since migrants are cared for by private sponsors, bypassing public structures. Additionally, the fact that the programme is little known and publicised has led to a situation in which the process underpinning its functioning is not very much known and monitored.[81]

C. Humanitarian Corridors in Belgium

In 2011, Belgium decided to develop its first state-led resettlement programme, despite the lack of specific legal provisions on resettlement in the Belgian legislation.[82] This decision was based on pilot experiences of ad hoc resettlement schemes from Iraq and Libya. The quotas are pledged yearly by the Belgian government. In 2014 the size of the quota amounted to 100 individuals per year. However, the beginning of the civil war in Syria triggered larger pledges, 300 in 2015, reaching a peak of 1,150 resettlement places available in 2018.[83]

Prompted by the Syrian refugee crisis and following the successful Italian and French experiences, Belgium too decided to set up its first humanitarian corridor in 2017.[84] The first memorandum of understanding was signed on 22 November 2017. The signatories of the memorandum were the Secretary of State for Asylum and Migration, for the Belgian state,[85] and several religious organisations, namely,

[79] ibid, 79.

[80] ibid, 83. The author quotes D Fassin, *La raison humanitaire: une histoire morale du temps present* (Paris, Éditions de l'EHESS/Gallimard/ Seuil, 2010).

[81] ibid.

[82] Provisions on resettlement are not included in the Law of 15 December 1980 (Aliens Act) (Loi du 15 décembre 1980 sur l'accès au territoire, le séjour, l'établissement et l'éloignement des étrangers, available at: www.ejustice.just.fgov.be/eli/loi/1980/12/15/1980121550/justel).

[83] UNHCR Resettlement Handbook, 'Country chapter: Belgium', available at: www.unhcr.org/uk/media/unhcr-resettlement-handbook-country-chapter-belgium, 2. In addition to state-led resettlement, Belgium runs a higher education pathway, which was established in 2022, as a pilot programme organised by the University of Leuven, Fedasil and Caritas International. Three students so far have been welcomed. For more information on this point see Share Network, above n 3.

[84] Belgium has also introduced a Community Sponsorship Programme in 2020. This will be examined in section IX of this chapter.

[85] The signature of the Secretary of State, Théo Francken, came as a surprise, as he was known for his harsh positions against immigration. Professor Jan de Volder, who was at the negotiating table for St Egidio, is convinced that the reason why the programme was accepted by Belgium was the security guarantees that the programme offers. Indeed, the programme allows full security checks and

the Community of St Egidio, as the promoter, in partnership with the Anglican Commission, the Bishops' Conference, the Muslim Executive of Belgium, the Central Israelite Consistory of Belgium, the United Protestant Church of Belgium and the Orthodox Church. The role of the St Egidio Community was, once again, crucial. Indeed, it was St Egidio that took the initiative of gathering together different churches and religious organisations operating in Belgium, to share the humanitarian corridor initiative in the country.[86]

The aim of the corridor was to allow safe passage and entry into Belgium for 150 Syrians, from Lebanon and Turkey.[87] As is noticeable from the list of the signatory organisations, unlike the Italian and French experiences, the Belgian humanitarian corridor is characterised by the involvement of non-Christian organisations.[88]

The negotiations between the religious organisations and the government began with a letter directed to the Belgian Prime Minister, the Minister of Foreign Affairs, and the Immigration Minister, on 23 January 2017.[89] In the letter, the organisations broadly delineated their respective commitments: Belgium should agree to issue the necessary entry visas and to look at the asylum requests favourably, while the associations, in exchange, would provide financial and emotional support for the sponsored families for one year, and would cover their transportation costs to Belgium.

The format of the memorandum is similar to the Italian and French ones. The selection criteria are listed in Article 2 and include families with children, men, women and children who are disabled or have health issues, elderly people, people belonging to a threatened religious, cultural or ethnic minority, and people with existing links to Belgium. The latter is a desirable but not an essential requirement. As with the Italian and French protocols, this requirement was included in the hope of avoiding secondary movements (onward migration) outside the Belgian territory.

screening before the immigrants effectively reach the Belgian territory. On this point see L Bernard, 'Le couloir humanitaire conduit en Belgique par la communauté de Sant' Egidio, entre alternative face à la gestion migratoire européenne et instrumentalisation au service du politique?' 2018–19 thesis written at Université de Liège, Faculté de Droit, Science Politique et Criminologie under the supervision of Professor Geoffrey Grandjean, 46.

[86] ibid, 44. It did so through the network established via the recently born inter-denominational platform 'Together in Peace'. It is important to note that the platform was used as a way to facilitate the introduction of the humanitarian corridors in Belgium but it was not originally funded for this purpose. Indeed, it was originally created to support the international march 'Together in Peace – Liberty and Respect', which took place in Brussels on Sunday 15 March 2015. See *The Brussels Times*, 'Around 3,500 people march under the slogan "Together in Peace, Liberty and Respect"' 16 March 2015, available at: www.brusselstimes.com/news/belgium-all-news/31976/around-3-500-people-march-under-the-slogan-together-in-peace-liberty-and-respect.

[87] The numbers of the visas to be granted were subdivided into 75 visas for Syrians coming from Turkey and 75 visas for Syrians coming from Lebanon.

[88] The Centre d'Action Laic, a prominent secular group operating in Belgium, refused to take part in this project. The group refused, partly because of the fear that the corridor would benefit mainly Christians. Moreover, the group also argued that projects concerning resettlement are tasks that should be performed only by the state. On this point see Bernard, above n 85, 44.

[89] ibid. Bernard refers to the letter, which can be found at: www.santegidio.be/wp-content/uploads/2019/01/2017-Lettre-Gouvernement-Couloir-Humanitaire-23-01-2017.pdf.

The selection is carried out in the host state, according to the listed criteria. As far as the first protocol is concerned, the selection is performed by the Community of St Egidio in Lebanon, and by the Orthodox Syrian Church in Turkey.[90] In Lebanon, the selection takes place through St Egidio's partners, such as the Red Cross, Unicef, Médecins sans frontières, Terre des Hommes, Save the Children, Caritas Liban, Assomud, Amel, JRS, Arcenciel and other local organisations.[91] In Turkey, the interviews and selection are run by the Orthodox Syrian Church, in collaboration with Caritas International and the International Catholic Migration Commission (ICMC).[92] The local partners conduct a minimum of three interviews, but there are usually more. In the first interview the local organisation meets potential candidates in a neutral place, such as a church, to establish a first connection. The second meeting, instead, takes place at the candidate's residence. This is important to allow the local partner to effectively understand the conditions of vulnerability of the potential beneficiaries of the programme. Finally, the third interview takes place at the Belgian embassy. On that occasion the plans for the trip to Belgium are discussed.[93]

Just as for the Italian and French protocols, it is the consulate that runs the first official security checks. If the screening is successful the candidates are issued humanitarian visas, based on Article 25(1)(a) of the Visa Code, that allow them to enter Belgium.[94] Once in Belgium, the beneficiaries of the programme have to apply for asylum and, if successful, are granted refugee status or subsidiary international protection.

From entering Belgium to being granted refugee status or subsidiary protection, the beneficiaries cannot rely on any form of state subsidy.[95] All the costs, including travel expenses, housing, food, language courses, etc are covered by the religious organisations. The financial responsibility of the organisations lasts for a maximum of one year.[96] The sponsored families only have access to urgent medical care, at the expense of the state, until they are granted refugee status or subsidiary protection, when they finally have access to the national health care system.[97] The religious organisations are also responsible for the emotional support of the

[90] Art 3(a)(b) Text of memorandum of understanding Belgian humanitarian corridor, 22 November 2017, available at: www.santegidio.be/wp-content/uploads/2019/01/D%C3%A9claration-dintention-Couloirs-Humanitaires.pdf.

[91] See 'Note sant'egidio sur le projet "couloirs humanitaires" (2017–18) pour l'audition a la commission affaires interieures de la chambre 5 février 2019', available at: www.santegidio.be/wp-content/uploads/2019/02/2019-Note-CH-Audition-Commission-AI-Chambre-5-fe%C4%9Bvrier.pdf, 3.

[92] ibid, 4.

[93] Bernard, above n 85, 51. The author highlights how the survey carried out regarding the beneficiaries of the programme in the city of Antwerp has shown that society's perception of this scheme is very positive. See also p 55.

[94] For a deep insight into the application of Art 25 in Belgium and European case law see S Bodart, 'Humanitarian Admission to Belgium' in MC Foblets and L Leboeuf (eds), *Humanitarian Admission to Europe* (Baden-Baden, Nomos/Hart publishing, 2020) 225.

[95] Text memorandum of understanding, above n 90, Art 10.

[96] ibid.

[97] ibid, Art 12.

resettled families.[98] This work is done by the volunteers of the various associations, and the Community of St Egidio acts as coordinator.[99]

A second protocol was signed on 25 December 2021. The framework of the scheme is very similar to that of the first. However, the second protocol has considerably broadened the category of potential beneficiaries, in being open to people coming from different regions of the Middle East, Africa and Asia. Moreover, more visas are now issued through the latest protocol, entitling 250 refugees in vulnerable conditions to enter the country.[100]

Some positive aspects of the Belgian application of humanitarian corridors can be seen. For example, it has been noted that in Belgium integration is improved by the partnership of Caritas with local ecumenical communities, as the capillary reach of these communities offers an undeniable advantage to the beneficiaries of programme.[101] However, some of the respondents who were interviewed in a study carried out to assess the success of the Belgian programme have raised some legitimate doubts. For instance, the issue of inequality has been raised, both in relation to those refugees that did not participate in the corridors and who thus have to apply for asylum directly in Belgium,[102] and in relation to those who do not belong to the religious faiths represented by the promoters of the project.[103] It has also been argued that the programme has been instrumentalised to achieve aims that are not strictly humanitarian. Indeed, some consider the Belgian corridor as a political tool in service of anti-immigration policies. As a matter of fact, the corridors allow the sponsors and their representatives to make a list of people that they consider eligible for the programme, while Belgium has the final say as to whether the selected people are entitled to enter its borders or not, but this whole process happens outside Belgian borders. Indeed, it has been suggested that this pattern allows the state to give a perception of humanitarian care, while being detrimental to others who choose to claim asylum in Belgium, by entering the country legally or illegally.[104]

D. Humanitarian Corridors in Andorra

The experience of the humanitarian corridors in Andorra broadly follows the patterns already described for Italy, France and Belgium. The origins of the corridor

[98] ibid, Art 13.
[99] ibid, Art 14.
[100] St Egidio, 'There is a new humanitarian corridor for 250 refugees, who are in their most vulnerable condition, in Belgium' 25 December 2021, available at: www.santegidio.org/pageID/30284/langID/en/itemID/45781/There-is-a-new-humanitarian-corridor-for-250-refugees-who-are-in-their-most-vulnerable-condition-in-Belgium.html.
[101] Bernard, above n 85, 55.
[102] ibid, 50–51.
[103] ibid, 56.
[104] ibid. This criticism is confirmed by the fact that the then secretary of state, Théo Francken, would approve these schemes, while still adopting more general anti-immigration policies.

in Andorra are to be found in a memorandum of understanding signed with the St Egidio Community in 2018, to help refugees living in Lebanon. Although the text of the memorandum is not publicly available, we know that in the Andorran scheme the potential candidates are selected in loco by the representatives of the community, interviewed, screened by the local embassies and issued a visa of territorially limited validity, according to Article 25 of the Visa Code, by either France or Spain, depending on where the refugees land.[105] Indeed, in order to take advantage of Article 25 of the EU Visa Code, France and Spain act as a transit bridge between the first hosting country and the final destination. The migrants, who would normally undergo many police checks procedures, are instead greeted by the Andorran authorities, who hand them a residence permit. As a matter of fact, the beneficiaries are immediately granted a permit of entry and residence,[106] that can eventually be converted into a classic '*permiso de residentia y trabajo ordinario*'. Under these permits, the beneficiaries of the programme are granted a furnished house and have their utility bills paid, depending on whether the person has a salaried job and dependants living with them.[107] Moreover, the beneficiaries of the programme have access to medical services, social services, education, employment and training.[108] Like the protocols in Italy, France and Belgium, the sponsoring organisation, in this case the Community of St Egidio, is involved in the selection process. The Community of St Egidio also trains the volunteers and provides a network to help the beneficiaries to integrate quickly into their new society. However, unlike the Italian, French and Belgian schemes, the Principality of Andorra supports the refugees by meeting the majority of the costs of hospitality.[109] So far, 20 people have benefitted from the scheme.

E. Concluding Remarks on Humanitarian Corridors

With Andorra we have concluded the analysis of the phenomenon of humanitarian corridors, seen as tools for resettlement. In the next chapter, other versions of humanitarian corridor schemes will be discussed, particularly focusing on

[105] Information gathered from the conversation with Daniela Pompei, manager of the St Egidio Community's services for migrants, 17 June 2022.

[106] Since Andorra is not a signatory of the Geneva Convention the classic routes to residence of Andorra did not foresee, up until 2018, the granting of permits for entry and residence of refugees. However, in order to allow the humanitarian corridors to operate within its borders, Andorra passed the Llei 4/2018, 22 de març Llei de protecció temporal i transitòria per raons humanitàries, available at: www.consellgeneral.ad/fitxers/documents/lleis-2018/llei-4-2018-de-proteccio-temporal-i-transitoria-per-raons-humanitaries. See also Sant' Egidio, 'Al via ai primi corridoi umanitari ad Andorra' 25 October 2018, available at: https://www.santegidio.org/pageID/30284/langID/it/itemID/27776/SantEgidio-al-via-i-primi-corridoi-umanitari-ad-Andorra.html.

[107] Llei 4/2018, above n 106, Art 9.

[108] ibid, Art 10, Art 11, Art 12.

[109] Catt.Ch, 'Profughi, Sant'Egidio; anche Andorra apre i corridoi umanitari' 8 May 2018, available at: www.catt.ch/newsi/profughi-santegidio-anche-andorra-apre-i-corridoi-umanitari/.

the experiences of the Vatican City, Portugal and St Marino, which support relocation within the EU. This further discussion will outline the versatility of these programmes, which have the capacity to adapt and support different forms of entry.

III. Short-Lived Experiments: Private Sponsorship in Poland, Czech Republic and Slovakia

During the Syrian crisis, the EU asked all the Member States to admit Syrian refugees, to share the migration burden, aimed at relieving the pressure on Greece, Italy and Spain. A relocation plan was agreed in 2015,[110] in response to the large influx of asylum seekers. The EU agreed to relocate 160,000 asylum seekers, subdividing them into quotas among Member States, based on each state's wealth and size. The Czech Republic, Poland, together with Hungary, were found to be in non-compliance with the legal obligations of the relocation plan and were taken to the Court of Justice of the European Union for an alleged breach of EU law.[111]

However, despite the disengagement with relocation, two of these countries – Poland and the Czech Republic – with the addition of Slovakia, adopted some ad hoc private sponsorship programmes for the resettlement of refugees. The programme formats for these countries were quite similar and, for this reason, a general account will be given for all of them together. These were short-lived experiments and are currently no longer running.

In July 2015, Poland implemented the ad hoc sponsorship initiative, in cooperation with the Estera Foundation and with the help of the Barnabas Fund, to welcome 158 Syrian Christians. Slovakia adopted an ad hoc resettlement programme in December 2015, where the humanitarian admission was supported by an NGO, to admit 149 Iraqi Christians from the refugee camp in Erbil. Under a similar programme, the Czech Republic admitted 153 Iraqi Christians from the Erbil camp, between January and April 2016, through the help of the NGO Generation 21 and the Barnabas Fund. Political lobbying was carried on by the NGO Generation 21 in this country in order to have the programme approved. The Czech government eventually agreed to introduce a private sponsorship of refugees programme, as long as the NGO Generation 21 would take on most of the financial responsibility. The agreement between the NGO and the government was completely informal, with no official law upon which the programme was based.[112]

[110] For more information see European Commission, 'Relocation: EU solidarity in practice', available at: home-affairs.ec.europa.eu/policies/migration-and-asylum/migration-management/relocation-eu-solidarity-practice_en.

[111] In 2020, the Court of Justice of the European Union ruled that the Czech Republic, Hungary and Poland had failed to comply with the 2015 relocation programme. For more details see the judgment in Joined Cases C-715/17, C-718/17 and C-719/17 *Commission v Poland, Hungary and the Czech Republic*, ECLI:EU:C:2020:257.

[112] See M Jelínková, 'A Refugee Crisis Without Refugees: Policy and media discourse on refugees in the Czech Republic and its implications' (2019) 13 *Central European Journal of Public Policy* 33, 35.

In relation to the eligibility criteria, all three programmes targeted people persecuted for religious beliefs, with a particular focus on Christians. For instance, the Slovakian and the Czech programmes targeted persecuted Christians in Iraq. Likewise, Poland introduced the vulnerability criterion within its scheme, and opened it to Syrians escaping a threat to life.[113] The Polish programme was promoted by the Estera Foundation and agreed by the then Prime Minister. Beneficiaries were chosen by selected churches acting in loco. To enter the country, the beneficiaries had to be able to provide their baptism certificate, a recommendation letter from the local priest and their health records.[114] While not adopting a strict approach in terms of naming, it seems that the promoter NGOs and the foundation had the freedom to select whomever they considered appropriate, within the remits of the eligibility criteria agreed with the state. While the agreed quotas counted towards the pledges of the state-led resettlement programme for the Czech Republic, these private schemes were the only route to resettlement in the case of Slovakia and Poland.[115]

Quite similarly to many of the humanitarian corridors already seen, the beneficiaries arrived in Slovakia, the Czech Republic and Poland with a national visa of territorially limited validity. This allowed the candidate to apply for asylum and, if successful, to be granted the status of refugee or recipient of subsidiary protection. In all the three programmes, costs such as travel, housing, household and other extra expenses were covered by the sponsors. In particular, in Slovakia the sponsor provided a monthly allowance for each person sponsored, to be increasingly reduced over time.[116] Similarly, in Poland the sponsor had to provide monthly support to cover the costs of housing, food and other general expenses.[117] In the Polish programme, medical care was provided by the state.[118]

[113] S Fratzke and B Salant, 'Tracing the Channels Refugees Use to Seek Protection in Europe' (2017), available at: www.migrationpolicy.org/sites/default/files/publications/MPI-EPIM_ChannelsOfEntry_FINALWEB.pdf, 15.

[114] *Financial Times*, 'Poland favours Christian refugees from Syria' 21 August 2015, available at: www.ft.com/content/6edfdd30-472a-11e5-b3b2-1672f710807b.

[115] The Czech Republic started its national resettlement programme back in 2008, when 43 Burmese refugees from Malaysia were resettled. It was repeated in 2010 and 2012, where two other groups of refugees were resettled. The Czech Republic also participated to the EU Resettlement Programme in 2015, when they pledged to resettle 400 refugees by 2017. This did not happen, as numbers were much lower. The programme was officially suspended in 2017. For more information see UNHCR Resettlement Handbook, 'Country chapter: Czech Republic', available at: www.unhcr.org/4e2d65a79.pdf, 1–2. By amending the relevant legislation, Poland began to allow resettlement of refugees from third countries in 2011. On this point see A Fihel, P Kaczmarczyk and R Stefańska, 'Recent Trends in International Migration in Poland' (2012) 1 *Central and Eastern European Migration Review* 69, 72. However, according to UNHCR data, no refugees were resettled (or relocated) in Poland between 2014 and 2018. See UNHCR factsheet, Poland, available at: www.unhcr.org/ceu/wp-content/uploads/sites/17/2019/09/Poland.pdf.

[116] European Migration Network, 'Resettlement and Humanitarian Admission Programmes in Europe- what works?' (2016), available at: home-affairs.ec.europa.eu/system/files/2020-09/emn-studies-00_resettlement_synthesis_report_final_en_0.pdf., 40.

[117] ibid.

[118] ibid.

As mentioned above, these were short-lived experiences. The difficulties faced by the immigrants and by their sponsors to promote successful integration was probably one of the main causes that triggered the failure of the programmes. For example, the beneficiaries of the Czech programme faced a variety of difficulties after arriving in the country, due to integration issues and lack of pre-departure expectations setting. This led to an early departure from the country towards, in most cases, neighbouring Germany, often seen as a better place in terms of life opportunities. This triggered rapid disengagement of the sponsors and the locals involved in these projects and gave an opportunity to the government to support the argument that the programme should not be renewed because refugees do not want to settle in the Czech Republic.[119] This was also the case for the Slovak and Polish programmes, where people moved to other countries in search of better conditions.

These programmes were highly criticised for including in the selection criteria the requirement of belonging to a Christian religious group. In particular, it was argued that the schemes discriminated against people of Islamic faith, who were also victims of the civil war in Syria. To this criticism Poland answered that only Christians were at risk of persecution in Syria by ISIS and, for this reason, the programme targeted only them.[120] Other arguments in support of the narrow scope of the programmes suggested that the schemes were not intentionally discriminatory but, on the contrary, were properly tailored to take into account both the needs of the sponsors and the beneficiaries. For example, it was suggested that in countries with a majority Christian population, with no mosques and pre-existing Muslim networks, the beneficiaries would struggle to integrate.[121]

IV. Community Sponsorship in Portugal: A Pilot

At the UNHCR Global Refugee Forum of 2019 Portugal pledged the introduction of a pilot private sponsorship programme, roughly based on the Canadian and Irish experiences,[122] by 2020. Initially, the project encountered difficulties and delays. This was due to the fact that, originally, the project was supposed to be supported by the Portuguese High Commission for Migration (ACM) but, due to red-tape issues and the sudden outbreak of the Afghan and Ukrainian crises, this did not happen.[123] After an initial period of inactivity the task was taken up, at the beginning of 2021, by the Portuguese Refugee Council (CPR), which initially

[119] Jelínková, above n 112, 35. Apparently, out of those who were admitted, only 35 stayed.

[120] *Financial Times*, above n 114.

[121] See B Brljavac, 'Refugee Crisis in Europe: The Cases Studies of Sweden and Slovakia' (2017) 3 *Journal of Liberty and International Affairs* 91, 99.

[122] See Pledges and Contributions Digital Platform, available at: globalcompactrefugees.org/pledges-contributions, GRF00888.

[123] Information gathered from the conversation with Barbara Oliveira and Clara Vaz from the Portuguese Refugee Council on 31 May 2023.

found help and support from the Open Community initiative in Ireland (The Open Community is now an independent organisation). The project was founded by the EU through AMIF (Asylum, Migration and Integration Fund). The fund was used to pay a small team of two people from the Portuguese Refugee Council to devote their time to the groundwork of initial research, subsequent development of a plan, and reporting to the government. The first phase of the project comprised research and development, public consultation and development of the key materials. This was followed by the second phase, the outreach, which was finally reached by the end of 2022. In this phase the project was publicised to the wider community to raise awareness, explain what Community Sponsorship consists of and how to become involved. The end of 2022 and beginning of 2023 were dedicated to capacity-building of the sponsors. In April 2023 the first testing of the programme started, with a family of refugees included in the state resettlement quotas of Portugal. In the testing phase the Portuguese Refugee Council selected a less vulnerable family, with the most potential for inclusion. If the testing results are successful, it is hoped that proper piloting will start in 2024, with half a dozen of families.[124]

Community Sponsorship has been designed as a complementary scheme to resettlement. A naming stream within the project has recently found a way through. An Afghan refugee already living in Portugal contacted the CPR denouncing the dangerous situation in which some of their family members in Iran found themselves. Within two months the supporting group was formed and trained, and the family members were able to enter Portugal on 7 November 2023.[125] It is worth noting that, as things stand now, there is no specific guidance in terms of requirements of who can be named. Indeed, the CPR is currently supporting the entry of 10 Afghan activist women, on the request of an Afghan sponsor already residing in Portugal who is unrelated to them.[126]

Additionality is not envisaged yet. However, the Portuguese government promised, subject to the pilot working, to expand its resettlement quotas and dedicate some to private sponsorships. There is not (yet) a specific primary or secondary piece of legislation that crystallises the introduction of the programme for refugees in Portugal. As a matter of fact, at the moment, the proposed scheme is based on the legislation authorising government resettlement, which can be found at Article 35 of Asylum Law 27/2008. Like some other schemes already analysed, the beneficiaries are granted a temporary visa under Article 25 of the Visa Code and, once in Portugal, they can apply for asylum.[127]

In relation to sponsors, the option that has been chosen is the group-of-five rule – a minimum of five people that join together to share the various financial and emotional responsibilities. It is necessary that the sponsors are connected to

[124] ibid. Information gathered on 30 January 2024.
[125] ibid.
[126] ibid.
[127] ibid, information gathered on 31 May 2023.

a local recognised organisation or NGO in order to be granted the status of sponsor. The CPR provides training and capacity-building to people that are interested in becoming sponsors and those that have already been accepted as sponsors. The training is nationally accredited as vocational training and is composed of seven modules, six e-learning and one in person, that have to be attended and completed.[128]

In order to understand the extent of the sponsor's financial responsibilities, it is important to first explain how resettlement is financed in Portugal. Portugal does not spend funds from its national budget to support resettlement, not even for the state-led programme. As a matter of fact, Portugal receives a lump sum for every resettled migrant from the European Commission (around 10,000 euros) and some extra money from AMIF. When the government receives this money, it acts as a mediator between the EU and the CPR, which is in charge of managing the funds according to the needs of each resettled individual. Funds from the EU are also allocated for community sponsorship beneficiaries to the Portuguese Refugee Council.[129] However, since the financial protocols can only be signed and paid after the beneficiaries arrive in Portugal, it is important for the sponsors to fundraise to ensure the coverage of initial expenses, like housing and other goods that may not be available through donation collection. Similarly to other European programmes, sponsors will be asked to cover rental expenses, utility bills, food and, if possible, extras. Health and education are accessible through the Portuguese state system.[130]

The programme lasts for 18 months. Safety nets in case of sponsorship break-downs have also been considered. In case of sponsorship break-down, the Portuguese Refugee Council will step in to mediate.

At the time of writing, two families have already been welcomed by Portugal under the pilot. Data on the successful application of the sponsorship are not yet available, since the programme still needs to be properly piloted on a larger number of families. However, based on the experience so far, it has been noted that the inclusion achieved is far better than that provided by the mainstream government programme. However, the CPR has acknowledged that successful integration could be an issue in terms of cultural and work integration. To address this potential problem, sponsors are encouraged to work with their local networks and seek the help and support of local industries and local authorities. Moreover, with the aim of achieving faster integration, it is the intention of the Refugee Council to undertake a pilot outside of Lisbon, where communities are smaller and costs are more contained.[131]

Finally, it should be noted that currently two other similar pilot private sponsorship schemes are currently being tested in Sweden and Finland. While these

[128] ibid.
[129] ibid.
[130] ibid.
[131] ibid.

schemes seem to operate more as 'buddy programmes', where sponsors do not take on any specific commitments, apart from helping the beneficiaries to get accustomed and integrate in the new local community,[132] it will be interesting to assess their success in the near future.

V. The UK Community Sponsorship Scheme

The UK started its first state-led resettlement programme in 1995, known as the Mandate Resettlement Scheme. This scheme is still running and concerns the resettlement of close family members of refugees who are already established in the UK and who can provide accommodation and financial support for them. There is no official quota for this scheme, and numbers, over the years, have been quite small.[133]

In 2004, the UK introduced its second most successful resettlement scheme, called the Gateway Protection Programme. The scheme, as well as the subsequent resettlement programmes, has its legal grounding in the Nationality, Immigration and Asylum Act 2002, section 59, which states that 'The Secretary of State may participate in a project which is designed to … (e) arrange or assist the settlement of migrants (whether in the United Kingdom or elsewhere)'. The initial quota of 500 refugees to be admitted on a yearly basis was extended to 750 in 2008.[134] The annual case load is decided at ministerial level, after having consulted the UNHCR Projected Global Resettlement Needs document and following discussion with other departments within the UK government and with the UNHCR.[135] The beneficiaries are selected using the UNHCR refugee criteria. To be resettled in the UK, the potential beneficiaries must also have been living as refugees in the first country of refuge for a period of five years, unless there is a compelling urgent need for resettlement.[136]

A third programme, known as the Vulnerable Persons Resettlement Scheme (VPRS), was launched in 2014. This programme initially targeted Syrians but its scope was extended in 2017, to include refugees of any nationality that fled Syria because of the conflict. The aim of the programme was to resettle 20,000 refugees by the end of 2020, assessed against the UNHCR refugee criteria.[137] Two years later, in 2016,

[132] MB Zanzuchi, N Dumann, F Tissot and A Skodo, 'Attracting, Retaining, and Diversifying Sponsors for Refugees in Community Sponsorship Programmes' September 2023 Migration Policy Institute, available at: www.migrationpolicy.org/sites/default/files/publications/mpie-caps-eu_sponsor-recruitment-2023_final.pdf, 5.

[133] Independent Chief Inspector of Borders and Immigration, 'An Inspection of UK Refugee Resettlement Schemes' (November 2019–May 2020), available at: assets.publishing.service.gov.uk/government/uploads/system/uploads/attachment_data/file/933956/An_inspection_of_UK_Refugee_Resettlement_Schemes.pdf, 15.

[134] ibid.

[135] ibid, 16.

[136] ibid.

[137] ibid.

a similar programme for the resettlement of vulnerable children – the Vulnerable Children's Resettlement Scheme (VCRS) – was launched. The scheme was open to vulnerable children and their families in Egypt, Iraq, Lebanon and Turkey, when resettlement was assessed to be in the best interest of the child by the UNHCR.[138]

Both the VPRS and VCRS programmes came to an end in early 2021. A new resettlement programme, known as the United Kingdom Resettlement Scheme (UKRS), was launched in February 2021. This scheme replaced the previous VPRS and VCRS and the Gateway Protection Programme. The new scheme is open to refugees deemed to fall within the UNHCR protected category groups. Global resettlement needs and the capacity of local authorities are taken into account to ascertain whether refugees can be resettled in the UK.[139]

The latest resettlement programme, called the Afghan Citizens Resettlement Scheme, opened on 6 January 2022, following the official conclusion of the war in Afghanistan on 31 August 2021. This is an ad hoc programme prioritising people that in Afghanistan helped the UK in standing up 'for democracy, women's rights, freedom of speech, and rule of law, and vulnerable people, including women and girls at risk, and members of minority groups at risk (including ethnic and religious minorities and LGBT+)'.[140]

Against this background, the UK was also one of the first states to experiment with sponsorship of refugees. A private sponsorship of refugees programme, known as Community Sponsorship Scheme, was initially launched in July 2016 as part of the VPRS scheme. However, with the birth of the new UKRS in 2021, the UK Community Sponsorship became an independent scheme. On this occasion, the UK government agreed that the quota of refugees resettled via Community Sponsorship would become additional to those resettled by the UK government.[141]

The UK Community Sponsorship Scheme was initially born out of the frustration of many British people who wished to do more for Syrians fleeing the civil war in their country. The scheme relies on section 59 of the Nationality, Immigration and Asylum Act 2022.[142] 'Otherwise, the formal legal framework

[138] ibid, 17.

[139] See Home Office, 'UK Refugee Resettlement: Policy Guidance' August 2021, available at: assets.publishing.service.gov.uk/government/uploads/system/uploads/attachment_data/file/1011824/Resettlement_Policy_Guidance_2021.pdf, 6.

[140] See Gov.UK, 'Afghan citizens resettlement scheme' 17 October 2023, available at: www.gov.uk/guidance/afghan-citizens-resettlement-scheme.

[141] While still part of the VPRS scheme the refugees resettled via Community Sponsorship counted towards the state-pledged quotas.

[142] The only express reference to the scheme is a ministerial arrangement under the Equality Act 2010 s 23 (1)(d). The Equality (Community Sponsorship) Arrangement 2016, available here data.parliament.uk/DepositedPapers/Files/DEP2016-0667/Equality__Community_Sponsorship__Arrangement_2016_-_dated_11.07.2016.pdf, states that the program focused only on Syrian nationals and individuals affected by the Syrian conflict. More details on Community Sponsorships in the UK are outlined by policy documents, guidelines and application forms published by the Home Office.

enabling resettlement is silent on the introduction of community sponsorship'.[143] The first official reference to introducing private sponsorship of refugees to the UK occurred during Theresa May's speech at the Conservative Party Conference of 2015:[144]

> I know the whole country was proud of the generosity of spirit shown by the British businesses and families who offered to shelter Syrian refugees in their own properties this summer. So, to help turn these acts of humanity into reality … we'll develop a community sponsorship scheme, like those in Canada and Australia, to allow individuals, charities, faith groups, churches and businesses to support refugees directly.

Whether this was an already developed project or an embryonic idea at that time, it is difficult to know.[145] However, after less than a year from Theresa May's initial announcement, on 19 July 2016, the new Home Secretary at the time, Amber Rudd, and the Archbishop of Canterbury, Justin Welby, stood together at Lambeth Palace to launch the new Community Sponsorship Scheme. On that occasion, the first family was warmly welcomed to live in a cottage within Lambeth Palace grounds.[146]

At the very beginning the scheme took shape quite informally. Apparently, in its early days, the official template of the application forms for charities wishing to be involved in the project was not drafted, and training for the sponsors was not yet available. As a matter of fact, everything was initially prompted by the Home Office, that sought help from charities and faith communities in terms of how to organise the scheme and the various framework documents.[147] In the early years the scheme only managed to resettle a small numbers of refugees, and this was in part to due the lack of staff and organisation, to be able 'to capitalise on the initial public enthusiasm'.[148]

Despite the initial organisational gap, the Home Office quickly managed to set up a rigorous application process, with the aim of making sure that sponsors could financially cope with the needs of the beneficiaries of the scheme, and that the programme could survive as a stand-alone project after the expiry of the VPRS,[149]

[143] J Bond and A Kwadrans, 'Resettling Refugees through Community Sponsorship: a Revolutionary Operational Approach Built on Traditional Legal Infrastructure' (2019) 35 *Refuge: Canada's Journal on Refugees* 87, 91.

[144] Theresa May, 'Theresa May's speech to the Conservative Party Conference – in full' 6 October 2015 *The Independent*, available at: www.independent.co.uk/news/uk/politics/theresa-may-s-speech-to-the-conservative-party-conference-in-full-a6681901.html.

[145] It looks like the project was not yet developed or thought through at the time of the conference. Information gathered from the conversation with Carly Whyborn, Interim Executive Director at Refugees at Home, on 9 February 2022.

[146] *Church Times*, 'At Lambeth Palace, Amber Rudd pledges more help to settle Syrian refugees' 19 July 2017, available at: www.churchtimes.co.uk/articles/2017/14-july/news/uk/rudd-pledges-more-help-to-settle-syrian-refugees.

[147] Whyborn, above n 145.

[148] See Independent Chief Inspector of Borders and Immigration, above n 133, 26.

[149] ibid. It also refers to the report Independent Chief Inspector of Borders and Immigration, 'An Inspection of the Vulnerable Persons Resettlement Scheme' (August 2017–January 2018), available at: assets.publishing.service.gov.uk/government/uploads/system/uploads/attachment_data/file/705155/VPRS_Final_Artwork_revised.pdf.

an objective that has been effectively achieved. In particular, soon after the official launch of the scheme, the Home Office published some guidance for prospective sponsors.[150] The guidance requested that the sponsor should provide a minimum of £9,000 to support integration for the refugees and offer suitable accommodation for at least two years.[151] This feature of Community Sponsorship is a key difference from the UKRS programme and the Mandate Resettlement Scheme, where accommodation and support for those who are resettled are offered directly by the local authority.[152] Nevertheless, it is important to note that the programme has been tailored to be delivered in close collaboration with local authorities. For instance, refugees are allocated to a community group that has been approved as sponsor, but the sponsorship will not take place in the place where the community group is located, unless the local authority gives its consent.[153]

As far as the financial responsibility is concerned, the Home Office has made quite a lot of funding available, both to the individual sponsors and to the local authorities where the refugees will be resettled. Examples are funding used to cover 'property void' costs, ESOL language classes, education, health, social care, making changes to a property to improve accessibility and even exceptional costs.[154] This approach is similar to that adopted by the UKRS programme. In this instance the Home Office provides 'full tariff' funding and education to the local authorities for the first year and decreased tariff funding from year two to year five.[155] Also, in case of default by the sponsor, following an assessment of the situation of the family and their needs, the local authority is allowed to provide support. Indeed, following a positive assessment of the situation, the government will entrust the local authority with tariff funding for years two to five.[156] The beneficiaries of the scheme are also entitled to national social security benefits (universal credit) and have access to local state schools and to the National Health System. The money that the sponsor provides to the beneficiaries is used towards integration support and, sometimes, to top up rent costs, which otherwise has to be afforded by the family.[157] It is important to note that the money is not handed over by the sponsor to the family but rather

[150] See Gov.UK, 'Apply for community sponsorship' 16 August 2023 available at: www.gov.uk/government/publications/apply-for-full-community-sponsorship.

[151] Independent Chief Inspector of Borders and Immigration, above n 133, 88.

[152] See Home Office, above n 139, 8. Offers for accommodation are sometimes identified at a regional level through the Strategic Migration Partnership (SMP). There are 12 SMPs in the UK. They are funded by the Home Office, although independent from it. Their task is to coordinate and help with the delivery of national programmes for the support of refugees and asylum seekers.

[153] ibid, 90.

[154] Reset, 'Available sources for funding-key things to do' 17 November 2021, available at: training-resetuk.org/application-process/available-sources-funding-key-things-do. On this point see also Gov.UK, 'Funding Instructions for local authorities in support of the United Kingdom's resettlement schemes (accessible)' 1 November 2023, available at: www.gov.uk/government/publications/uk-resettlement-programmes-funding-instruction-2023-to-2024/funding-instruction-for-local-authorities-in-the-support-of-the-united-kingdoms-resettlement-schemes-accessible.

[155] Home Office, above n 139, 9.

[156] ibid.

[157] Information gathered from the exchange of emails with Amina Khanom, Programmes Manager at Reset Communities for Refugees on 1 February 2024.

the sponsors use the money to pay for what they have to provide to the beneficiaries of the scheme.[158] The latter is equal to what would be offered to resettled refugees via the other government programmes, and includes meeting the refugees at the airport, help to get access to the social and health services, English classes and, more generally, support towards finding a job and becoming independent.[159]

In 2020, a safety net was also introduced to alleviate the financial responsibility that sponsors may face in case of default or of other unforeseeable circumstances. The Shapiro Foundation donated £1,000,000 to the UK sponsorship initiative. This fund was utilised to provide grants to charities and community interest companies to cover their financial exposure if issues arose.[160]

As far as the selection procedures are concerned, the UK works in close collaboration with the UNHCR. Indeed, it is the UNHCR that has the responsibility to run the selection and case-work activities in relation all the existing resettlement programmes currently available in the UK, including Community Sponsorship Scheme. People that are normally referred for Community Sponsorship qualify as refugees but do not live in UNHCR refugee camps but rather in urban areas, where situations of serious vulnerability mostly occur. The activity of the UNHCR is subdivided into different phases. First, the UNHCR will check the identity of the members of the family and the family composition.[161] Then, the UNHCR officers will interview the family, to assess their resettlement needs and vulnerability.[162] They will then make a refugee status determination assessment, by which it will be determined whether the potential beneficiaries can be considered refugees under the Geneva Convention. Finally, before sending the names of the potential candidates to the UK authorities for consideration, the UNHCR officers will interview them again, for a final assessment of whether the refugees meet the UNHCR criteria for resettlement.[163]

Once the potential beneficiaries have been identified, the UNHCR applies its checks to each individual. This is done against the Geneva Convention exclusion clauses stated at Article 1(f).[164] In any case, the UK can still refuse entry on security

[158] ibid.

[159] Home Office, above n 139, 12–13.

[160] The Community Sponsorship Backstop Fund was only guaranteed until January 2022.

[161] Whyborn, above n 145. Please note that there is no legal requirement stating that the beneficiaries of the UK scheme have necessarily to be families. However, in practice, the majority of the resettled refugees in the UK are groups of families. This is also because the benefits granted by the government (Universal Credit) to an individual alone would not be sufficient to cope with all their expenses.

[162] ibid.

[163] Home Office, above n 139, 5–6. The categories for eligibility are: Legal and/or Physical Protection Needs; Survivors of Violence and/or Torture; Medical Needs; Women and Girls at Risk; Family Reunification; Children and Adolescents at Risk; Lack of Foreseeable Alternative Durable Solutions.

[164] Art 1(f) states that: 'The provisions of this Convention shall not apply to any person with respect to whom there are serious reasons for considering that: (a) he has committed a crime against peace, a war crime, or a crime against humanity, as defined in the international instruments drawn up to make provision in respect of such crimes; (b) he has committed a serious non-political crime outside the country of refuge prior to his admission to that country as a refugee; (c) he has been guilty of acts contrary to the purposes and principles of the United Nations'.

or other grounds.[165] After having passed the security checks run by the UK, the beneficiaries of the programme also have to undergo pre-entry health assessments, to understand whether the individual needs health assistance and, if so, which treatment is needed. If assistance is needed, the UK works towards resettling the individual in an area that can offer the appropriate health facilities. The beneficiaries are also offered immunisation and they are checked for fitness to travel.[166]

Before departure, travel assistance and cultural orientation are provided by the International Organization for Migration (IOM). In relation to travel assistance, the IOM helps with visa applications, with accompanying refugees to the UK visa centres for their biometric appointments, with booking flights, exit permits from the country of first refuge and with providing appropriate confirmation that the refugee can travel. As far as cultural orientation is concerned, refugees aged 14 years and above are invited by the IOM to a pre-departure meeting to gather the key information they need before entering the UK and to set expectations.[167]

The beneficiaries of the programme are granted six months' Leave Outside the Rules visas prior to departing the country for the UK. These visas are rare and are only issued on compelling compassionate grounds.[168] IOM relies on these visas to obtain exit permits from the country of first refuge and to make all the appropriate travel arrangements.[169] Once in the UK, resettled refugees are granted indefinite leave to remain and refugee status,[170] and they can apply for British Citizenship after five years.[171]

In order to become a sponsor, the group of people interested in sponsoring refugees should be a charity (or should be able to organise one and register it), or should work with one, or should be a Community Interest Company.[172] The sponsor is approved by the Home Office and approval is sought for each family that a group decides to sponsor.[173] A named individual within the organisation is nominated as the Lead Sponsor. The Lead Sponsor is normally someone holding a senior position within the organisation and is the person that holds full

[165] See Home Office, above n 139, 8.

[166] See Home Office, Public Health England, IOM, 'Health Protocol, Pre-entry health assessments for UK bound refugees' June 2020, available at: assets.publishing.service.gov.uk/government/uploads/system/uploads/attachment_data/file/892799/Badged_HA_protocol_IOM_HO_PHE_-_June_2020.odt.pdf, 2–3.

[167] Home Office, above n 139, 10.

[168] Home Office, 'Leave outside the Immigration Rules' 29 August 2023, available at: assets.publishing.service.gov.uk/media/64eef28f13ae1500116e3013/Leave_outside_the_Immigration_Rules.pdf, 5.

[169] See Home Office, above n 139, 11.

[170] *Indefinite* leave to remain has been granted to resettled refugees since October 2021. Before then, individuals resettled through VPRS or VCRS were granted refugee status with five years' leave to remain on arrival. After five years, they were able to apply for indefinite leave to remain.

[171] Share Network, above n 3.

[172] For a definition of Community Interest Company in the UK see Gov.UK, 'Setting up a social enterprise', available at: www.gov.uk/set-up-a-social-enterprise.

[173] See Gov.UK, 'Community sponsorship: guidance for prospective sponsors' 16 August 2023, available at: www.gov.uk/government/publications/apply-for-full-community-sponsorship/community-sponsorship-guidance-for-prospective-sponsors.

responsibility for the plan with the Home Office. Once the sponsor has been approved, to get final consent from the Home Office, the sponsor has to be able to prove that enough money – at least £9,000, as mentioned above – has been made available towards the sponsorship, that proper housing has been found,[174] and that the local authority has given its consent.[175] Sponsors, co-aided by various volunteers, are responsible for the family for 12 months and have to provide housing for at least two years.[176]

Unlike what happens for the humanitarian corridors and for the expired examples of Poland, Slovakia and the Czech Republic, where the particular beneficiaries are selected by the representatives of the sponsoring organisations in loco, the UK programme does not envisage naming among its key features, since, as mentioned above, it is the Home Office that chooses the beneficiaries from the UNHCR lists and matches them with the sponsors. To facilitate the matching exercise, it is important that both the local authority and the sponsor, in the application, specify what they can offer to the resettled refugees. This entails, for example, whether they can provide someone speaking the native language of the beneficiaries. The Home Office will do the matching in accordance with the information available. The Home Office will then propose the match, sometimes disclosing sensitive information to the sponsors, such as trauma, divorce, past experiences, health conditions,[177] and specifying the household composition and, if necessary, the language spoken. Based on this information, the local authority and the sponsor can then accept or refuse the sponsorship.[178] In case of refusal, the family will be resettled somewhere else.

The sponsor needs to be able to provide a comprehensive plan for resettlement, and to show that robust safeguarding and complaints policies are in place.[179] The sponsor has also to undergo proper training. While no training was available at the

[174] ibid.

[175] ibid. As mentioned before, local authorities play a crucial role in the resettlement of refugees. Local authorities have to give consent for the sponsorships to take place within their area, as they have to take into account the impact of resettling additional families. In addition, local authorities also check that the sponsor is suitable to support the resettled families. In particular, the grounds upon which the consent could be refused are the inability to provide the necessary local services (for example, lack of school places), community tensions within the proposed housing area, or the local authority having strong reasons to believe that the sponsor is not suitable to take on the responsibility of the Community Sponsorship.

[176] Share Network, above n 3.

[177] Khanom, above n 157.

[178] Whyborn, above n 145. The Home Office will send an anonymous description of the family, specifying just some key information such as the number of the family members, the language spoken, and medical needs.

[179] Gov.UK, 'Community sponsorship: guidance for prospective sponsors', above n 173. These have to be properly drafted by the sponsor (templates are available on the government website). As far as safeguarding is concerned, the policy is put in place to test the good character of the sponsor. The complaints policy has to be made available to the resettled family so that they are able to escalate concerns, should they arise.

beginning, since 2018 Reset has become the organisation that provides training and support to all the sponsors that have been approved by the Home Office.[180] If all the above requirements are fulfilled, the Home Office approves the application and the Lead Sponsor has to sign a formal agreement.[181] Sponsor groups and beneficiaries have the option to contact each other before the latter's arrival in the UK.[182] As previously mentioned, the first version of the UK Community Sponsorship programme was embedded within the VPRS scheme. No additionality was originally envisaged, and the numbers of sponsored refugees counted towards those pledged within the VPRS programme. Since 2021, additionality has become a key feature of Community Sponsorship. However, the fulfilment of additional quotas through the scheme was postponed during Covid, because of the queue of people waiting to fulfil the previous pledges. It is likely that additionality will be capped, as the Government is looking into introducing a cap on resettlement in the Illegal Migration Act 2023.[183]

The UK sponsorship scheme has proven to be particularly flexible and has inspired related initiatives. In 2017, King's College London applied to participate in the scheme and, in collaboration with the UNHCR, the Home Office and Citizens UK, acted as a sponsor to welcome a Syrian family.[184] Building on this experience, a University Sponsorship Model was created by King's College London, in collaboration with The Open University, Newcastle University and the University of Leicester, to implement a parallel scheme to Community Sponsorship, to welcome displaced Ukrainian students and academics to allow them to continue their studies and work from a safe place in the UK.[185]

[180] In 2018 the Home Office called for bids to provide training to potential sponsors. The bid was won by the newly established organisation Reset, which was awarded £1 million by the Home Office. Reset is an organisation that is funded 90 per cent by the Home Office and the remainder by philanthropic organisations. Training covers the early phases, from the preparation of the application to the welcoming of the refugee family in the UK. Reset also supports local authorities and Lead Sponsors, while preparing alongside the group. Reset also commissions research, to evaluate the development of the schemes, and undertakes advocacy activities to ensure the further expansion of the scheme. See, in particular, Reset, 'About Reset', available at: resetuk.org/about/about-reset.

[181] The template for the agreement relating to the provision of community sponsorship can be found at: assets.publishing.service.gov.uk/government/uploads/system/uploads/attachment_data/file/1096343/Agreement_Version_5.0.pdf.

[182] Khanom, above n 157.

[183] ibid. See also Electronic Immigration Network, 'No new routes proposed in the Home Office's Illegal Migration Act report on safe and legal routes to the UK' 11 January 2024, available at: www.ein.org.uk/news/no-new-routes-proposed-home-offices-illegal-migration-act-report-safe-and-legal-routes-uk.

[184] Share Network, above n 3.

[185] For more information see WONKHE, 'Ukraine one year on: how the HE sector can support those displaced by conflict' 24 February 2023, available at: wonkhe.com/blogs/ukraine-one-year-on-how-the-he-sector-can-support-those-displaced-by-conflict/, and King's College London, 'University Sponsorship: Providing sanctuary for Ukrainian students and academics' 21 February 2023, available at: www.kcl.ac.uk/university-sponsorship.

Important academic studies on the UK scheme have already been advanced.[186] Research has shown the importance of the role of positive affective and reactive emotions for the sustainability of private sponsorship programmes in the UK. In particular, the study emphasises how, for the majority of the sponsoring volunteers involved in the schemes, this experience brought positive affective emotions towards the refugees and other members of the group and positive reactive emotions, such as pride in what has been achieved as a group and by the refugees, and shows the importance of maximising these positive emotions for the success of the scheme.[187] The programme has also helped to operationalise some British Values in a concrete manner, particularly in relation to tolerance. Indeed 'reflecting on approaches such as sponsorship, which promotes human interaction, understanding and tolerance, is one way to start addressing these problems through practical measures'.[188] Finally, research has also pointed out that the work of sponsors is having an impact on the UK governance of migration and raising awareness of resettlement issues.[189]

Nevertheless, despite the overall success of the scheme, some shortcomings are still experienced. One key issue relates to the mismatching of refugees to geographical areas. Indeed, this can become sometimes problematic due to the diverging expectations of the refugees and their job skills.[190] Social and cultural differences can also be an issue, and both sponsors and refugees may be unprepared, particularly in relation to socialising and gender relations.[191] The programme seems also to suffer from lack of expectation management, which has become more and more evident in the relationship between sponsors and beneficiaries.[192] Another issue that seems to cause frustration is the slow pace of achieving financial independence, which is difficult to accomplish in only 12 months.[193] This is also triggers anxieties connected to the lack of affordable accommodation in the UK, for those that have to leave the property they were resettled into, after the two-year tenancy comes to an end.[194] Furthermore, it has been argued that Community Sponsorship

[186] See in particular J Phillimore and M Reyes, 'Community Sponsorship in the UK: from application to integration' July 2019 interim report, available at: www.birmingham.ac.uk/documents/college-social-sciences/social-policy/misc/cs-uk-iris-june-2019.pdf.

[187] See J Phillimore, M Reyes-Soto, G d'Avino and N Nicholls, 'I Have Felt So Much Joy: The Role of Emotions in Community Sponsorship of Refugees' (2022) 33 *VOLUNTAS: International Journal of Voluntary and Nonprofit Organisations* 386, 394. See also M Reyes-Soto, 'It's About the Power of Little People': the UK Community Sponsorship Scheme, a New Space for Solidarity, Civic Engagement and Activism' (2023) 24 *Journal of International Migration and Integration* 1939.

[188] J Van Selm, 'Community based sponsorship of refugees resettling in the UK: British values in action?' in EM Gozdziak, I Main and B Suter (eds), *Europe and the Refugee Response: a Crisis of Values?* (London, Routledge, 2021) 185, 198.

[189] Reyes-Soto, above n 187, 1952.

[190] Phillimore, Reyes, above n 186, 38.

[191] ibid.

[192] Khanom, above n 157. See also IriS, 'Expectations and Understanding of Community Sponsorship before Refugee Arrival' (2017), available at: www.birmingham.ac.uk/Documents/college-social-sciences/social-policy/iris/2020/1-expectations-and-understanding-policy.pdf.

[193] Phillimore and Reyes, above n 186, 39.

[194] Khanom, above n 157.

'marks the withdrawal of the state from the responsibility of care for refugees'.[195] While this statement may have found more grounding under the previous version of Community Sponsorship, where additionality was not yet contemplated, the fact that the UK seems reluctant to publish a target both for UKRS and Community Sponsorship, and the risk that the quotas of government programmes might be reduced in favour of private sponsorship's targets, seem to make this criticism still valid. Finally, from a broader perspective, research has shown that the reason why the Community Sponsorship Scheme coexists with antagonistic legislation towards immigration in the UK is the fact that the former seems to have been introduced more as a way to manage immigration, rather than to promote international protection.[196]

VI. Germany and the 'New Start in a Team' or 'Nest' Programme

Germany has had a resettlement programme since 2012.[197] The commitment to a permanent state-led resettlement programme, in collaboration with the UNHCR, is a recent initiative, since Germany has had a long history of ad hoc admission programmes.[198] The programme became institutionalised in 2014. The resettlement numbers pledged per year were 300, which rose to 500 per year in 2015. Numbers have drastically increased again more recently. Indeed, Germany pledged 6,500 places for 2023 and 13,100 for the biennium of 2024–25, under the EU resettlement and humanitarian admission scheme.[199]

Resettlement in Germany has its legal basis in section 23(4) of the Residence Act.[200] This section states that the Federal Ministry of the Interior in agreement with the federal States, can order the Federal Office for Migration and Refugees to grant admission permits to asylum seekers selected for resettlement. On arrival, they will be granted resident permits for three years, which can then be

[195] See D Dajani, 'Refuge under austerity: the UK's refugee settlement schemes and the multiplying practices of bordering' (2020) 44 *Ethnic and Racial Studies* 58, 67.

[196] On this point see G D'Avino, 'Framing Community Sponsorship in the context of the UK's hostile environment' (2022) 42 *Critical Social Policy* 327, 347.

[197] A pilot started in 2011, prompted by the Save Me campaign of 2008. For more information see P Endres de Oliveira, 'Humanitarian Admissions in Germany – Access vs Rights?' in MC Foblets and L Leboeuf (eds), *Humanitarian Admission to Europe: The Law between Promises and Constraints* (Baden-Baden, Nomos, 2020) 199, 210. For a broad overview of refugee protection systems in Germany see A Korntheuer, 'Germany Refugee Protection System' in A Korntheuer, P Pritchard and DB Maehler (eds), *Structural Context of Refugee Integration in Canada and Germany* (Köln, GESIS, 2017) 37, 38.

[198] Endres de Oliveira, above n 197, 210.

[199] Information gathered via e-mail from Theresa Schmidt, Coordinator Civil Society Contact Point for the German Community Sponsorship Programme NesT on 9 February 2024.

[200] Admissions in Germany are also allowed through s 22 of the Residence Act (*Aufenthaltgesetz*), which targets individuals, outside the quota system of s 23, 'in accordance with international law or on urgent humanitarian grounds'. For more details see Endres de Oliveira, above n 197, 202.

extended.[201] Section 23 gives no option to apply for individual admission and its application is based on admission orders. The orders give details on the procedure to be followed for different entry schemes and the criteria that the potential beneficiaries must fulfil to be admitted to Germany.[202] The admission of foreigners for resettlement in Germany is based on referrals from the UNHCR.

Within this legislative context sits the New Start in a Team or NesT programme.[203] This programme is the first nationwide private sponsorship of refugees programme in Germany. It started as a pilot project[204] to offer protection to up to 500 vulnerable refugees who had left their countries and sought refuge in Ethiopia, Egypt, Jordan or Lebanon.[205] The programme was designed by German government agencies in collaboration with the UNHCR, some members of the civil society such as Caritas, the German Red Cross and the Evangelical Church of Westphalia, and with the support of the Bertelsmann and Mercator Foundations.[206] Also this programme has its roots in section 23(4) of the Residence Act and in the admission order,[207] which states that the beneficiaries of the scheme will be resettled in Germany relying on the above legislative background. Based on this legislation, the beneficiaries of NesT are granted a residence permit and the status of resettled refugees.

The negotiations that gave birth to the NesT programme began in 2018. Some of the shortcomings of the previous private sponsorship experiences in Germany seem to have shaped the way in which NesT was originally tailored.[208] It was the German Ministry of the Interior of the time that approached civil society, with

[201] Schmidt, above 199. She also specified that it is in the admission orders that information about residence conditions can be found. See, in particular, the admission order for 2023, available at: www.bmi.bund.de/SharedDocs/downloads/DE/veroeffentlichungen/themen/migration/humanitaere-aufnahmeprogramme/resettlement/aufnahmeanordnung-bes-2023-02-15.pdf;jsessionid=7216EC46D41E037ECABB99890ACFDF46.live862?__blob=publicationFile&v=2, under point 6.

[202] Endres de Oliveira, above n 197, 204.

[203] The NesT programme had already some precursors in Germany. The most notable are the *Länder* admission programmes and Syrian refugee sponsors (more in Chapter four of this book). For more information see V Pohlmann and H Schwiertz, 'Private sponsorship in refugee admission: Standard in Canada, trend in Germany?' (2020) research brief 1, available at: km4s.ca/wp-content/uploads/Private-sponsorship-in-refugee-admission-Standard-in-Canada-trend-in-Germany.pdf, 2.

[204] NesT ran as a pilot programme until the end of 2022. NesT became a regular programme of the German federal government on 1 January 2023. The Federal Office for Migration and Refugees, an agency under the Ministry of the Interior, published a report that assessed the success of the programme, available in German at F Tissot, N Dumann and M Bitterwolf, 'Das Aufnahmeprogramm „Neustart im Team": Studie zur Programmumsetzung' (2003) 44, available at: www.bamf.de/SharedDocs/Anlagen/DE/Forschung/Forschungsberichte/fb44-evaluation-nest.pdf?__blob=publicationFile&v=8.

[205] Pohlmann and Schwiertz, above n 203, 3.

[206] Endres de Oliveira, above n 197, 214.

[207] In the admission order the government indicates how many people per year can enter Germany under different routes and schemes. As far as NesT is concerned, the target is 500 refugees per year. See for example the admission order of May 2021, available at: www.bmi.bund.de/SharedDocs/downloads/DE/veroeffentlichungen/themen/migration/humanitaere-aufnahmeprogramme/nest-neustart-im-team/ao-nest-2021.pdf?__blob=publicationFile&v=3, under point 1.

[208] Endres de Oliveira, above n 197, 209.

the aim of creating a federal programme that would apply to the entire German territory.[209] The pilot programme was then officially launched in May 2019.

The NesT programme is implemented by the Federal Ministry of the Interior, for Building and Community, the Federal Government Commissioner for Migration, Refugees and Integration and the Federal Office for Migration and Refugees.[210] As far as the selection of the beneficiaries is concerned, NesT is available to individuals that have already been recognised as refugees by the UNHCR. Like the UK Community Sponsorship Scheme, naming is not a feature of NesT. However, the programme is additional to state resettlement quotas, with 200 NesT places pledged in 2023 and 500 places pledged for the 2024–25 biennium.[211] The government, in particular the Federal Office for Migration and Refugees (BAMF), is in charge of the vetting procedures and has the final say on who is entitled to enter the country.[212] The refugees admitted are mostly family units. It is uncommon to see single people accessing the scheme, since sponsors want to offer support to more than one person.[213]

The Civil Society Contact Point consists of representatives of Caritas Germany, the German Red Cross and the Evangelical Church of Westphalia. They are the first point of contact for parties and mentoring groups that are willing to participate in supporting the beneficiaries of the programme.[214] Their role is to work together with the sponsors, guide them through the whole process, and provide them with training and supervision. The involvement of these organisations is very important, as it has been noted that the commitment of well-known civil society actors contributes to greater public acceptance of refugee protection in Germany.[215]

Any institution, organisation or individual can become a mentoring sponsor. However, similarly to participants in the Canadian private sponsorship of refugees scheme, individuals interested in becoming sponsors have to join together in a group of at least four members.[216] Sponsors will have then to participate in a one-day event that explains how the programme runs and how it is organised.[217] Afterwards, the groups have to apply to the Federal Office for Migration and

[209] Information gathered from the conversation with the anonymous contributor at Civil Society Contact Point for the German Community Sponsorship Programme NesT on 14 March 2022.

[210] A Kreienbrink, 'Jahresbericht 2019 des Forschungszentrums Migration, Integration und Asyl' (2020) (Jahresbericht / Bundesamt für Migration und Flüchtlinge (BAMF) Forschungszentrum Migration, Integration und Asyl (FZ)), Nürnberg, BAMF and FZ, available at: www.ssoar.info/ssoar/handle/document/71250, 23.

[211] Schmidt, above n 199.

[212] NesT, 'NesT-New Start in a Team: working together to help refugees', available at: resettlement.de/wp-content/uploads/nest_broschuere_quadratisch_auflage_EN_v03.pdf, under 'What is NesT?'.

[213] Schmidt, above n 199.

[214] Kreienbrink, above n 210, 23.

[215] ibid.

[216] Schmidt, above n 199. The minimum number of sponsors/mentors was reduced to 4 people in 2022 to make participation in the programme easier.

[217] This event is organised by the national Contact Point for Civil Society (Zivilgesellschaftliche Kontaktstelle, ZKS). For more information on ZKS see Endres de Oliveira, above n 197, 215.

Refugees, to become officially recognised as sponsors. The Civil Society Contact Point helps the sponsors through the application process more generally.[218]

Once the sponsor group is accepted (NesT calls it a mentoring group), the Federal Office for Migration and Refugees proceeds with the family matching. The group will be notified that the beneficiaries have been matched to them. Although the letter contains anonymised information about the beneficiaries, some key information will be conveyed, particularly in relation to the language spoken by the family.[219] The sponsors will be able to accept or not accept the matching. If the sponsoring group agrees, the beneficiaries will be asked to agree to the NesT scheme.

The first meeting between the beneficiaries of the scheme and the mentoring group takes place in Friedland or Doberlug-Kirchhain, under the supervision of Caritas.[220] The duties of the various groups are listed in the admission order.[221] Overall, the mentoring groups have to cover the costs of adequate accommodation for one year[222] and non-material support aimed at the integration of the beneficiaries of the programme for one year.[223] The costs of utilities, travel, food and language classes are borne by the state through social benefits. As far as integration support is concerned, sponsors assist with appointments at government offices, schools, training and jobs.[224] Particularly in relation to training and jobs, sponsors encourage the beneficiaries to engage with migration counselling centres. In these centres the refugees receive advice and counselling on available jobs, to help the beneficiaries achieve independence.[225] If independence is not achieved after one year, the state intervenes to pay rent and continues to provide social assistance through benefits, which will last for an undetermined period of time, until the refugees are capable of providing for themselves.[226]

Unlike the UK scheme, and more similarly to the Italian one, the local authorities cannot veto the arrival of the NesT beneficiaries within their area. The Federal Office will notify the local authority about the arrival of a beneficiary family and the local authority can only accept. In reality, in the majority of cases, the local authority will already be aware of the arrival of a NesT family, as the sponsor group

[218] NesT, above n 212, under 'How do refugees find sponsors?'. Schmidt (above 199) also pointed out that sponsors have to gather the documents themselves. The Civil Society Contact Point only supports, explains and vets the application papers before forwarding them to the authorities.

[219] Although the matching process is totally run by the Ministry of the Interior, the sponsor group is able to put some criteria in the application that can influence the matching process. Anonymous contributor, above n 209.

[220] Endres de Oliveira, above n 197, 214.

[221] See, for example, the admission order of 2021, above n 207.

[222] The cost of net rent has to be deposited in advance in a fiduciary bank account, to make sure that all the funds are effectively available. See NesT, above n 212, under 'Who can participate and what sponsors do?'.

[223] This was previously two years. See Share Network, above n 3.

[224] ibid.

[225] Anonymous contributor, above n 209.

[226] Schmidt, above n 199.

normally liaises with the local offices to sort out issues such as school availability, healthcare, etc.[227]

Refugees arriving in Germany through NesT immediately receive a residence permit of three years, without having to apply for asylum. This can be renewed, and after five years they can apply for a permanent residence permit.[228]

Not a great deal of research has been conducted on this specific programme yet. However, some of the advantages and disadvantages of the scheme have been highlighted by Endres de Oliveira. In particular, NesT, compared to other German forms of private sponsorship of refugees such as the *Länder* schemes (which will be analysed in Chapter four), puts less financial burden on the sponsors. On the other hand, however, it is feared that the additionality element that characterises NesT could lose its impact if the programme is used to replace parts of the annual resettlement quotas.[229]

In June 2023 the BAMF research centre evaluated the NesT programme.[230] The results were based on the period from the start of the pilot in 2019 to the end of 2021. Data, which was collected through interviews, show the crucial role played by the mentoring sponsor groups in the integration phase of the beneficiaries of the scheme. The report also highlighted how NesT proved to be an important expansion of the German routes to welcome refugees,[231] and hence an important addition to the protection of larger numbers of vulnerable people. However, the report has also raised some concerns about the risk of low participation by the civil society, mostly due to financial pressures, including problems with the housing market, long waiting times and lack of prior information about the refugees to be resettled and to be cared for by the sponsor group.[232] The matching criteria are also an aspect that was raised as something needing to be rethought; data show that one primary criterion used in this process was the size of the apartment offered, while preferences, language, etc were left as secondary.[233]

VII. Community Sponsorship Ireland

Resettlement in Ireland has its legal foundations in section 59 of the International Protection Act 2015. Refugee quotas are pledged on a yearly basis and vary. As to 2018, the resettlement admission target was of 600 individuals. The annual quota

[227] Unlike the UK scheme however, school or hospital availability do not seem to be an issue to be raised by the local authorities.

[228] Share Network, above n 3.

[229] Endres de Oliveira, above n 197, 215.

[230] See Tissot, Dumann and Bitterwolf, above n 204.

[231] ibid, 80.

[232] ibid, 76.

[233] ibid, 79.

is determined by government and decisions regarding the country of origin and country of first asylum are made by the Minister for Justice, in collaboration with the Department of Foreign Affairs and Trade, and with UNHCR.[234]

Following the experience of the family reunification programme for Syrian families, which will be better analysed in Chapter four, Ireland introduced a private sponsorship programme, named Community Sponsorship Ireland (CSI), in November 2019. The launch of the programme by the Minister of State with special responsibility for Equality, Immigration and Integration, David Stanton, followed the highly successful experience of the pilot scheme,[235] operating since December 2018, in the counties of Cork, Waterford and Meath.[236] The programme was born owing to the collaboration between the government of Ireland, Refugees and Citizenship Canada (IRCC), and organisations such as the UNHCR, the Irish Red Cross, Nasc (Migrant and Refugee Rights), the Irish Refugee Council and Amnesty International Ireland.[237]

CSI is grounded in the Irish Refugee Protection Programme (IRPP), which was established in 2015 by the government[238] to help respond to mass migration that was experienced in Southern Europe. Under the programme, the Irish government pledged to accept 4,000 immigrants via different routes such as intra-EU relocation, refugee resettlement and some other mechanisms. CSI is included by the IRPP under the category of resettlement,[239] which also covers the state-led Irish resettlement programme in cooperation with the UNHCR. CSI numbers count towards the quotas pledged by the government for resettlement; hence the scheme is not additional.[240] Moreover, the scheme is not characterised by the naming element either, as the beneficiaries of the programme are people already registered with the UNHCR as refugees in the first hosting country.

From a practical point of view, it is the UNHCR that provides the Irish Department of Justice (formerly Department of Justice and Equality) with detailed information about any potential beneficiary for resettlement. It is this department

[234] See UNHCR Resettlement Handbook, 'Country chapter: Ireland', available at: www.unhcr.org/protection/resettlement/3cac29da4/unhcr-resettlement-handbook-country-chapter-ireland.html, 3.

[235] The pilot CSI programme commenced in December 2018. During this phase five refugee families were warmly welcomed by host community groups. Another family was welcomed in Dublin in December 2018.

[236] See Gov.ie, 'Minister Stanton launches Refugee Community Sponsorship Ireland', available at: www.gov.ie/ga/preasraitis/3c1fbe-minister-stanton-officially-launches-refugee-community-sponsorship-i/.

[237] ibid.

[238] Gov.ie, 'Background to the Irish Refugee Protection Programme', available at: www.gov.ie/ga/foilsiuchan/fec0a-background-to-the-irish-refugee-protection-programme/.

[239] For more information about IRPP see Gov.ie, 'Irish Refugee Protection Programme', available at: www.gov.ie/en/publication/ede36-irish-refugee-protection-programme/.

[240] However, the government has committed to additionality in the medium- to long-term. See NF Tan, 'Community Sponsorship in Europe: Taking Stock, Policy Transfer and What the Future might Hold' (2021) 3 *Frontiers in Human Dynamics*, available at: www.frontiersin.org/articles/10.3389/fhumd.2021.564084/full, 5. At the moment, it represents 10% of the resettlement quota. See Share Network, above n 3.

that takes a final decision on whether the candidates can be admitted to Ireland. The staff of IRPP carry out face-to-face interviews, where they try to assess whether the information held on file is accurate, to gather extra details, to talk about duties and responsibilities and to manage expectations.[241] Before making a final decision, the Department of Justice ensures that all the potential beneficiaries undergo a full Garda[242] security assessment and interview.[243]

It is the IRPP staff who, after the refugees have been referred to Ireland for resettlement by the UNHCR and after having conducted the necessary interviews, decide whether the candidates will be selected for resettlement via CSI. The option is communicated to the candidates, who can decide to refuse.[244] If the candidates accept being resettled via this route, the IRPP staff will ask them their permission to share some information about their needs and health conditions, to make sure that appropriate matching with the right sponsors is carried out.[245] Once the matching has been done, the Community Sponsorship Group (CSG) and the Regional Support Organisation (RSO) are immediately notified.

The beneficiaries of the scheme are given programme refugee status, which grants them the same rights and entitlements as those classified as refugees under the Geneva Convention. In particular, refugee status gives them the right to reside in Ireland for at least three years and this can be renewed.[246] At the end of the three years the beneficiaries of the programme are also entitled to apply for Irish Citizenship.[247]

Sponsors are normally people from different backgrounds and might come from different organisations, such as religious ones, sport associations, a trade union or simply a group of friends or neighbours. The minimum requirements are that the group should be composed of at least five people and that these people should be at least 18 years old.[248] Sponsors, like the beneficiaries, have to undergo Garda vetting and will have to engage with an RSO, in order to receive support during the application phase, and proper training.[249] As a matter of fact RSOs, such as the Irish Red Cross, the Irish Refugee Council and Nasc Ireland, to mention some, are organisations that, by entering into an agreement with the Department of Justice, are allowed by the latter to offer guidance to sponsors.[250]

[241] See Department of Justice and Equality, 'Community Sponsorship Ireland: Initial Policy Framework', available at: www.redcross.ie/wp-content/uploads/2019/03/CSI-Policy-Framework-WEB.pdf, 9.

[242] Garda is the National Police and Security Service of Ireland.

[243] Department of Justice and Equality, above n 241, 9.

[244] ibid.

[245] ibid, 10.

[246] See s 53 of the International Protection Act 2015.

[247] Share Network, above n 3.

[248] Department of Justice and Equality, above n 241, 7.

[249] ibid.

[250] Their responsibility consists in organisational responsibilities for support and coordination of the sponsoring groups and vetting. ibid, 11.

Sponsors, with the help of the chosen RSO, have to develop a meticulous and detailed resettlement plan, including spelling out their financial and non-financial commitments. In particular, as far as the financial commitment is concerned, the sponsoring group has to agree to commit to providing paid accommodation for two years, and financial support for 18 months. The sponsoring group has to show that they own at least 10,000 euros per family, to be made available in case of exceptional needs or specialist costs to be covered for physical, mental and/or dental health, transport, interpretation and/or translation, language training, housing, employment preparation and job seeking, start-up needs such as household supplies and furnishings, clothing, and cultural and social activities.[251] As far as general health, education, and employment issues are concerned, the sponsored immigrants will benefit from the social protection offered by the state.[252]

The scheme also provides alternatives in case of sponsorship breakdown. Since the state-led resettlement and CSI are both encompassed under the umbrella of IRPP, in case of a breakdown of the sponsorship due to financial or other issues, the links between the sponsor and the sponsored family will be severed and the latter will continue their programme under the state scheme.[253]

By 2021, around 50 people were welcomed in Ireland under the CSI scheme. By the end of 2023 100 people per year are expected to be welcomed through this programme.[254] Recently there have also been suggestions to ramp up the scheme, by making more resources available, in order to respond to the Ukrainian crisis. Although this is evidently a good result, the fact that the numbers count towards state quotas and are not additional is an evident limitation on the potential of the programme. Indeed, since community sponsorship should not replace the state's responsibilities on resettlement,[255] 'additionality should remain at the forefront of discussions on community sponsorship, to avoid the effective outsourcing of government responsibilities'.[256]

[251] ibid, 7.

[252] ibid, 8.

[253] Before declaring the breakdown of the sponsorship the RSO will act as mediator and, if necessary, the National Support Organisation may also decide to get involved. If the sponsorship cannot be continued IRPP will have the final say on the matter. ibid, 13.

[254] See Irish Refugee Council 30 Years, 'Community Sponsorship', available at: www.irishrefugeecouncil.ie/listing/category/community-sponsorship.

[255] On this point see AL Hirsch, K Hoang and A Vogl, 'Australia's Private Refugee Sponsorship Program: Creating Complementary Pathways or Privatising Humanitarianism?' (2019) 35 *Refuge: Canada's Journal on Refugees* 110.

[256] Quoting Hirsh, see NF Tan, 'Community Sponsorship, The Pact and The Compact: Towards Protection Principles' in S Carrera and A Geddes (eds), *The EU Pact on Migration and Asylum in light of the United Nations* Global Compact on Refugees (Florence, European University Institute, 2021) 71, 76, available at: cadmus.eui.eu/handle/1814/70600.

VIII. Private Sponsorship in Spain: The Basque Country's Auzolana II Programme

A UNHCR resettlement programme was introduced in Spain only in 2009.[257] Before that, Spain had engaged in ad hoc resettlements since 1999, when it welcomed Albanians from Kosovo through the UNHCR Humanitarian Evacuation Programme. The UNHCR resettlement programme has its legal basis in Law 12/2009 of 30 October on the Right to Asylum and Subsidiary protection.[258] The law introduces the idea of resettlement, describing it as programmes prepared by the national government, in collaboration with the UNHCR, and other relevant international organisations. The law specifies that the Council of Ministers, at the proposal of the Ministers of the Interior and of Labour and Immigration, after hearing the Interministerial Commission for Asylum and Refuge, will annually agree on the number of people who may be resettled in Spain. The quota is currently 100 people per year.

The idea of introducing a private sponsorship of refugees scheme in Spain started in the wake of the many deaths in the Mediterranean, following the Syrian immigration crisis of 2015. Witnessing the struggles of desperate migrants, civil society started to pressure the central government to introduce safe and legal paths of entry into Spain. This action was also reinforced by a visit to Spain of a Global Refugee Sponsorship Initiative delegation, that organised meeting with institutional representants and members of the civil society in November 2017.[259] Soon after, in January 2018, the Basque regional government signed the first Auzolana agreement with the Spanish central government. The purpose of the agreement was to complement the reception and integration efforts of the central government in relation to refugees and asylum seekers.[260] With the change of government in June 2018, the new Prime Minister began to implement a less intransigent and more humane immigration policy. In July 2017 Spain, together with the UK, Argentina, New Zealand and Canada, signed a document to reiterate their commitment to the introduction of community sponsorship of refugees.[261] In the month after, the government announced the launch of a new community sponsorship of refugees pilot project: Auzolana II. The scheme was created as a collaboration between the central government, the Basque regional government and the UNHCR.[262] The

[257] UNHCR, 'UNHCR welcomes establishment of Spain's resettlement programme', available at: www.unhcr.org/news/briefing-notes/unhcr-welcomes-establishment-spains-resettlement-programme.

[258] Ley 12/2009, de 30 de octubre, reguladora del derecho de asilo y de la protecció n subsidiaria, available at: www.boe.es/buscar/act.php?id=BOE-A-2009-17242.

[259] C Manzanedo, 'Community-Based Refugee Sponsorship in Spain: What Are the Experiences?' (2019) Q&A Trending Issues on Migration (Budapest, Friedrich Ebert Stiftung, 2019), available at: https://library.fes.de/pdf-files/bueros/budapest/15599.pdf, 2.

[260] ibid.

[261] ibid, 3.

[262] ibid.

final agreement was signed on 29 June 2019 by the General Secretariat for Human Rights, Coexistence and Cooperation of the Basque Government, the Department of Integration and Humanitarian Support, with the UNHCR and some social organisations such as Cáritas Diocesana Bilbao, Cáritas Diocesana Vitoria, Cáritas Diocesana Sebastián and the Ignacio Ellacuría Social Foundation.[263]

The Auzolana II private sponsorship experience is characterised both by public and private involvement. On one hand, the programme falls within the Spanish National Resettlement Programme, because its numbers count towards state resettlement quotas and are not additional. Moreover, it is the UNHCR that selects the potential beneficiaries of the scheme, hence excluding naming from this programme. The Spanish state has the final say on whether the UNHCR-chosen candidates can be admitted and, once the refugees enter the territory, the Basque government takes charge of them.[264] On the other hand, once the people are redistributed in the cities of Bilbao, Donostia and Vitoria, the local administration has to support the programme.[265] Practically speaking,

> public administrations from various regions interact with third sector entities and organised civil society groups acting under the umbrella of these. Local administrations in the regions touched by the experience may also engage, though they are not signatories to the agreement.[266]

During the first phase of the pilot, Caritas and the Jesuits were asked to collaborate. Due to their experience in resettling refugees, they were asked to form and train local groups that would act as sponsors to the resettled families.[267] These two catholic organisations also had to spell out and provide the government with an integration strategy, which included the names of the sponsors that are directly in touch with the refugees and that have the responsibility for the success of the scheme, proof of appropriate housing, a minimum of 10,000 euros in their bank account for the beneficiaries' subsistence expenses and a plan targeted towards integration and independence,[268] which is expected to be achieved in between 18 and 24 months.[269]

In the event of sponsorship breakdown, protection is given by the general national admission system for refugees.[270] The expenses of health care, education,

[263] See General Secretariat of Human Rights, Coexistence and Cooperation, 'Auzolana II Pilot Community Sponsorship Experience – Evaluation Report', available at: static1.squarespace.com/static/61701919c9cd9200cd8e6ccc/t/61ba033d142a2518f09b6cd2/1639580483721/Basque+Country-+Pilot+Community+Sponsorship+Evaluation+_Full+report_EN.pdf, 19.

[264] Manzanedo, above n 259, 3. The identification of the families occurs in Jordan. The names are submitted to the Spanish government for final approval.

[265] ibid.

[266] General Secretariat of Human Rights, above n 263, 20.

[267] Manzanedo, above n 259, 3–4.

[268] For more details on the plan see General Secretariat of Human Rights, above n 263, 21.

[269] ibid.

[270] ibid, 36.

and the salary of a part-time social worker, are covered by the Basque government for two years.[271]

Having arrived at the airport, the beneficiaries of the scheme receive a copy of the resolution verifying their international protection status. They are also granted long-term residency, but they have to process the application for such residency at the local police station within 15 days of arrival.[272]

In March 2019, with the launch of the pilot, Spain welcomed 29 Syrian refugees – five families – all coming from Jordan. Five local groups, coordinated by the Ellacuría Foundation and Caritas, were created and each of them assigned to one family.[273]

The success of the Auzolana programme triggered the expansion of the initiative to Valencia in 2021 through a new pilot that helped the admission of 25 Syrian refugees from Lebanon.[274] The initiative was promoted by the Ministry of Inclusion, Social Security and Migration (MISSM), the Generalitat Valenciana and UNHCR in Spain, together with some church organisations such as Servicio Jesuita a Migrantes España, Cáritas Diocesana Orihuela-Alicante, Cáritas Diocesana Segorbe-Castelló and Cáritas Diocesana Valencia, which organised and promoted the initial pilot.[275] The Valencia pilot programme is very similarly run and organised, and displays the same characteristics in terms of naming and additionality, as the Auzolana II one. Once the refugees arrive in Spain, having been hosted in the MISSM facilities, they move to the host municipalities within the Valancia area. The beneficiaries are granted accommodation, food, language tuition, legal advice and integration support and are provided for by the local community sponsorship group, under the supervision of the religious organisations and with the collaboration with the local municipalities and the Vice-Presidency and Regional Ministry of Equality and Inclusive Policies.[276]

A similar programme was also introduced in the Spanish autonomous region of Navarre.[277]

In a country that is relatively new to managing immigration of refugees, the Auzolana II programme was a success, and was exported to other areas within Spain. The most interesting aspect is that the programme relies on the collaboration of different layers of public institutions – central government, regional government and local authorities – with civil society actors, both at organisational and individual level. This is a remarkable aspect of this programme, as coordination

[271] Manzanedo, above n 259, 4.

[272] General Secretariat of Human Rights, above n 263, 26.

[273] ibid.

[274] See in particular European website on integration, 'Spain: Pilot programme for the reception and integration of refugees', available at: ec.europa.eu/migrant-integration/news/spain-pilot-programme-reception-and-integration-refugees_en.

[275] ibid.

[276] ibid. See also M Siegel 'Community (Private) Refugee Sponsorship Programs Around the World', available at: www.youtube.com/watch?v=VAy2tUI7hMU&t=809s, from minute 13.34 to 16.47.

[277] Share Network, above n 3.

among these stakeholders has developed and improved through this scheme.[278] Other positive elements that have been identified include the extra support given to private sponsors by the introduction of a part-time social worker to the scheme, who coordinates the work of local sponsor groups and refugee families. Equally, the extra financial support to the family given by the Basque government has eased the financial responsibility of sponsors.[279] Nevertheless, it has to be noted that the scheme could have reached higher goals if the government allowed it to feature additionality. Although originally conceived as an additional scheme, before the launch the Spanish government decided to use the scheme only for those that had already been selected under state quotas.[280] This decision defeated one of the key aims of the initiative, which was opening up more spaces for people in need of resettlement.[281] Although perhaps understandable during the pilot phase, it has been argued that this decision should be reconsidered, also to better align the scheme with the objectives of the New York Declaration of 2016.[282]

IX. Community Sponsorship in Belgium[283]

This chapter has already discussed how Belgium was involved in the humanitarian corridor initiative. However, in 2020, Belgium also introduced Community Sponsorship. This programme was established owing to the collaboration of the State Federal Reception Agency for Asylum Seekers (Fedasil) and Caritas Internationalis.[284] This programme is not additional to state quotas, as it counts towards state resettlement numbers, and does not envisage naming within its core characteristics, as the identification of beneficiaries is done by the UNHCR, while the selection is processed by the Belgian government, through the Commissioner General for Refugees and Stateless Persons (CGRA).

Sponsors are composed of a group of four or five volunteers. Only family units are accepted onto the programme, for 12 months, which can be extended for further 12 months. The financial responsibility of the sponsors is limited. Indeed, sponsors have to cover the costs of the family only between arrival and the receipt of social benefits, which are normally issued between one and two months after arrival. The initial costs are estimated at between 3,000 and 5,000 euros.

[278] Manzanedo, above n 259, 4–5.

[279] See Share Network, 'Regional governments piloting Community Sponsorship Programmes – Evaluating the Basque Country Programme (2019–2021), available at: www.share-network.eu/articles-and-resources/story1.

[280] General Secretariat of Human Rights, above n 263, 32.

[281] ibid.

[282] ibid.

[283] The programme is not yet well advertised. The key information about this programme currently available can be found in Share Network, above n 3. It is also mentioned in Fedasil, 'Community Sponsorship', available at: www.fedasil.be/en/resettlement/community-sponsorship.

[284] This programme does not stand upon a strong legislative background, but this is not surprising since state-led resettlement is also not mentioned in the Belgian law.

In addition to the initial financial support, sponsors are responsible for helping the family during the integration process, by helping them to build networks, improve language skills and become accustomed to Belgian culture. The family, in parallel with the sponsors, also receives the support of public services, through social assistants.

Before departure, the families are also subject to medical screening. If this final screening is successful, the families are offered a place in the programme, which they accept by signing the consent form to the agreement. After having agreed to participate in the programme, the beneficiaries are invited to take part in an orientation course called BELCO. This course is delivered by Fedasil and includes an explanation of the programme and of life in Belgium.

As mentioned earlier, naming is not allowed by this programme. In its place Fedasil carries out an informal and anonymous matching between sponsors and beneficiaries. Sponsors have no say in deciding who they can support, as only basic information is shared with them, such as, family composition, age and language. The matching normally pairs sponsors and beneficiaries based on profiles and capacities, ruling out preferences.

As soon as the beneficiaries arrive in Belgium, they are greeted by their sponsors, Fedasil and Caritas, and immediately transferred to their homes. They also have to apply for refugee status immediately, and a positive outcome is guaranteed. Upon obtaining that status, social benefits are granted, together with an initial five-year residence permit.

Between 2020 and 2022, 39 people have been welcomed through this programme. Belgium also pledged the entry of further 50 people in 2023, through this scheme. Critics have pointed out that these numbers are quite low, compared to the initial pledges made by Belgium, where the target was set at 100 refugees to be resettled by the scheme on a yearly basis.[285] A recent survey has also pointed out the difficulty that the programme is facing in retaining sponsors. Indeed, it has been found that even after a positive sponsorship experience, some sponsors will need some time before repeating the experience, with many that do not show an openness to the idea of sponsoring again.[286]

X. A Final Assessment of Private Sponsorship as a Resettlement Tool

This overview of private sponsorship of refugees programmes as resettlement tools has hopefully shed light on which countries in Europe currently run schemes of this kind and how these schemes are organised and function. Each programme, to a lesser or greater extent, has been both praised and criticised.

[285] Zanzuchi, Dumann, Tissot and Skodo, above 132, 6.
[286] ibid, 9.

Positive and negative appraisals are sometimes recurrent in more than one of the programmes that have been analysed. For instance, quite a few programmes have been praised for allowing vulnerable people, beyond the numbers already pledged by the states through national resettlement schemes, to reach Europe in a safe manner. The role played by private sponsorship in this respect is even more appreciated when considering that the involvement of private sponsors often means fewer costs for the state.

The crucial role played by sponsors is indeed something that has also been highlighted and appreciated. Indeed, achieving higher levels of integration, compared to state-led resettlement programmes, seems easier when private sponsors are involved. Recent research has also pointed out the importance of positive affective and reactive emotions, as a trigger that incentivises the involvement of the sponsors, and as something to be welcomed. Some positive feedback has also been collected in relation to the ability of the sponsor, granted by few schemes, to directly select the beneficiaries. This is because people who would not otherwise be entitled to resettlement, since they do not strictly fulfil the Geneva refugee definition, are nevertheless allowed to seek protection under some schemes (mainly the humanitarian corridors). More broadly, private sponsorship of refugees schemes have been recognised in some states as being potentially capable of strengthening national values and igniting a positive change in immigration governance and policy at state level.

At the same time, quite a few common lines of criticism seem to be recurrent in many of the adopted schemes, almost symmetrically to the accolades. To put it simply, it is as if every aspect of private sponsorships that is worthy of praise entails an opposite side that is potentially problematic. For example, the fact that quite a few private sponsorship schemes promote safe entry of refugees beyond state quotas, has been subject to fierce criticism, as it was argued that the impact of additional sponsorship programmes could be drastically impaired if private sponsorships are utilised to cover parts of the annual state resettlement quotas. More precisely, it is argued that the presence of these schemes could lead states to simply 'use private sponsorship as a means of privatised resettlement – that is, it might simply "substitute and subsidize" the refugees they would otherwise resettle through publicly funded programmes'.[287] Indeed, where there is additionality, it could be argued that the state is simply shifting the costs of resettlement onto well-meaning individuals and groups.

Furthermore, the freedom left to the sponsors, in some of schemes, to select the beneficiaries, also seems to come with its shortcomings. Particularly in relation to the experience of the humanitarian corridors, the option left to the sponsor to

[287] M Bradley and C Duin, 'A Port in the Storm: Resettlement and Private Sponsorship in the Broader Context of Refugee Regime' in S Labman and G Cameron, *Strangers to Neighbours: Refugee Sponsorship in Context* (Montreal, McGill-Queens University Press, 2000) 74, 79.

select the beneficiaries of the programme risks of jeopardising equality. Indeed, the representatives of the sponsoring organisations seem to have quite a lot of discretion within the selection process. Critics suggest that this approach runs the risk of an arbitrary categorisation of refugees as more worthy or less worthy of protection, without relying on objective standards. This could likely be raised as objection to the Portuguese scheme, when and if the pilot is approved and numbers start to swell. The naming issue leads to further criticism, directed also in particular at the Belgian humanitarian corridor scheme and the expired schemes of Poland, Slovakia and the Czech Republic. In these instances, the option of selecting led to arguments that the programmes were unfair, since the sponsors were permitted (or forced, in the case of Poland, Czech Republic and Slovakia) to sponsor those belonging to their own religion. Interestingly however, in programmes such as NesT, where matching criteria are utilised, the criticism related to the lack of information made available to the sponsors about the people to be resettled. This suggests that introducing the possibility of selecting beneficiaries within a scheme is a controversial choice all round, and one that needs to be further debated.

While being praised for their work and for being the real strength of private sponsorship programmes, sponsors' role in the integration phase can also be problematic. Despite the importance of sponsors in helping beneficiaries to reach independence and integration, in the analysis of quite a few schemes it was mentioned how there are still remarkable difficulties in promoting integration, particularly in relation to helping the refugees to achieve emotional and financial autonomy. This can happen, regardless of external factors such as the decision to resettle refugees in areas that do not offer many job opportunities, because the sponsors lack the necessary training or expertise, or because of the heavy and prolonged financial burdens deriving from the sponsorship itself (when, for example, the beneficiaries struggle in learning the language and in becoming financially independent within the timeframe given by the sponsorship). These problems, as found in the analysis of the Belgian Community Sponsorship scheme, can negatively influence the experience of the sponsors, to the extent that they might not be open to the idea of repeating the sponsorship experience again.

Finally, some criticism concerns the fact that these programmes can lead to broader discrimination issues. For example, in the case of humanitarian corridors, the differences between those who participate to the schemes and those that do not benefit from the schemes and apply for asylum in the country instead, have been highlighted. In particular, the former can benefit from significant support, guidance and help from the sponsors, unlike the latter. Sometimes discrimination can also be triggered by the type of permit that is issued to those that have been resettled through private sponsorships compared to those that have applied for asylum within the country. Different treatment of people in similar situations creates double standards. From a broader perspective, this is linked to the fact that private sponsorship of refugees programmes have also been challenged for endorsing an unfair immigration system, where refugees that patiently wait to be resettled are rewarded, while those applying for asylum after having endured treacherous journeys are penalised. This is the reason why further criticism suggests that these schemes are effectively a façade or concession for the public, to hide other stringent and fortress-based immigration policies.

The above reflections suggest that the key challenges to private sponsorship of refugees schemes as tools for resettlement relate to issues of additionality, naming, the role of the sponsor and discrimination. These will be addressed in greater detail in Chapter five.

4

Private Sponsorship of Refugees Schemes as Different Forms of Admission

I. Introduction

The previous chapter provided an overview of the key European private refugee sponsorship schemes that are oprationally similar or linked to resettlement. Following the distinction proposed in Chapter two, we now move on to look at schemes that advance and enhance different ways, other than resettlement, of welcoming foreigners into the host country. Most of the schemes that are going to be analysed are now expired. Nevertheless, it is still important to understand how they functioned, since quite a lot of people are now safely living in Europe owing to these programmes and because, if necessary, in the future they could be replicated.

As with the previously analysed programmes, most of these private schemes began to be piloted in answer to the outbreak of the Syrian civil war. Indeed, the expired German, Irish and Swiss family reunification/humanitarian admission programmes, for instance, precisely targeted the Syrian family members of applicants living in the host state, whether they still resided in Syria or had moved to neighbouring countries. As the Syrian emergency slowly stabilised, relocation programmes with elements of private sponsorship were introduced to target other nationalities, as in the case of Portugal, the Vatican and St Marino. More recently, due to the outbreak of the war in Ukraine in February 2022, the UK introduced the Homes for Ukraine scheme, a temporary humanitarian form of admission that targets Ukrainian nationals fleeing from the war.

While these schemes amount to different forms of legal admission (family reunification and/or humanitarian admission, relocation), this chapter suggests that each of them is also characterised by components of private sponsorship, such as the financial support and /or integration and emotional support provided by the sponsor during the reception and integration phase.

The chapter will first look at the now expired German *Länder* family reunification schemes, at the Swiss and Irish family reunification schemes, which have also expired, and at the UK Homes for Ukraine programme, still functioning. Brief accounts will be also offered of the St Marino scheme, not yet tested, which effectively consists of relocation by allowing the admission of unaccompanied minors to be fostered by local families, and finally of the Portuguese and Italian/Vatican humanitarian corridor programmes, which entailed the relocation of vulnerable migrants from European immigration centres.

These schemes will be analysed in turn. At the end of the chapter some conclusions will be drawn. As in the previous chapter, the conclusion will identify the advantages and shortcomings that characterise these particular programmes, in order to identify the broader issues to learn from. This will be particularly useful for the analysis proposed in Chapter five.

II. The Expired *Länder* Programmes in Germany

In 2013 temporary admissions schemes at *Länder* (State) level were introduced in Germany.[1] These schemes began as a response to the Syrian refugee crisis and were additional to the quotas reserved to the state-run schemes.[2] The programmes involved all the German States, with the exception of Bavaria, and consisted of family reunification schemes for extended family members. The majority of these programmes were not renewed after 2016. The programmes in Berlin, Brandenburg, Hamburg, Schleswig-Holstein and Thuringia remained in force longer,[3] with Thuringia being the last programme to close-down, in December 2022.

These programmes, as will be soon seen, were conceived within the framework of humanitarian admissions. For this reason, the underpinning rationale of these programmes was that the beneficiaries only needed 'temporary protection', rather than durable solutions. This came, as will be soon highlighted, with the burden of granting fewer rights to the beneficiaries of the programme, compared to those who, for example, are admitted through the NesT programme.

The schemes were designed to target Syrians with first- or second-degree relatives in Germany. The programmes were grounded in section 23(1) of the German Residence Act. According to this provision, the beneficiaries of the programme were granted a residence permit for up to two years with the possibility of

[1] These private sponsorship programmes ran in parallel to the German state-led resettlement programme, to the Humanitarian Admission Programme for 20,000 Beneficiaries of Protection from Syria, its Neighbouring Countries, Egypt and Libya (HAP Syria) and to the Admission Procedure for Afghan Local Staff (AP Afghanistan). For more information on these programmes see J Grote, M Bitterwolf and T Baraulina, 'Resettlement and Humanitarian Admission Programmes in Germany: Focus-Study by the German National Contact Point for the European Migration Network (EMN)' (2016), BAMF working paper no 68, available at: www.ssoar.info/ssoar/bitstream/handle/document/67691/ssoar-2016-grote_et_al-Resettlement_and_Humanitarian_Admission_Programmes.pdf?sequence=1&isAllowed=y&lnkname=ssoar-2016-grote_et_al-Resettlement_and_Humanitarian_Admission_Programmes.pdf.

[2] It has been argued that Germany, in comparison to other countries, has offered a relatively high level of protection to Syrians, owing to the multitude of programmes run at national and federal level. See in particular N Ostrand, 'The Syrian Refugee crisis: a comparison of responses by Germany, Sweden, the United Kingdom, and the United States' (2015) 3 *Journal of Migration and Human Security* 255.

[3] P Endres de Oliveira, 'Humanitarian Admission to Germany – Access vs Rights?' in MC Foblets and L Leboeuf (eds), *Humanitarian Admission to Europe: the Law between Promises and Constraints* (Baden-Baden, Nomos, 2020) 199, 208.

extension pursuant to section 8 of the Act. A permanent residence permit was granted after five years at the earliest, after high thresholds relating to language skills and financial support had been fulfilled.[4] The residence permit allowed the sponsored family members to take on employment to contribute to their living expenses,[5] although with some limitations, which will be discussed below.

These schemes, despite effectively being family reunification/humanitarian admission programmes, have been categorised as private refugee sponsorship, 'since the main requirement is a "declaration of commitment" (*Verpflichtungserklung*) from a private sponsor in Germany undertaking to cover the accommodation and living expenses of the applicant'.[6]

These programmes were not subject to overall State quota to be fulfilled (some States initially introduced quotas but later removed them).[7] The sponsor was entitled to apply to support more than one beneficiary but for every person that was admitted a separate declaration of commitment was required. The commitment that the sponsor was supposed to take on was spelled out in section 68(1) of the German Residence Act, and consisted of bearing the living expenses and reimbursing the public funds expended on the sponsored family member's living expenses 'including the provision of living space, medical care in case of illness and any required nursing care, and including any such expenditure which is based on a legal entitlement of the foreigner'.[8] The declaration of commitment also set the level of responsibility towards the sponsored beneficiaries.[9] While the legislation did not specify the sponsor's minimum income, in practice it was the individual State that dictated the figures.[10] The timeframe of the declaration of commitment was initially unlimited.[11] However, this requirement was found to put too much strain on the sponsors.[12] The law was eventually changed on 7 July 2016, and reduced the limit of commitment to five years.[13]

The sponsors could be Syrian citizens, German citizens or citizens of any Member State, who were family members of the potential beneficiaries. Some

[4] This is in contrast to schemes aimed at resettlement, where a permanent residence permit can be granted after just three years. The difference is due to the fact that these schemes were conceived as temporary, while those based on resettlement are aimed at reaching a permanent solution. See Endres de Oliveira, above n 3, 218. These schemes also do not include a clear path to citizenship. The acquisition of citizenship is left at the discretion of the government. See European Commission, 'Study on the feasibility and added value of sponsorship schemes as a possible pathway to safe channels for admission to the EU, including resettlement' final report (2018), available at: op.europa.eu/en/publication-detail/-/publication/1dbb0873-d349-11e8-9424-01aa75ed71a1, 69.

[5] Grote, Bitterwolf and Baraulina, above n 1, 45.

[6] Endres de Oliveira, above n 3, 207–8.

[7] Urban Justice Center, 'Models of Private Sponsorship: Past and Present Programs, and How the Private Sector Can Create Alternative and Complementary Pathways or Expand Resettlement for Refugees' (2018), available at: refugeerights.org/news-resources/models-of-private-sponsorship, 15.

[8] Grote, Bitterwolf and Baraulina, above n 1, 41.

[9] European Commission, above n 4, 75.

[10] ibid, 53. 'For example, Berlin fixed income thresholds for sponsors ranging from 2,210 EUR per month for single persons to 3,365 EUR for married couples with one child acting as sponsors'.

[11] Endres de Oliveira, above n 3, 209.

[12] ibid.

[13] ibid. Section 68(1) sentence 4 Residence Act.

States, however, even allowed third parties to make a declaration of commitment.[14] The sponsors had to be resident in the State at least for one year, or six months, depending on the scheme.[15]

Unlike other private sponsorship of refugees schemes, the beneficiaries did not necessarily have to be located outside their state of origin (neighbouring Syrian country or Egypt). Indeed, beneficiaries could also apply from within Syria. The groups that were targeted, apart from Syrians, were also stateless people who had lived in Syria for three years.[16]

As far as the beneficiaries are concerned the schemes included, as a key selection criterion, the presence of family ties within Germany. German States not only opened the scheme to core family members but also to extended ones, such as grandparents, grandchildren, siblings and their spouses and their minor children.[17] Under certain circumstances, such as the need of preserving the family unit, further primary carers of minor children could be included. However, some States went even beyond this and also included unrelated carers of children.[18]

The selection process was simple. The sponsor had to express his interest in hosting a family member to the competent foreign authority or, during the initial phase of the programme, through a telephone hotline. To approve the application, the relevant authority had to check the family ties between the sponsor and the potential beneficiary and the financial standing of the sponsor and be satisfied with it. As far as the financial solvency of the sponsor was concerned, this could be tested in different ways, depending on the individual State.[19] However, since the financial burden was found to be too onerous on the sponsor, a debate on how this burden could be eased was initiated among the States. Eventually, on top of reducing the sponsor's financial commitment to five years, it was also agreed that, from 1 July 2014, medical care would be supported by the State and a declaration of commitments could be made by the *Länder* within their humanitarian admission scheme quotas,[20] effectively increasing the State's responsibility for the financial aspect of the scheme. Furthermore, in case of insolvency of the sponsor, the government would step in, retaining the right to be reimbursed by the sponsor at a later stage.[21]

Once the application was approved, the request was transferred to the relevant consular authority, which would contact the beneficiary directly to book an in-person interview and start the visa procedures. Security screening was undertaken by the diplomatic authorities before issuing a visa.[22] International

[14] Grote, Bitterwolf and Baraulina, above n 1, 41.
[15] Originally, these schemes required that the sponsors had to have been resident in Germany at least since 2013. See Grote, Bitterwolf and Baraulina, above n 1, 41.
[16] ibid. Admissions from other countries were also possible but it was at the discretion of the State.
[17] ibid.
[18] European Commission, above n 4, 62.
[19] Grote, Bitterwolf, Baraulina, above n 1, 43–44.
[20] ibid, 44.
[21] Urban Justice Center, above n 7, 16.
[22] Grote, Bitterwolf and Baraulina, above n 1, 41.

organisations were not involved in the implementation of the programme and UNHCR-recognised refugee status was not required.[23]

The residence permit was issued under section 23(1) of the Residence Act. The duration of the residence permit was temporary, due to the humanitarian nature of the scheme. Indeed, it spanned between two and three years, depending on the provision of the admission order, and permanent residence could only be granted after five years, subject to a very high threshold linked to language proficiency and proof of economic independence.[24]

The temporary residence permit allowed the beneficiaries of the programmes to pursue employment. The permit also entitled pre-school children who had been admitted through the scheme, to access state-funded *Kindergarten*, and school and university education for those who were older.[25] However the residence permit did not grant the beneficiaries access to orientation courses which they were only able to attend if financed by the sponsor, or if no individual from another preferred group would attend.[26] Moreover, social welfare assistance was only available at a reduced level.

These programmes were quite successful in Germany. As of 2021, over 24,000 individuals were granted admission through these schemes.[27] It has been noted that, although the programmes did not necessarily target the most vulnerable refugees, nevertheless they did manage to create a safe way to enter Germany for those that faced difficult circumstances in Syria and needed to flee.[28] The choice of opting for family reunification/humanitarian admission with a strong private sponsorship component had the advantage of speeding up integration for the beneficiaries, owing to the strong family, emotional and financial support networks provided as soon as they entered the country. Moreover, the reach of the programmes was further expanded due to the intentionally broad definition of family members, which in some cases was able to encompass those not necessarily linked to the sponsor by a blood relationship. In a nutshell, it seems that the flexible family reunification format was certainly one key component which was conducive to the success of the programme. Moreover, it is also worth noting that the lack of State quotas on the numbers of family members[29] allowed to enter, was also likely conducive to the growth and success of the scheme.

Despite the success of the programmes, some challenges became evident over time. The key problem was triggered by the existence of several other programmes targeting the same group of beneficiaries.[30] As seen before, in comparison to other

[23] ibid.
[24] Endres de Oliveira, above n 3, 218.
[25] Grote, Bitterwolf and Baraulina, above n 1, 46.
[26] European Commission, above n 4, 72.
[27] Endres de Oliveira, above n 3, 208.
[28] Urban Justice Center, above n 7, 15.
[29] ibid.
[30] For an exhaustive account on this matter see C Tometten, 'Resettlement, Humanitarian Admissions and Family Reunion: the Intricacies of Germany's Legal Entry Regimes for Syrian Refugees' (2018) 37 *Refugees Survey Quarterly* 187.

programmes available in Germany – eg those aimed at permanent solutions such as resettlement or admission of foreigners through the classic asylum route – the beneficiaries of these schemes were entitled to fewer rights. These differences led many beneficiaries of these programmes to believe that they had been treated unfairly.[31] Consequently, many beneficiaries of *Länder* schemes – almost half of those admitted – decided instead to apply for refugee protection, in order to be granted better rights. The discrepancy in the level of protection and rights offered by the different routes, eventually not only created confusion among the beneficiaries of the programmes, but also increased the workload of the relevant administrative authorities, which not only had to engage directly with the migrants in trying to make clear their entitlements, but also had to deal with the increased numbers of asylum applications.[32]

Looking more closely at shortcomings in relation to the specific rights granted to those that benefitted from the *Länder* schemes, it is worth noting that these schemes offered far less protection than the German standard resettlement programme in relation to family reunification and access to work, due to their temporary nature. Individuals admitted through private sponsorship schemes at *Land* level had few options to reunify with their family members that were left behind. Indeed, under section 29(3) of the German Residence Act, family reunification with members of the nuclear family may only be granted 'for reasons of international law, on humanitarian grounds or in order to safeguard political interests of the Federal Republic of Germany'. This stands in striking contrast to the rights granted to resettlement refugees and Convention refugees, who have the right to reunify with their nuclear family.[33] Moreover, in relation to access to work, although the beneficiaries of the private sponsorship scheme could take up employment, their right was subject to several limitations, compared to the rights granted to the beneficiaries of other programmes – such as, for example, having to apply for a separate work permit in order to be able to work. Moreover, freelance (self-employed) jobs were allowed to this category of sponsored individuals only in exceptional circumstances.[34]

III. Ireland's Syrian Humanitarian Admission Programme

Both Ireland and Switzerland implemented short-lived programmes as a way to allow applicants to reunify with their extended Syrian families. The Irish programme, known as the Syrian Humanitarian Admission Programme (SHAP),

[31] Grote, Bitterwolf and Baraulina, above n 1, 49.
[32] ibid.
[33] Endres de Oliveira, above n 3, 220–21.
[34] ibid, 219.

was introduced outside the established refugee resettlement programme.[35] The scheme was a short-term programme and was introduced by the Minister for Justice and Equality of the time – Alan Shatter – on 14 March 2014, with the deadline for applications falling on 30 April 2014. The scheme was not grounded in any legislation, but consisted of a simple administrative arrangement.[36] Also, the scheme was not subject to any quota[37] but to a temporal limitation of six weeks to allow the time to submit the applications.

The programme allowed Irish naturalised citizens of Syrian birth and Syrians lawfully resident in Ireland to sponsor family members of Syrian nationality residing in Syria or who fled to neighbouring countries to escape the civil war. The sponsor was allowed to apply for admission of up to four 'of their most vulnerable family members'.[38] Priority would normally be given to two family members,[39] and normally to applications made on behalf of elderly parents, children, mothers and their children, single women and girls and disabled family members.[40] The humanitarian scheme was effectively tailored as a family reunification programme, and it was described as a private sponsorship scheme, since it was open to extended family members, based on their vulnerability, and because of the sponsor's financial responsibility, as it was the sponsor that had to cover the expenses of the beneficiary to avoid the latter becoming a burden on the state, and broader emotional responsibility during the integration phase.

As far as the procedure was concerned, the requests were received and processed by the Family Reunification Unit in the Irish Naturalisation and Immigration Service (INIS).[41] The decisions were notified in writing, with no possibility of appeal.[42] However, as mentioned above, INIS showed flexibility and some applications were left under review until the conditions were met, even after the expiry of the deadline, to allow individuals to benefit from the programme.[43] The estimated time to process the requests was envisaged as a maximum of 12 weeks. However, in reality, the process took longer, in some cases up to seven months.[44] Potential beneficiaries went through security checks and had to provide evidence of being vaccinated against or screened for certain diseases.[45]

[35] Up until 1998, Ireland engaged with resettlement of refugees through ad hoc programmes. In 1998 Ireland started to collaborate with UNHCR in the UNHCR-led Refugee Resettlement Programme, with the programme being officially up and running in 2000. In 2005, Ireland agreed to resettle 200 people every year. In 2015, the Irish Refugee Protection Programme (IRPP), in response to the refugee crisis, was established. Resettlement is regulated by the amended Refugee Act 1996, s 24. See S Arnold and E Quinn, 'Resettlement of Refugees and Private Sponsorships in Ireland' (2016) EMRI Research Series no 55, available at: emn.ie/files/p_201612120402502016_Resettlement%20Report.pdf, 19 and 23.

[36] ibid, 22.

[37] ibid, 46.

[38] ibid, p ix.

[39] ibid. However, the authors note that the authorities were allowed to apply a flexible approach, and that once they effectively allowed five family members to enter and reside in Ireland.

[40] ibid, 45–46.

[41] ibid, ix.

[42] ibid, 46.

[43] ibid.

[44] ibid, 47.

[45] ibid.

Prior to arrival, the beneficiaries were granted a visa that would allow safe passage and entry into Ireland. Once arrived, they had to submit their passports, which were issued with a SHAP authorisation stamp, and register with the Garda National Immigration Bureau.[46] The SHAP stamp and the certificate of registration constituted their residence permit[47] and granted them temporary residence rights for two years. Although the programme did not envisage the possibility of automatically extending the residence permit, the authorities confirmed that the residence permit would be renewed on a case-by-case basis for a further two years, subject to good character, vetting and identity checks.[48]

The beneficiaries of the programme held the right to seek work, either as an employee or as an employer, by establishing a business.[49] Sponsored family members also had access to the national health system, but only for essential medical treatments.[50] They could also access state nurseries and state primary and secondary schools.[51] Finally, they could access English classes and labour support, but not all of the integration services that are normally offered to resettled refugees were available to the beneficiaries of SHAP.[52]

The scheme was characterised by a strong private sponsorship component. Indeed, the sponsor had to take on the responsibility of supporting and maintaining all the family members that were allowed to benefit from the programme. The key requirement of the programme was that the sponsored family member should not be a burden on the state. For this reason, the beneficiaries of the scheme had no access to social welfare payments, social housing or housing allowance. Moreover, the application costs (SHAP stamp and certificate from the Garda National Immigration Bureau[53]) and maintenance had all to be borne by the sponsor for the entire length of the sponsorship.[54]

In total, 119 people were granted the right to reside in Ireland under the SHAP programme.[55] This is quite a remarkable number, considering that the programme operated for only six weeks. Once it was terminated, practitioners and scholars advocated for the introduction of new private sponsorship of refugee programmes, modelled after SHAP.[56] This denotes that, despite the evident limitations of SHAP,

[46] ibid.

[47] ibid.

[48] ibid, 48.

[49] ibid.

[50] ibid.

[51] ibid.

[52] ibid.

[53] €60 fee per person for the Irish entry visa and €300 per person for the GNIB certificate.

[54] Arnold and Quinn, above n 35, 48–49. Beneficiaries were entitled to take up a job activity. However, this was not a feasible option for some of the beneficiaries who were elderly or sick. In this case, unless the beneficiary pursued other routes of protection – such as applying for asylum, which grants access to social benefits – the responsibility of the sponsor was not time limited. See p 50.

[55] A total of three-hundred and eight people applied. See Arnold and Quinn, above n 35, p ix, which refers to Parliamentary Question 24 November 2015 [41635/15]. See also S Arnold, C Ryan and E Quinn, 'Ireland's response to recent trends in international protection applications' (2018) ESRI Research Series no 72, available at: www.tara.tcd.ie/bitstream/handle/2262/83795/RS72.pdf?sequence=2.

[56] The current Community Sponsorship scheme was analysed in Chapter 3 of this book.

the idea of collaboration between the private and the public sector to answer to the problems faced by refugees was welcomed by Irish society. This fact has indeed been proved by the more recent legislative developments, with the introduction of Community Sponsorship Ireland, which, despite working on a very different model from SHAP, shares its core purpose.

Considering the SHAP's shortcomings it should be noted that, despite being welcomed, the programme was also highly criticised for more than one reason. First, as briefly hinted at above, the temporary nature of the programme, with a residence permit limited to two years and not automatically renewable, caused insecurity for the beneficiaries and led them to apply for asylum, for fear of being deported. Equally, the unlimited financial responsibility of the sponsor for the family members benefitting from the programme, created an incentive for the latter to apply for asylum before the end of the two-year period.[57] The temporary nature of the programme also had consequences for employment prospects. Indeed, the UNHCR denounced the fact that it led to difficulties in accessing work and adult higher education.[58] Finally, UNHCR also noted that the short time-frame for application did not allow sponsors enough time to put together their applications and prevented the scheme from being properly advertised and becoming well known among the public.[59]

IV. Switzerland's Expired Private Sponsorship Family Reunification Programme

A facilitated family reunification/humanitarian admission programme was introduced in Switzerland on 4 September 2013 by the Federal Department of Justice and Police.[60] The scheme was created to extend protection to a broader group of Syrian nationals, following the deteriorating situation in Syria, by replacing the

[57] Arnold and Quinn, above n 35, 50.

[58] ibid, 49.

[59] ibid, 47.

[60] Directives establishing the 'Facilitated procedure for the issuance of visitor visa for relatives of Syrian nationals living in Switzerland' published on 4 September 2013 (reference number: COO.2180.101.7.266789 / 322.213/Syrien/2010/03648). Since the ratification of the Geneva Convention of 1955, Switzerland has welcomed refugees for resettlement. The resettlement and humanitarian schemes adopted in Switzerland are all grounded on Federal Council Decrees. The first government-led resettlement pilot project began in September 2013, when the Federal Council approved the admission of five 500 particularly vulnerable individuals, already recognised as refugees by the UNHCR, up until 2015. In 2015 the humanitarian action plan HUMAK was introduced. This plan envisaged the admission of further 3000 refugees, within the following three years. Under this programme, some refugees entered via resettlement and others under a humanitarian visa scheme. In 2016 the Resettlement II programme, which targeted Syria, and the Resettlement III programme in 2018, targeting people that had reached Libya, were introduced. The Federal Council approved three other resettlement frameworks, one for 2020/2021, another for 2022/2023 and finally one for 2023/2024. For more information on this topic see State Secretariat for Migration SEM, 'Resettlement Programmes since 2013' (2023), available at: www.sem.admin.ch/sem/en/home/asyl/resettlement/programme.html.

previous Directives issued in 2012. As a matter of fact, the 2012 Directives were supposed to facilitate the obtaining of visas for certain categories of people affected by the Syrian civil war but ended up not being utilised by many applicants.[61]

Like the Irish private sponsorship scheme, the Swiss programme was not grounded in any law, but implemented administratively.[62] The programme targeted Syrian nationals, allowing those with existing refugee status or permanent residence in Switzerland to be joined by their Syrian extended family residing in Syria, in other neighbouring countries and Egypt, and by those who had fled Syria to those countries due to the outbreak of the civil war.[63] The original version of the programme was amended on 4 November 2014, to include requirements for proof of sufficient funds and living space by the sponsor, to be able to lodge a successful application on behalf of their relatives.[64] The programme was then terminated abruptly on 29 November 2013, less than three months from its launch.[65]

A key characteristic of this programme, similar to the German and Irish ones, was the possibility given to the sponsor to selecting from a broad pool of family members.[66] This element allowed the programme to go beyond the category of core family members characterising the classic family reunification route. As a matter of fact, the Swiss programme ended up including also relatives in the ascending and descending lines and their core family members and siblings.[67]

[61] Facilitated procedure for the issuance of visitor visa for relatives of Syrian nationals living in Switzerland' published on 4 September 2013 (reference number: COO.2180.101.7.266789 / 322.213/ Syrien/2010/03648).

[62] European Commission, above n 4, 44.

[63] Directives 2013, above n 60, section I(b). In order to be eligible, beneficiaries could not hold a valid residence permit from any of these third countries.

[64] J Kumin, 'Welcoming Engagement: How Private Sponsorship Can Strengthen Refugee Resettlement in the European Union' (2015) Brussels, Migration Policy Institute Europe, available at: www.migrationpolicy.org/research/welcoming-engagement-how-private-sponsorship-can-strengthen-refugee-resettlement-european, 33.

[65] The reasons underpinning the termination of the programme are complex and multifaceted. In the Communication by the Swiss Federation of 29 November 2013, which announced the termination of the programme, it was argued that the scheme was terminated because 'It is likely that most people in a situation of immediate distress and eligible to obtain such a visa have in the meantime made use of this possibility'. However, the same document stated that difficulties had arisen due to the number of visa applications submitted. In particular, it was reported that some consulates, for example Istanbul, experienced long waiting times and that was considered to be in contradiction to the spirit of the programme, originally intended to be *ad interim* and to provide a quick response. See Le portail du Gouvernement Suisse, 'Octroi Facilite de visas aux parents de ressortissants syriens vivant en Suisse: levee de la mesure provisoire' (2013), available at: www.admin.ch/gov/fr/start/dokumentation/medienmitteilungen.msg-id-51180.html.

[66] European Commission, above n 4, 44.

[67] ibid, 62. These relatives would have otherwise missed out on the opportunity to join their families since they would not have qualified for the classic family reunification route. Directives of 4 September 2013, at section I(a), state that 'The family relationship must be credibly and clearly demonstrated, even if the visa applicant is unable to produce official civil status documents due to the difficult situation in Syria. The family relationship must appear likely on the basis of information provided by the applicant(s), taking into account the specific circumstances. A DNA test should only be ordered in exceptional cases following consultation with the FOM'. See Directives 2013, above n 60.

The private sponsorship nature of the scheme meant that the sponsor had quite a few responsibilities to undertake, such as financing the travel of their family members to Switzerland and 'providing the costs of housing, living expenses, and health insurance for the first 3 months after arrival'.[68]

Following the naming of the potential beneficiaries, the relevant consulate would check the application against certain requirements, listed in the Directive. It is interesting to note that these requirements were much looser than those applied in other similar schemes. For instance, as far as the security checks to be applied to the potential beneficiaries of the programme were concerned, the Directive stated, at section II(d), that it was up to the Swiss authorities to decide whether or not authorise the entry, even for people that had been issued 'a national entry ban or who [were] listed in the Schengen Information System (SIS) as being barred from entering the Schengen Area'. Moreover, 'the intention to leave the territory of Switzerland before the expiry of the visa' and the 'detailed verification of personal and direct danger' were not checked either.[69]

After the application was approved by the relevant state representative, a visa on humanitarian grounds would be issued. The visa was of type D – limited territorial validity (valid only for Switzerland) – in accordance with the Schengen Visa Code. This visa would last 90 days and would allow safe passage and entry into Swiss territory.[70] Unlike the German and Irish programmes, the Swiss sponsorship scheme required that the family member would apply for a protected status after arrival. Within 90 days, before the expiry of their entry visas, the family members had to submit an application for international protection.[71] This element of the scheme, compared to the temporariness of the German, Irish and, as will be soon seen, UK/Ukrainian programmes, likely provided a better sense of stability to its beneficiaries.

The programme was seen as being effective in achieving its aim.[72] On 29 November 2013, the day on which the programme was terminated, 719 people entered Switzerland, including 475 women and children. Furthermore, nearly 5,000 additional people made an appointment with a Swiss government representative to apply for a visa under the scheme.[73] Eventually, the total number of visas issued under this scheme totalled 4673.[74]

However, despite its successes, some limitations were also apparent. For instance, it was assumed that the limited commitment of the sponsor in terms

[68] ERN scoping paper 'Humanitarian Admission Programmes in Europe: expanding complementary pathways of admission for persons in need of international protection' (2018), available at: www.iom.int/sites/g/files/tmzbdl486/files/documents/ERN%2Bscoping-paper-Humanitarian-Admission-Programmes-in-Europe.pdf, 17. See also European Commission, above 4, 75.

[69] Directives 2013, above n 60, section II(a).

[70] European Commission, above 4, 67.

[71] ibid, 68.

[72] Le portail du Gouvernement Suisse, above n 65. However, it was also argued that the programme, rather than being terminated because its aim was achieved, was a victim of its own success. See European Commission, above n 4, 67.

[73] Le portail du Gouvernement Suisse, above n 65.

[74] European Commission, above n 4, 44.

of financial responsibility – only 90 days – increased uncertainty.[75] In particular, scholars advanced that this short time window during which the sponsor was financially responsible for the beneficiary, topped by the fact that the sponsors did not necessarily need to be legal residents in Switzerland, triggered a high level of ambiguity which eventually led to the termination of the programme.[76] Indeed, stakeholders seem to support models of sponsorship that impose longer time commitments on the sponsors, since the long-term aim of private sponsorship of refugees is integration, and that cannot be achieved in a short period of time.[77] Finally, it was also argued that the fact that the beneficiaries did not receive a work permit upon entry into Switzerland, unlike the beneficiaries of other Swiss immigration routes, affected the success of the policy.[78]

V. The UK Homes for Ukraine Scheme

Following the outbreak of the war in Ukraine, the UK put in place a series of humanitarian schemes targeting Ukrainian nationals. The UK government introduced the Ukraine Extension Scheme, which allows Ukrainians already in UK territory to extend their stay up to three years.[79] The government also introduced the Ukraine Family Scheme,[80] which allows UK citizens, citizens of other nationalities, as long as they are settled in the UK, and others[81] to reunify with their Ukrainian relatives who would not normally qualify under the classic family reunification route. Finally, the UK also introduced the Homes for Ukraine scheme. Unlike the family reunification scheme, the UK Homes for Ukraine targets Ukrainians that do *not* have established family links in the UK. These three programmes offer a generous general level of protection, quite similar to that provided by the EU.[82]

[75] D Bertram, A Maleki and N Karsten, 'Factoring in Societal Culture in Policy Transfer Design: The Proliferation of Private Sponsorship of Refugees' (2019) 21 *Journal of International Migration and Integration* 253, 263.

[76] ibid, 266.

[77] European Commission, above 4, 75. However, at the same time stakeholders highlighted how the sponsors' commitment should not be too lengthy either.

[78] D Bertram, A Maleki and N Karsten, above n 75, 266.

[79] Gov.UK, 'Apply to stay in the UK under the Ukraine Extension Scheme' 19 February 2024, available at: www.gov.uk/guidance/apply-to-stay-in-the-uk-under-the-ukraine-extension-scheme. This scheme closed for applications on 16 May 2024.

[80] Gov.UK, 'Apply for a Ukraine Family Scheme Visa' 19 February 2024, available at: www.gov.uk/guidance/apply-for-a-ukraine-family-scheme-visa. This scheme closed for applications on 19 February 2024.

[81] In addition, the sponsors can also be refugees, persons with humanitarian protection, or EEA or Swiss citizens with pre-settled status under the EU Settlement Scheme (where this is based on residence in the UK before the end of the transition period). See Gov.UK, 'Immigration Rules' 31 January 2024, available at: www.gov.uk/guidance/immigration-rules/immigration-rules-appendix-ukraine-scheme.

[82] M Benson, N Sigona and E Zambelli, 'Humanitarian visas in a hostile environment: historical legacies, geopolitical ties and everyday experiences' Migzen Research Brief no 5, available at: zenodo.org/

This section focuses on the Homes for Ukraine scheme only. This is because this is the only programme that features a strong private sponsorship component,[83] as will be soon seen.

The UK launched this scheme on 14 March 2022. The scheme, currently still in operation, is open to all Ukrainians that were resident in Ukraine before 1 January 2022. The scheme is also open to their immediate family members, who could also be of other nationalities.[84] Applicants can apply from Ukraine or from any other third country.[85] The beneficiaries are only issued a three-year visa to stay in the UK. After the three years, the beneficiaries of the scheme, if they intend to stay in the UK, will have to apply for a study visa or work visa, or successfully apply for asylum.

Sponsors can be British Nationals or simply be entitled to reside in the UK (indefinite leave to remain, refugee status, humanitarian protection, EU settled status or EU pre-settled status). To register their interest, sponsors have to be willing to offer the beneficiary a spare room or a home for at least six months. Sponsors are allowed to name the individuals that they would like to support. Those that do not have a named individual in mind can record their interest in becoming a sponsor and they will be matched with a candidate.[86] There is no limit to the numbers entitled to entry.[87]

The role of the sponsors in this programme is very important as they are the ones that have to provide suitable accommodation for six months, or for up to three years when unaccompanied children are involved.[88] Their role is also important from an emotional point of view, as they are the first contact for people that normally do not have any previous link to or network in the UK.

The government has an active involvement in the programme and provides support to recipients. Sponsors are supported by the government with a tax-free monthly 'thank you' payment of £350, limited to one per household. The payment

records/10571433, 6. For a better understanding of what happens at EU level in terms of protection of Ukrainians fleeing the war, see Council Implementing Decision (EU) 2022/382 of 4 March 2022 establishing the existence of a mass influx of displaced persons from Ukraine within the meaning of Article 5 of Directive 2001/55/EC, and having the effect of introducing temporary protection, ST/6846/2022/INIT, OJ L 71, 4.3.2022.

[83] Unlike the expired family reunification schemes that have already been analysed, under which the sponsors had to be able to provide for a certain period of time the Ukraine Family Scheme came with the right to claim benefits, in addition to the right to study and work, and no specific financial requirement to be borne by the sponsor. See Free Movement, 'Can Ukrainians take refuge in the UK? The Ukraine Family Scheme and other routes', available at: freemovement.org.uk/can-ukrainians-take-refuge-in-the-uk-immigration-concessions-and-asylum-policy/.

[84] Gov.UK, 'Homes for Ukraine scheme: frequently asked questions' 29 July 2022, available at: www.gov.uk/guidance/homes-for-ukraine-scheme-frequently-asked-questions.

[85] ibid.

[86] ibid. In Scotland and Wales, people that have expressed an interest in becoming sponsors will be matched through the Scottish and Welsh Devolved Government Sponsorship Schemes.

[87] R Machin, 'The UK – a home for Ukrainians? An analysis of social security and housing policy' (2023) 31 *Journal of Poverty and Social Justice* 298, 299.

[88] ibid.

is increased to £500 monthly, when the guest has been in the house for at least 12 months.[89] Furthermore, the government grants immediate access to means-tested, non-means-tested and disability benefits, on condition that the beneficiaries of the scheme left Ukraine after 24 February 2022 and resided in Ukraine immediately before 1 January 2022.[90] Beneficiaries have also free access to the National Health Service, schooling system, they are given domestic fee status if applying for university studies and are eligible to apply for social benefits and homelessness assistance.[91]

Despite the slow start and early delays, the numbers indicate that the programme has been successful, with 154,500 arrivals by the end of 2022.[92] However, some researchers have expressed concern that the scheme could increase the already deep-rooted issues associated with the UK's Universal Credit system. Indeed, payment delays, mismatching with job coaches, etc are more likely to be experienced 'by Ukrainians, who are newly arrived to the UK and often lack professional support'.[93] Moreover, concerns have also been raised in relation to sponsors that are entitled to social benefits, as a change in the household composition could trigger a review of the sponsor's Universal Credit claim.[94] Concerns about housing have also been shared, as the end of the sponsorship could leave the beneficiaries of the scheme without suitable accommodation, despite the measures of including Ukrainians within the social housing and homelessness assistance.[95] Finally, the temporariness of the scheme is detrimental to the beneficiaries' sense of stability and capacity to make long-term plans.

VI. Fostering of Unaccompanied Minors: Private Sponsorship in St Marino

The experience of private sponsorship of refugees in the Republic of St Marino is quite recent. St Marino became initially involved with the St Egidio humanitarian corridor initiative in 2017 when the Republic welcomed two refugees to its territory. In this case, the local Italian embassies issued a visa of limited territorial validity, according to Article 25 of the Visa Code. The beneficiaries did not undergo police check procedures once they landed in Italy, but were instead greeted by the St Marino authorities, who handed them a residence permit to reside in the Republic. It is not clear whether the costs of maintenance and integration of the migrants were covered by the Community of St Egidio or by the St Marino state itself, as information on this point is not readily available.

[89] ibid.
[90] ibid, 301.
[91] ibid.
[92] Share Network, 'Resettlement and Community Sponsorship across Europe', available at: www.share-network.eu/articles-and-resources/sponsorship.
[93] Machin, above n 87, 300.
[94] ibid, 302.
[95] ibid. There are long waiting lists in most local authority areas for suitable social housing for families.

Likely due to the limited geographical capacity of the Republic, the humanitarian corridor initiative never grew substantially. However, the humanitarian corridor scheme, despite not being hugely successful in terms of numbers, strengthened collaboration between the Republic and the Community of St Egidio and paved the way for the introduction of a new initiative targeting unaccompanied migrant minors. In April 2021 a bill was unanimously approved that enabled individuals and families to host unaccompanied foreign minors living in migrant centres or in hosting facilities,[96] known as Law of 30 April 2021 nº 79 on welcoming unaccompanied minors.[97] The scheme is expressly targeted toward the relocation of unaccompanied minors, who are to be welcomed into foster care. Following the approval of the law, the Community of St Egidio and the Republic of St Marino signed a memorandum of understanding to facilitate the entry and relocation of unaccompanied minors located in Greece.[98] Like for the corridors discussed in the previous chapter, this memorandum allows representatives of the Community of St Egidio in loco to take care of the selection process of the potential beneficiaries. However, Article 4 of Law of 30 April 2021 nº 79 refers to 'Authorised organisations' who are involved in caring and protecting unaccompanied minors, both in Italy and abroad. This suggests that, once the scheme has been properly tested and implemented, the Community of St Egidio might not be the only organisation involved in identifying the potential beneficiaries, but other organisations could also be involved.

On this point, the scheme introduces an implicit shared partnership between private stakeholders: on one side there are the families, who will take on the emotional and financial responsibility for the beneficiaries, even covering the expenses of the trip to St Marino from the state of current residence,[99] and on the other side there is the Community of St Egidio and other associations, which will engage with the selection of the beneficiaries.

The scheme is designed as potentially being able to go beyond relocation of unaccompanied minors. Indeed, if the unaccompanied minors find themselves in a third country, the authorities will work to issue a transit visa through Italian territory.[100] The local Italian embassies will issue a visa of limited territorial validity, according to Article 25 of the Visa Code. The beneficiaries, once landed in Italy, will then be escorted to St Marino, where a residence permit will be granted.

[96] Info Migrants, 'San Marino approves legislation to host unaccompanied minors' (2021), available at: www.infomigrants.net/en/post/31968/san-marino-approves-legislation-to-host-unaccompanied-minors.

[97] Legge 30 Aprile 2021 nº 79 Disposizioni in materia di accoglienza di minori stranieri non accompagnati, available at: www.consigliograndeegenerale.sm/on-line/home/scheda17172327.html.

[98] Sir Agenzia d'informazione, 'Corridoi umanitari: Capitani reggenti di San Marino in visita a Sant'Egidio. Firmato memorandum per accogliere minori stranieri non accompagnati' (2021), available at: www.agensir.it/quotidiano/2021/5/26/corridoi-umanitari-capitani-reggenti-di-san-marino-in-visita-a-santegidio-firmato-memorandum-per-accogliere-minori-stranieri-non-accompagnati/. The text of the memorandum is not publicly available.

[99] Art 7 Legge 30 Aprile 2021 nº 79.

[100] ibid, Art 10.

Article 6 of the Law outlines the requirements that should be fulfilled by the foster family and, among those, the financial capacity to provide for the minor is, of course, included. However, it is important to note that Article 14 allows the institution of a dedicated fund, to which private donations can be made with the aim of financially sustaining the families involved in the project.

Finally, according to Article 17, in case of revocation of the foster care agreement, the Republic of St Marino will continue to take care of the minor, through the financial support of the Institute for Social Security.

The practical implications of this initiative have not been tested yet. Indeed, at the time of writing no applicant families have yet expressed an interest in fostering.[101] The slow response from civil society may be simply coincidental or could indicate that, perhaps, the programme should be better promoted or rethought to create incentives to enhance broader participation.

VII. Portugal: Private Sponsorship to Support Intra-EU Relocation

One of the private sponsorship schemes that ran in Portugal was part of the intra-EU relocation scheme programme.[102] This programme ran in parallel to the UNHCR resettlement state programme, which commenced in 2007.[103] Portugal initially experimented with private sponsorship of refugees within the intra-EU relocation programme, rather than resettlement. However, as was seen in Chapter three, there is now a refugee sponsorship pilot programme that was established to support resettlement.

[101] Information gathered from a conversation with Dr Giulia Muratori, legal expert of the Directorate of Legal Affairs in the Republic of St Marino, 18 April 2023.

[102] The intra-EU relocation scheme – a burden-sharing plan for relocation – was approved within the European Agenda on Migration initiative. The Agenda also includes activities that aim to reduce the migratory phenomenon, such as strengthening patrols within the Mediterranean, acting against smugglers, improving deportation and the asylum system, together with new facilities for administrative confinement, identification and expulsion. On this topic see F Vacchiano, 'On marginal inclusion: refugees at the fringes of citizenship in Portugal' in S Aboim, P Granjo and A Ramos (eds), *Changing Societies: Legacies and Challenges. Ambiguous inclusions: inside out, outside in*, vol 1 (Lisbon, Universidade de Lisboa, 2018) 99, available at: www.ics.ulisboa.pt/books/book1/full.pdf. For more information on the Portuguese relocation programme, see Alto Commissariado Para Migrações, Relatório de Avaliação da Política Portuguesa de Acolhimento de Pessoas Refugiadas (2017), available at: www.acm.gov.pt/documents/10181/27754/Relatorio_Acolhimento%2BPessoas%2BRefugiadas_Dez.2017.pdf/d21546b3-7588-483d-92a3-fa8185d61b5b.

[103] The annual UNHCR resettlement scheme was approved officially by the Council of Ministers in Portugal in 2007, following two ad hoc resettlement schemes in 2006, with an annual quota of 30 people submitted by UNHCR. The number of pledges was increased during the Syrian crisis. Resettlement in Portugal finds its legal grounding in Art 35 of Asylum Law 27/2008. For more information see P Kortsaris, 'The Syrian Refugee Crisis: Resettlement and Other Complementary Pathways of Admission to Third Countries as Part of the Response' (2018) 149 *Nação e Defesa* 134, 147, available at: core.ac.uk/download/pdf/322889116.pdf.

It is important to note that relocation and resettlement are two distinct solutions, proposed to very different categories of people. Indeed, while resettlement is a solution offered by third countries to qualified refugees, who are given the opportunity to move and 'resettle' on a permanent basis, relocation concerns asylum seekers, who are moved from EU countries under extreme migratory pressure to others within the EU, which will then take responsibility for assessing their claims.

The intra-EU relocation scheme was first implemented in 2016. This came after increasing numbers of migrants reaching Italian and Greek shores proved to be challenging for the immigration authorities of those states, particularly as far as the identification and initial reception of migrants were concerned.[104] Intra-EU relocation was introduced by the ad hoc Council Decisions of 14 and 22 September 2015[105] and it has its legal foundation in Article 78(3) TFEU.[106] The decisions set the numbers of immigrants to be relocated from Greece and Italy to the other Member States. The programme effectively introduced a derogation from the Dublin system, since the responsibility for a number of asylum applications, which normally lies with the state of first entry, was shifted from Greece and Italy to other Member States.[107]

The intra-EU relocation scheme worked in tandem with the Hot Spot European system. Indeed, migrants were relocated only after applying for international protection at the hot spots in the countries of first arrival, and after having been fingerprinted.[108] The migrants had no right to choose their state of destination.[109] Owing to this programme, 34,323 people were successfully relocated.[110]

Within this background, Portugal started participating in the intra-EU relocation scheme in 2015, relocating asylum seekers from Italy and Malta, and, since

[104] See F Maiani, 'Hotspots and Relocation Schemes: the right therapy for the Common European Asylum System?' 3 February 2016, *EU Immigration and Asylum Law and Policy Blog*, available at: eumigrationlawblog.eu/hotspots-and-relocation-schemes-the-right-therapy-for-the-common-european-asylum-system/.

[105] Council Decision (EU) 2015/1523 of 14 September 2015 establishing provisional measures in the area of international protection for the benefit of Italy and Greece, OJ L 239, 15.9.2015, 146–56 and Council Decision (EU) 2015/1601 of 22 September 2015 establishing provisional measures in the area of international protection for the benefit of Italy and Greece, OJ L 248, 24.9.2015, 80–94. According to the first decision, a total of 40,000 migrants had to be relocated from Italy and Greece. According to the second decision, a total of 120,000 migrants had to be relocated from Italy and Greece. Decision 2015/1601 was challenged by Slovakia and Hungary. Their challenge was rejected by the CJEU in Joined Cases C-643/15 and C-647/15 *Slovak Republic and Hungary v Council of the European Union* ECLI:EU:C:2017:631.

[106] Art 78(3) TFEU, read in conjunction with Art 80 TFEU, offers the legal grounds for the principle of solidarity. Art 78(3) states that 'In the event of one or more Member States being confronted by an emergency situation characterised by a sudden inflow of nationals of third countries, the Council, on a proposal from the Commission, may adopt provisional measures for the benefit of the Member State(s) concerned. It shall act after consulting the European Parliament'. See European Parliament, 'At glance: Emergency measures on migration: Article 78(3) TFEU' (2020), available at: www.europarl.europa.eu/RegData/etudes/ATAG/2020/649325/EPRS_ATA(2020)649325_EN.pdf.

[107] For more information on this topic see Maiani, above n 104.

[108] ibid.

[109] ibid.

[110] NF Tan, 'Community Sponsorship in Europe: Taking Stock, Policy Transfer and What the Future might Hold' (2021) 3 *Frontiers in Human Dynamics: Refugees and Conflict*, available at: www.frontiersin.org/articles/10.3389/fhumd.2021.564084/full, fn 7.

2020, relocating unaccompanied asylum-seeking minors from Greece.[111] Portugal pledged to receive a total of 4,775 relocated migrants.[112] Between 2015 and 2018, the Portuguese government implemented a temporary scheme to meet its relocation targets, where private sponsors would take on some responsibilities in relation to immigrants' needs, such as accommodation, food and clothing, support in accessing healthcare services, support in accessing the labour market, support in accessing education, and language courses.[113]

To make sure that the programme was properly implemented, the Portuguese government put together a special unit, known as the 'Working Group for the European Agenda on Migration'. This unit was presided over by the Immigration and Border Service, a department of the Portuguese national police – and was composed of representatives of the Ministries of the Interior, Education and Health; the National Institute for Employment and Vocational Training (IFPPT); the National Institute for Social Security; and the High Commissioner on Migration (ACM).[114] Its task was to coordinate a system for reception of immigrants, where the public and private sector would cooperate together.[115]

Two of the key principles enshrined in the programme were 'giving value to the reception potential of territories of middle and low density, preventing the concentration of people' and 'ensuring the gradual acquisition of autonomy by refugees'.[116] Indeed, the reception phase was set up and supported not just in urban but also peripheral areas.[117]

The appeal of the Working Group for the European Agenda on Migration was embraced by a number of public and private bodies throughout Portugal.[118] As far as a sponsor's eligibility was concerned, a key player was the Institute of Father António Vieira (IPAV). This is a non-governmental organisation of Catholic background that launched the Refugee Support Platform (PAR) in September 2015.[119]

[111] UNHCR, Portugal: Relocation and Humanitarian Admission, available at: help.unhcr.org/portugal/relocation/.

[112] R Atanasova, 'Portugal as a state of relocation under the Provisional EU Relocation Scheme' (2016) 13 *Revista Migrações – Número Temático Planos de Integração para Migrantes* 109, 114, available at: www.om.acm.gov.pt/documents/58428/569795/Portugal+as+a+State+of+Relocation+under+the+Provisional+EU+Relocation+Scheme+-+Rositsa+Atanasova.pdf/7178aec3-b14a-48dd-89bb-2517bd714dde. This was a very generous approach, compared to other countries such as Hungary, Slovakia, Poland and the Czech Republic. It has been argued that Portugal's engagement in the matter was influenced by the strong power of the Catholic Church, which took 'its lead from Pope Francis' pro-refugee stance, bolstering national support'. On this point see PM Costa and L Sousa, 'Portugal's Openness to Refugees Makes Demographic and Economic Sense' 10 February 2017, available at: deeply.thenewhumanitarian.org/refugees/community/2017/02/10/portugals-openness-to-refugees-makes-demographic-and-economic-sense.

[113] European Commission, above n 4, 132.

[114] Vacchiano, above n 102, 102.

[115] ibid.

[116] ibid.

[117] F Vacchiano, 'Camouflaging borders: relocation, neglect and disciplines of emplacement in Portugal' (2019) 5 *International Journal of Migration and Border Studies* 273, 277.

[118] ibid.

[119] E Challinor, 'Refugee Hospitality Encounters in Northern Portugal: "Cultural Orientations" and "Contextual Protections"' (2018) 96 *Migration and Society* 96, 101.

This platform created a website where organisations could apply in order to offer to host a refugee family.[120] PAR also provided training to the various organisations willing to become sponsors.[121] Simultaneously, the Portuguese Jesuit Refugee Service established a network of volunteers, such as banks, companies and universities to mobilise various resources to welcome large numbers of people.[122]

The reception of the relocated migrants was highly decentralised and carried out in 99 different municipalities, by different institutions and organisations, both public and private. These bodies were responsible, in partnership with the Portuguese government, for managing the reception and integration process.[123]

In order to be eligible as a sponsor, an individual had to show proof of independent and adequate accommodation.[124] Interestingly, families that were hosted and helped by an organisation via PAR were given support for two years, while families that were hosted outside PAR, for example through the Red Cross, were granted a shorter contract of 18 months.[125] As seen above, the financial responsibility of the sponsoring institution covered accommodation, food and clothing. For all the other expenses the beneficiaries could rely on 6,000 euros for each person received through the relocation programme. Moreover, adults were entitled to 150 euros a month and 75 euros per child.[126] At the end of the 18-month or two-year period, the beneficiaries of the programme continue to enjoy subsidiary protection or refugee status rights, respectively, for three and five years. If the migrants continue to need support at the end of the reception programme, perhaps because they are still unemployed, support will come from the Instituto de Solidariedade e Segurança, the Portuguese social security system.[127]

As far as the beneficiaries of the programme are concerned, the migrants were selected according to the criteria set out in Council Decisions 2015/1523 and 2015/1601, on Intra-EU relocation. Paragraph 27 of Decision 2015/1523 states that the applicants entitled to relocation are those in clear need of international protection, and among those, priority should be given to 'vulnerable applicants within the meaning of Articles 21 and 22 of Directive 2013/33/EU of the European Parliament and of the Council', which include respectively

> minors, unaccompanied minors, disabled people, elderly people, pregnant women, single parents with minor children, victims of human trafficking, persons with serious illnesses, persons with mental disorders and persons who have been subjected to torture, rape or other serious forms of psychological, physical or sexual violence, such as victims of female genital mutilation.

[120] ibid.
[121] European Commission, above n 4, 82.
[122] Vacchiano, above n 102, 102.
[123] See C Constantino and M Minas, 'My new home? Strategies and challenges of refugee integration programs in Portugal' (2022) 50(8) *Journal of Community Psychology* 3792, 3796.
[124] European Commission, above n 4, 54.
[125] Challinor, above n 119, 101.
[126] ibid.
[127] ibid.

and 'applicants with special reception needs'.[128]

The beneficiaries of the programme were granted a temporary entry permit and had to apply for protection status on arrival, via the regular asylum route. They were granted the same rights as other asylum seekers.

The relationship between sponsors and beneficiaries was constantly monitored. The Jesuit Refugee Service was appointed to this task and regularly visited the beneficiaries of the scheme and made sure that the relationship was running smoothly. If any issue was identified on the side of the sponsors, help could be sought via their working group. Equally, if the beneficiaries faced some difficulties, they could seek help through a hotline established by the High Commission for Migration.[129]

To the programme goes the honour of having triggered a real interest and involvement of civil society in trying to find feasible solutions to the issue of refugee protection. Owing to the intra-EU relocation experiment, Portugal also gained the confidence to pave the way for the introduction of the independent Community Sponsorship of refugees, which was analysed in more detail in Chapter three. However, it is important to note that the scheme also suffered from some quite serious issues. First of all, stakeholders raised an issue of discrimination within the programme itself. In particular, as mentioned above, families supported by the Refugee Support Platform received support for two years while those supported by other organisations, only got 18 months' support. This raised a criticism of double standards and unfair discrimination, based on the nature of the sponsor.[130] Moreover, although the stakeholders involved in the process were passionate and committed to the cause, and platforms and services dedicated to integration seemed well arranged and working well despite the lack of resources, some authors highlighted a variety of gaps and limitations, 'such as the lack of training and adequate preparation of professionals; the lack of planning for reception and integration by host institutions; the need for greater collaboration among all the stakeholders; the poverty of strategies to promote language learning'.[131] In October 2017, it was confirmed that almost half of the beneficiaries of the programme had left Portugal. This is probably because they never intended to go to Portugal in the first place, but also because of the conditions they encountered while there.[132]

VIII. Humanitarian Corridors for Relocation of Migrants from Greece and Cyprus

In 2016, in the midst of the refugee crisis, Pope Francis visited the Greek island of Lesbos. He left the island with three refugee families, a total of 12 people, and he

[128] Directive 2013/33/EU of the European Parliament and of the Council of 26 June 2013 laying down standards for the reception of applicants for international protection (recast) OJ L 180, 29.6.2013, 96–116.
[129] European Commission, above n 4, 85.
[130] ibid, 73.
[131] Constantino and Minas, above n 123, 3796.
[132] Vacchiano, above n 117, 278.

brought them back with him to the Vatican.[133] This gesture triggered the beginning of a new series of humanitarian corridors from Greece and Cyprus to Italy. These corridors however, unlike those described in the previous chapter, are not aiming to support resettlement but rather are private sponsorships that support intra-EU relocation procedures, as in the above-cited case of Portugal.

The memoranda allowing the introduction of these humanitarian corridors were signed by the Community of St Egidio and the Italian Ministry of the Interior to mainly welcome people located in Greece (first from the islands and now Athens).[134] In particular, the first pilot corridor between St Egidio and the Italian Ministry of the Interior was signed in 2016, after the papal visit to Lesbos, and allowed the entry of 67 migrants from there. The Vatican was involved in this initiative through the Vatican Office of Papal Charities, which sponsored the entry of some of these migrants, who were then hosted and received support from the representatives of the Community of St Egidio on Italian territory.[135] This memorandum was followed by another one signed in 2019, for the entry of 33 refugees. On 23 September 2020 another memorandum was signed between St Egidio and the Italian Minister of the Interior for the entry of 300 migrants from the Lesbos camp of Moira.[136] Among this group, unaccompanied minors were also accepted.[137]

As far as Cyprus is concerned, a humanitarian corridor was established through an agreement between the Vatican Secretary of State, and the Italian and Cypriot authorities, in collaboration with the Vatican migrants and refugees unit and the Community of St Egidio, in December 2021,[138] after the Pope's visit to the island.[139] The Holy See requested the cooperation of the Community of St Egidio in relation to the selection of the candidates in most need of relocation, the organisation of the trip to Italy, and the process of integration into Italy, to be guaranteed for at least one year or for the longer period needed for the beneficiaries to become independent. The operation is entirely financed by the Vatican and a total of 50 people have already been welcomed to Italy under this scheme.

From a juridical point of view, the relocation corridors resemble the classic ones aimed at resettlement in terms of the selection procedure and the breadth and duration of financial and emotional support. Despite the still relatively limited

[133] H Smith, 'Pope Francis takes refugees to Rome after Lesbos visit' 16 April 2016, *The Guardian*, available at: www.theguardian.com/world/2016/apr/16/pope-francis-flies-to-lesbos-to-highlight-humanitarian-crisis-in-europe.

[134] Information gathered from a conversation with Daniela Pompei, manager of the Community of St Egidio's services for migrants, 17 June 2022.

[135] ibid.

[136] Ministero Interno, '300 richiedenti asilo da Lesbo in Italia grazie a corridoio umanitario' 22 settembre 2020, available at: www.interno.gov.it/it/notizie/300-richiedenti-asilo-lesbo-italia-grazie-corridoio-umanitario.

[137] ibid.

[138] Vatican news, 'Un primo gruppo di rifugiati da Cipro in Italia con il sostegno della Santa Sede' 3 December 2021, available at: www.vaticannews.va/it/papa/news/2021-12/papa-francesco-cipro-accoglienza-migranti-vaticano.html.

[139] Rai news, 'Daniela Pompei, Comunità di Sant'Egidio: l'arrivo del papa a Cipro è una spinta per tutti' 2 December 2021, available at: www.rainews.it/archivio-rainews/articoli/daniela-pompei-corridoi-umanitari-santegidio-6d95acbc-e7d0-47cb-ad9d-050a81640ee9.html.

numbers, compared to the classic humanitarian corridors applied to refugees coming from third countries, these solutions are showing how private sponsorship initiatives can work efficiently within a repertoire of multifaceted and nuanced combinations. The examples of humanitarian corridor initiatives seeking to enhance relocation have shown that private stakeholders (St Egidio) and public stakeholders (the Vatican state) can share, respectively, integration and financial responsibilities for migrants that are welcomed in the territory of another state (Italy). This not only shows the malleability of the schemes but also the crucial importance of the collaboration between private sponsors and states.

IX. A Final Assessment of Private Sponsorship Schemes as Different Forms of Admission

As with the previous chapter, Chapter four has provided an overview of the past and present European experience of private sponsorship of refugees seen, this time, as different forms of admission from resettlement. This overview has hopefully helped the reader to understand how these private sponsorships work. Moreover, this analysis, like Chapter three, has tried to show, when possible,[140] the key reasons for each scheme's success or perceived failure.

Positive and negative appraisals are often recurrent in more than one of the programmes that have been analysed by this chapter.

Starting from private sponsorship schemes linked to humanitarian admissions/family reunification, the expired family reunification programmes of Germany, Ireland and Switzerland showed some evident common advantages. All three schemes broadened the normally strict categories of third-country national family members allowed to apply for reunification, by including extended family members and, in some cases, even members that were not strictly related by blood-ties. One could argue that the possibility of selecting, within predetermined but loose categories, from a broader pool of family members, has been conducive to the success of the schemes. Choosing to introduce programmes based on family reunification models and enhanced by a sponsorship component also offered the opportunity to the beneficiaries of the schemes to arrive in a country already supported by a strong, close-knit network. On top of the emotional support, sponsoring family members were asked to take on substantive financial commitment. Finally, these schemes did not apply the quota logic. Owing to this element, these programmes allowed more people to flee very precarious and dangerous situations quickly and in safety, while without these schemes this might not have been possible to such an extent and in such timely fashion.

[140] Please note that the St Marino scheme has not been tested yet. Reflections, at this stage, should only be taken within the realm of best guesses.

However, these schemes also had some downsides. In particular, the temporary nature of some of these schemes was a serious limitation in terms of beneficiaries' capacity to make long-term plans. Moreover, the beneficiaries of the three expired family reunification programmes seemed to experience discrimination, compared to those immigrants that were welcomed by the same states following other routes. Perhaps in order to compensate for some of the generous features of the schemes, the programmes wanted to add some stricter elements. For example, the German *Länder* family reunification programmes did not allow the beneficiaries to become sponsors themselves and to reunify with the people left behind, which is something that other standard routes permit. In Ireland the programme was characterised by an unlimited (time-wise) financial responsibility on the sponsor and a residence permit to family members that lasted for just two years. These features are in contrast with the classic Irish family reunification scheme. Finally in Switzerland, unlike the classic family reunification route, the beneficiaries of the Syrian scheme did not immediately receive a work permit. In relation to these schemes, streams of criticism have also been raised as far as the role of the sponsor is concerned, for different reasons. In particular, while in Ireland and Germany complaints arose in relation to the too heavy financial burden placed on the sponsor's shoulders, in Switzerland it was argued that the temporally limited financial responsibility of the sponsor caused uncertainty.

The UK Homes for Ukraine humanitarian programme also presents some positive and negative elements. Indeed, the programme, by including the possibility of selecting the beneficiaries without being subject to any quota, is allowing many more people to escape from the war and this is certainly a successful outcome. However, once in the UK, the Ukrainian beneficiaries of this programme struggle to integrate, due to delays in welfare provisions, job availability and the temporariness of the scheme.

In relation to the relocation programmes above described, it is evident how integration for relocated migrants is better supported when private stakeholders get involved. In the case of the privately sponsored relocation system of Portugal, the sponsors not only made financial provision by covering accommodation, food and clothing, but also provided a strong network of contacts and support. Equally, the Italian/Vatican humanitarian corridors from Cyprus and Greece offered strong financial support from the Vatican and substantive help from a myriad of volunteers, mostly connected to the Community of St Egidio, who dealt with the integration needs of the beneficiaries.

However, the crucial role played by the sponsor in the ancillary relocation schemes varies, depending on the specific programme. While the programmes involving the Vatican and Community of St Egidio seemed to be highly successful, the Portuguese relocation programme struggled in some aspects of its integration phase, mainly due to lack of training for the sponsors, who found themselves in difficulty when dealing with the needs of the families. Moreover, particularly as far as the Portuguese relocation scheme is concerned, the programme was accused of being discriminatory, due to the double standards applied to the beneficiaries, depending on the nature of the sponsor involved.

The above synthesis has shown the key strengths and challenges to private sponsorship of refugees seen as different forms of admission from resettlement. The possibility of selecting the beneficiaries and not being subject to state quotas – which we could refer to as naming and additionality for simplicity – seem to be particularly central for the success of the Homes for Ukraine scheme. Moreover, the fact that several other of these programmes were not subject to state quotas and allowed the sponsor to choose within a loose category of family members, or within a vast category of people potentially entitled to relocation, provided that they fulfilled the vulnerability criteria, is also broadly connected to the idea of naming and additionality and, again, seemed to be key to the success of the programmes. On the other hand, criticism of most of the schemes within this category seem to be focused on discrimination issues and the role played by the sponsor within the schemes.

The next chapter, owing to the analysis proposed in Chapters three and four, will address the question of how European private sponsorship schemes could be enhanced. This will be done first by looking at the features of naming and additionality, developing the argument using sponsorship programmes seen as tools for resettlement as key examples, because this is the category of sponsorship to which these elements are more easily connected and understood. The chapter will suggest a new possible way to conceptualise the relationship between the state and private stakeholders over state sovereignty. Based on this conceptualisation, the chapter will then make a proposal on how to enhance sponsorship schemes, by promoting the elements of naming and additionality. The practical limitations of this proposal will be analysed in the final part of the chapter. In that section the issue of discrimination and the controversial role played by the sponsor will also be discussed.

5

Expanding the Reach of Private Sponsorship of Refugees in Europe: A Proposal

I. Introduction

Up until now, the phenomenon of private sponsorship of refugees and how it has been embodied in Europe has been analysed and described. While the first chapter was dedicated to an historical overview and the second chapter was focused on a more detailed description of the phenomenon, the last two chapters have offered an overview of the specific European sponsorship programmes to date (some functioning, some already expired), focusing on their key features, strengths and challenges.

After having looked at the schemes, some of which operated and some of which still operate in Europe, this chapter now aims to take the discussion to a deeper level. Indeed, the key question that this chapter aims to address is whether there might be a way to enhance and ameliorate the work done by these programmes in Europe.

As things stand, considering only the numbers of the largest active private sponsorship schemes that support resettlement in Europe (the St Egidio humanitarian corridors in Italy, France, and Belgium, Community Sponsorship in the UK and the NesT programme in Germany), fewer than 6,000 people in total have benefitted from being the recipients of these private sponsorship schemes.[1]

[1] Data are currently quite difficult to collect. However, according to Sant'Egidio, 'Dossier sui corridoi umanitari in Europa' January 2022, available at: www.santegidio.org/pageID/34176/langID/it/Dossier-sui-corridoi-umanitari-in-Europa.html, 4,342 people were recipients of humanitarian corridor programmes as at January 2022; according to Gov.UK, 'Local communities welcome hundreds of refugee families' 16 August 2023, available at: www.gov.uk/government/news/local-communities-welcome-hundreds-of-refugee-families#:~:text=Over%201%2C000%20vulnerable%20refugees%2C%20fleeing,through%20the%20community%20sponsorship%20scheme, around 1,000 people were recipients of Community Sponsorship in the UK as at August 2023; and according to the Federal Office for Migration and Refugees, 'Humanitäre Flüchtlingsaufnahme im Programm "Neustart im Team" (NesT)' 21 June 2023, available at: www.bamf.de/SharedDocs/ProjekteReportagen/DE/Forschung/Migration/evaluation-resettlement-programm-nest.html?nn=447036, around 339 people benefitted from the Nest German scheme from 2019 to 2023. These numbers are also, roughly, confirmed by Share Network, 'Resettlement and Community Sponsorship across Europe', available at: www.share-network.eu/articles-and-resources/sponsorship.

While this is a remarkable achievement, it is small compared to the estimated 2.4 million refugees in need of resettlement in 2024.[2] The numbers achieved by these key European schemes are also minimal if we consider that in Canada the target for 2021, 2022 and 2023 was 22,500 for each year.[3] It is also worth noting that many of the private resettlement schemes seem to have 'fallen short of the annual admission targets'.[4]

It is also important to remember that many private European schemes offer protection only to UNHCR recognised refugees. However, it is well known that many migrants are in situations of extreme vulnerability, that is, nevertheless, unrelated to the conditions that would allow them to receive the UNHCR refugee status. For instance, migrants' need for protection can arise from factors that are not related to conflict or political persecution, such as 'climate change, environmental degradation, natural disaster or serious economic and social distress'.[5] Moreover, many migrants become extremely vulnerable while in transit, because they have been expelled, suffered violence or abuse of basic human rights or been caught in human trafficking.[6] For migrants that find themselves in this vulnerability limbo, there does not seem to be a clear option, either offered at state level or by private stakeholders. Given the data and evidence at hand, one might wonder whether there is a way to introduce enhanced and far-reaching programmes in Europe to improve upon the existing ones and to address the issues above.

This chapter will first focus on two key features of private sponsorships that have been identified as strengths, but also potentially problematic: naming and additionality. Since naming and additionality are features that more evidently pertain to sponsorship programmes seen as tools for resettlement, the argument of this chapter on how state sovereignty should step back to allow sponsors to operate will be developed referring mainly to this category of sponsorships. However, this proposal could also be applied to sponsorship seen as other forms of admission, as will be signposted throughout the chapter.

The chapter will initially look at naming and additionality in turn in section II, highlighting the reasons why these features should be promoted and facilitated within the European schemes, to allow an increase in numbers of people entering

[2] See UNHCR, 'UNHCR: Global refugee resettlement needs grow in 2024' 26 June 2023, available at: www.unhcr.org/news/press-releases/unhcr-global-refugee-resettlement-needs-grow-2024.

[3] See ISS of BC, 'Resources for Private Sponsorship of Refugees', available at: issbc.org/our-resources/resources-for-private-sponsorship-of-refugees/.

[4] MB Zanzuchi, N Dumann, F Tissot and A Skodo, 'Attracting, Retaining, and Diversifying Sponsors for Refugees in Community Sponsorship Programmes' September 2023 Migration Policy Institute, available at: www.migrationpolicy.org/sites/default/files/publications/mpie-caps-eu_sponsor-recruitment-2023_final.pdf, 6.

[5] A Betts, 'Towards a "soft law" framework for the protection of vulnerable migrants' (2008) Research Paper no 62 *New Issues in Refugee Research*, available at: www.unhcr.org/sites/default/files/legacy-pdf/48b7f9642.pdf, 2.

[6] ibid, 3.

a safe European host state and broaden the category of people that, despite not being classified as refugees, might benefit from protection due to their conditions of vulnerability.

The chapter will then argue that the state-centric approach that permeates current thinking over immigration is likely one of the reasons that prevents the utilisation of naming and additionality to their full potential. In order to allow naming and additionality to strengthen private sponsorship programmes and make a real difference for people in need of protection, this book will propose an alternative perspective on immigration, that is one that sees the state 'stepping back', allowing private stakeholders to step forward when they can show that they are capable of satisfying some of the state's key concerns over the protection of its territory and borders – welfare, integration and security. The chapter will conclude that European states should experiment more with naming and additionality in schemes that see the private sponsor taking on the responsibility for the welfare, integration and vetting costs of the beneficiaries.

The application of this proposal, however, is subject – as the chapter highlights in the concluding remarks – to a series of limitations.

To conclude, two points to note. In the previous two chapters it was noted that two other aspects that stirred criticism around private sponsorship schemes were the role played by the sponsor and the discriminatory nature of the schemes. These issues will be discussed when assessing barriers to the concrete application of the programmes and how they can be overcome.

Finally, the suggestions proposed by this chapter are mostly framed from a theoretical perspective, supported by some available data. This is a choice, since the purpose of this book was to fill a gap in the literature by describing how sponsorships have flourished in Europe and how they could be enhanced, based on the evidence and literature available so far. I am aware that what this chapter is suggesting should also be tested in reality. This could be done in the future through empirical studies based on the Italian St Egidio humanitarian corridors, as they most closely embody my proposal.

II. Sponsorship's Key Elements: Theoretical Analysis

A. Naming

This book has shown how naming is an element that characterises sponsorship schemes that work as tools for resettlement, and some examples have been given in Chapter three. Moreover, some schemes that support other forms of admission are designed in such way as to include a broad pool of beneficiaries, from which the sponsor is free to select whom to support.

As pointed out in Chapter one, naming is an intrinsic element of the private sponsorship programmes implemented by Canada following the Second World

War. Whilst at the beginning naming was informally applied, the procedures following the 1976 Immigration Act explicitly allowed sponsors to name the beneficiary or specify individuals belonging to particular affinity groups such as ethnic or religious groups.[7] The Canadian interest in naming fluctuated over the years, and while during the Southeast Asian crisis of the late nineteen seventies and early eighties there was more interest in the 'unnamed "sponsorship of a stranger"',[8] in the nineties interest in naming rose again.[9] The trend towards larger numbers of named sponsorship was analysed in several studies in the nineties, including the Canadian government's 1995 study report. The report recommended to continue allowing naming so as to maintain the collaboration with certain NGOs that demanded the right to name the beneficiaries of the schemes, and to take into account the fact that not all beneficiaries were family members but also, potentially, high-priority humanitarian cases.[10] This last point was confirmed in 2016 by the Government of Canada's full evaluation of the refugee resettlement programmes, where private sponsorships characterised by naming were considered to be aligned with Canada's resettlement programme, in terms of humanitarian support,[11] despite of their strong family reunification nature.[12]

As was seen in Chapter one, one of the reasons why sponsors were so eager to be granted the discretion to choose the beneficiaries of the programme is related to the fact that, unlike the government, sponsors were originally very concerned about welcoming the most vulnerable, rather than using integration and employability as the yardstick of their modus operandi. Although things might have changed over time, with the Canadian government getting more involved in international resettlement obligations and starting to campaign for vulnerability as a criterion too, it has been recognised, as mentioned above, that the family reunification aspect can affect the naming process but does not exclude the work that private sponsorship of refugees does towards humanitarian causes, and the two can often go hand in hand. Moreover, sponsors still consider the naming aspect important because selecting named refugees makes their impact on resettlement more significant. Indeed, naming is the best ally to a proper use of the feature of additionality, as named refugees do not normally come from the same pool as

[7] S Lerh and B Dick, '"Naming" refugees in the Canadian Private Sponsorship of Refugees Program: Diverse Intentions and Consequences' in S Labman and G Cameron (eds), *Strangers to Neighbours: Refugee Sponsorship in Context* (Montreal, McGill-Queens University Press, 2000) 42, 46.

[8] ibid.

[9] ibid, 47.

[10] ibid, 48. The authors refer to Citizenship and Immigration Canada, Corporate Review, Planning Review and Renewal, 'Study Report on the Review and Development of a Process for Matching Refugees and Sponsors' (Ottawa, CIC, February 1995). The report also suggested to introduce a matching system between sponsors and beneficiaries, to make unnamed sponsorships more attractive.

[11] ibid, 49.

[12] ibid. The authors note that the 2016 evaluation shows how 35% of people who entered Canada through GAR and 62% of people who entered Canada through PSR had already a family network.

those candidates benefitting from state-led resettlement schemes, hence there is 'a higher likelihood that privately sponsored refugees are not simply substituting for state resettlement'.[13]

Despite the evident support for naming by Canada, the Canadian government expressed concerns about the naming process for humanitarian reasons.[14] Lehr and Dick point out that in a system of private referrals, necessarily, the sponsor has to have a personal link with the potential beneficiary, either because the two have met before, perhaps in the country of the refugee, or because a family member in Canada proposed the candidate to the sponsor for sponsorship.[15] The authors point out that this amounts to an issue of fairness, because private sponsorships are effectively available only to those with connections in Canada.[16] Along the same lines, Lenard sees naming as problematic in private sponsorships due to fairness concerns. The author synthetises the problem with naming as follows: 'given the real unmet need with respect to resettlement spaces for refugees, the connection to a Canadian citizen or permanent resident gives refugees in need a significant advantage in the tragic competition to find a safe and permanent home'.[17] The author's reasoning builds upon the concept of fairness and the appropriate distribution mechanisms that should drive choices when dealing with highly scarce resources, such as resettlement places.[18] The author suggests that vulnerability should be the key criterion that should motivate the choice to sponsor because justice requires allocation of scarce places to the most in need. While the author accepts that having family links is a strong reason to prioritise admission in resettlement through private sponsorship schemes, and hence naming should be allowed in these cases, Lenard also suggests that private sponsors should be discouraged or even prevented from choosing potential beneficiaries for other reasons such as religion, culture, race, ethnic background, etc and that sponsors should draw from the UNHCR list of vulnerable refugees instead.[19] This is because in programmes where naming is allowed, the sponsor has a say on who to admit and their capacity to influence admissions interferes within the realm of justice.[20] The author concludes that naming should be allowed but restricted and, apart from family members, sponsors 'should be constrained to selecting among those who are most vulnerable'.[21]

[13] ibid, 51.

[14] ibid, 47–48. See, in particular, around the period of the post PSR review of 1990 and the government report of 1995.

[15] ibid, 52.

[16] ibid.

[17] PT Lenard, 'How should we think about private sponsorship of refugees, book on private sponsorship' in S Labman and G Cameron (eds), *Strangers to Neighbours: Refugee Sponsorship in Context* (Montreal, McGill-Queens University Press, 2000) 61, 64.

[18] ibid, 65.

[19] ibid, 66.

[20] ibid, 66–70.

[21] ibid, 70.

With all of the above considered, it is time to look at naming within the European context. As seen, some kind of freedom in choosing the beneficiaries is allowed in some of the schemes. Should this continue to be the case? Should one even be thinking about reinforcing or introducing the feature of naming, within the European schemes?

Naming is a feature that has not been experimented with to the full extent of the Canadian PSR in Europe. Freedom to select candidates was applied in the short-lived trials of sponsorship of refugees in Poland, the Czech Republic and Slovakia. A naming stream has just been opened in the Portuguese sponsorship pilot, although it has yet to be seen if many people will be able to take advantage of this possibility since the government, to date, has not finalised the operativity of the scheme. A diluted version of naming is also utilised in the humanitarian corridor schemes that were analysed in Chapter three. Here, it is a diluted version of naming in comparison to the Canadian use of naming because, as already seen, the memoranda of understanding governing the humanitarian corridor schemes contain a list of vulnerability criteria and sponsors have to select beneficiaries that fulfil such criteria.[22] Moreover, the selection is carried out by representatives of the community of St Egidio or of some other twin organisations in loco, and not by an individual or group of individuals. However, the informality that still characterises the humanitarian corridor experiences, with concrete possibilities for the organisation itself to select and choose who to welcome by interpreting and applying the criteria suggests that an element of naming is implicitly part of these schemes.

The latest data available show that, up to 14 January 2022, Italy welcomed 3,398 people from third countries,[23] France admitted 530 people from Lebanon, Belgium received 150 people from Lebanon and Turkey, and Andorra welcomed 16 people from Lebanon through humanitarian corridors. Most of these people have been chosen from the categories that go beyond the Geneva Convention definition of refugee.[24] These numbers may seem to be a drop in the ocean, but are considerable if one thinks that it is likely that many of these people would not have found a new home in Europe through state-led resettlement schemes or private sponsorships that do not allow naming.

As far as private sponsorship of refugees seen as tools for various forms of accession is concerned many European schemes – like the now expired family reunification schemes, the ongoing Homes for Ukraine scheme and the relocation humanitarian corridor by St Egidio and the Vatican State – have encompassed

[22] Sometimes the selection is even done in collaboration with the UNHCR, following their lists of vulnerable candidates.

[23] See St Egidio, 'Humanitarian corridors in figures' 14 January 2022, available at: www.santegidio.org//downloads/EN-Humanitarian-corridors-20220114.pdf. This number has been calculated by deducting from 3,632 those that entered through Greece and Cyprus, as those count towards relocation.

[24] Humanitarian Corridors, 'Corridoi umanitari: le procedure di implementazione per la loro estensione su scala europea'(2016), available at: www.humanitariancorridor.org/wp-content/uploads/2019/12/REPORT_ITA_WEB.pdf, 13.

a level of freedom in choosing the beneficiaries. Such freedom of choice may be within a broad group of family members, within the umbrella of the vulnerability criteria of the memorandum of understanding for the private schemes supporting relocation, or may be total freedom like in the Homes for Ukraine scheme. Numbers are remarkable, amounting to roughly 29,000 people that have benefitted from some privately sponsored family reunification schemes,[25] 234 from the relocation scheme run by the Vatican and St Egidio[26] and 186,800 visas issued for the Homes for Ukraine scheme.[27]

Recent studies on the European schemes have also pointed out how programmes that do not encompass the naming element, or some kind of more personalised matching mechanism, are more likely to dissuade sponsors from committing to the sponsorship cause.[28] The studies elaborate on the reasons behind this attitude, which seems due to potential sponsors' perception of having 'little ownership over the process, fears that they may feel less connected to refugees with whom they have little in common, and/or limited motivation to invest their time and resources in supporting someone they do not know'.[29] The Portuguese pilot sponsorship scheme seems to support these findings, as the numbers of interested sponsors swelled when the opportunity to name arose.[30] Numbers also seem to support this argument. For instance, two countries similar by population, Italy and the UK, within the same time window, the first running a scheme characterised by naming and the second not allowing it, welcomed 3,398 people versus 1,000 respectively.[31]

[25] 79 people benefitted from the SHAP programme in Ireland, see House of the Oireachtas, 'International Protection' debate 24 March 2022, available at: www.oireachtas.ie/en/debates/question/2022-03-24/341/, 4,000 people from the Swiss family reunification scheme targeting Syrians, see UNHCR, 'Finding solutions for Syrian refugees' 27 November 2014, available at: www.europarl.europa.eu/meetdocs/2014_2019/documents/libe/dv/8_1_syria_refugeees_unhcr_2014_11_27_/8_1_syria_refugeees_unhcr_2014_11_27_en.pdf, 1 fn 5, and 25,000 people from the *Länder* sponsorship schemes in Germany, see European Parliament, 'Community sponsorship schemes under the new pact on migration and asylum' (2021), available at: www.europarl.europa.eu/RegData/etudes/BRIE/2021/690675/EPRS_BRI(2021)690675_EN.pdf, 4.

[26] St Egidio, above n 23. The number comprises the people that have been admitted from Cyprus and Greece.

[27] Gov.UK, 'UK Family Scheme, UK Sponsorship Scheme (Homes for Ukraine) and Ukraine Extension Scheme visa data', as updated on 11 June 2024, available at: www.gov.uk/government/publications/ukraine-family-scheme-application-data/ukraine-family-scheme-and-ukraine-sponsorship-scheme-homes-for-ukraine-visa-data--2#:~:text=Sponsorship%20Scheme%3A%20220%2C700-,Total%20Ukraine%20Scheme%20visas%20issued%20to%20people%3A%20251%2C000,Ukraine%20Family%20Scheme%20visas%3A%2071%2C700. However, the number includes both those selected and those that entered through the matching mechanism.

[28] Zanzuchi, Dumann, Tissot and Skodo, above n 4, 17.

[29] ibid. The study supports this point with evidence coming, once again, from Canada, comparing the success of PSR, where naming is allowed, to the BVOR programme, which follows a matching system but struggles to meet its targets due to lack of sponsors' interest (p 17).

[30] Information gathered from the conversation with Barbara Oliveira and Clara Vaz, Portuguese Refugee Council, on 30 January 2024. However, as mentioned earlier, it remains to be seen whether the programme will be eventually approved by the government.

[31] Numbers available at Share Network, above n 1.

These considerations suggest that it seems reasonable to allow sponsors the option to name the beneficiaries of the private schemes and this is something that should be seriously contemplated by states that are thinking about piloting private sponsorship schemes for the first time, and by those that already have a private sponsorship programme in place and may want to enhance it. Moreover, given the success of programmes that allow sponsors to select and the fact that quite a few have now expired, the urgency of advocating for naming in private sponsorship of refugees is becoming more pressing.

However, if naming should be allowed and promoted, should it be limited? The criticism of the Canadian PSR scheme reported above suggests that naming, in its pure form of freely selecting beneficiaries, is unfair, if carried on outside family reunification instances. As seen, according to Lenard, while naming should not be precluded when relying on family links as selection criteria, it should be curtailed as far as other affinity criteria (eg race, religion etc) are concerned.

The concept of distributive justice, which concerns fairness in distributing benefits and costs within the community, can further shed light on Lenard's criticism. According to Finnis, distributive justice is one of the three elements of justice – together with general justice and commutative justice. One of the six characteristics, according to Finnis, of distributive justice, is what 'practical reasonableness requires of particular people'.[32] Indeed, each person, in the reality of their daily deliberations, cannot truly give 'equal weight or equal concern' to the interests of anyone anywhere in the world.[33] This is because each person lives in and comes from a community. As Finnis notes, they have family and personal relations, promises, debts of gratitude, and 'relations of interdependence with or assumption of authority in relation to ascertained persons or communities'.[34] However, he goes on to note that when it comes to

> the problem of assessing the extent of one's responsibilities in reason for the welfare of persons in other political communities … its resolution … is constantly threatened by the pull of unreasonable self-preference, group bias and lukewarmness about human good.[35]

The state and governing authorities have a decisive role[36] in fighting against these 'pulls' for the sake of distributive justice.

If we assume that affinity elements such as ethnic background, culture, resilience, etc belong to the 'pull of unreasonable self-preference' considerations, then the state should overcome them in favour of vulnerability, as Lenard suggests, when it comes to designating the pool of people whom private sponsors are allowed to choose from as beneficiaries of a private sponsorship of refugees scheme.

[32] J Finnis, *Natural Law and Natural Rights* (Oxford, Clarendon Law Series, 2011) 175.
[33] ibid, 177.
[34] ibid.
[35] ibid.
[36] ibid, 188. The author argues that the role of the state is decisive, although subsidiary, as the state only has to enforce duties that the community already has in the first place.

Most of the European schemes that encompassed or still encompass the possibility of selecting candidates seem to consider affinity criteria as unreasonable self-preferences. For example, the humanitarian corridor schemes allow freedom to the sponsoring organisation in selecting candidates, but that freedom is tempered by the vulnerability criteria of the memoranda of understanding.[37] One should not see the expired humanitarian/private family reunification schemes which allowed sponsors to choose from a broad category of family members, beyond vulnerability considerations, as a contradiction, since it should be remembered that freedom to select in family reunification cases is accepted as trumping instances of vulnerability.

Currently, the scheme that allows selecting candidates without specifying a precise list of vulnerability criteria is the Homes for Ukraine one, although, effectively, one could argue that all the beneficiaries of this scheme are in a vulnerable position, since they are escaping the war. However, there is also a scheme that could grow to potentially apply naming without necessarily or uniquely complying with vulnerability rules, and that is the Portuguese sponsorship pilot which, as things stand at the time of writing, does not have to follow a precise guideline in terms of vulnerability conditions that the named beneficiaries should fulfil. If the development of this sponsorship succeeded and went in this direction, this would imply that affinity choices could be seen as legitimate preferences, and not as unreasonable self-preferences. When considering this potential outcome, one should not disregard it as completely impossible as one should remember that reliance on affinity criteria is very common in immigration matters. As mentioned above, the reality of one's daily deliberations is affected by the ties with the communities one belongs to. The role of immigration networks, whether cultural, religious, etc has been the subject of many studies and has been shown to be an important determinant in people's choices about their immigration destinations.[38]

Could this scenario – naming detached from vulnerability, outside of family reunification instances – be accepted? To answer this question, it is important to remember that since private sponsorship schemes are programmes that have been created to bring people in danger to safety, their original aim should not be forgotten. For this reason, if some states in Europe were to include naming in a new sponsorship scheme, vulnerability should be paramount. However, as mentioned above, affinity is a criterion that is very commonly applied in

[37] The only exception seems to be the French humanitarian corridor scheme, where the criterion of resilience is coupled with that of vulnerability, effectively allowing sponsors to choose only among those people that are likely to be quickly integrated. On this point see M Ngombe, 'Les Couloirs Humanitaires: un régime d'exception pour gérer des réfugiés «désirables»' (2020) 1 *Revue internationale des études du développement* 65, 81.

[38] Among all see H Rose and J Saltzman Chafetz, *Religion across borders: transnational immigrant networks* (Walnut Creek CA, Altamira Press, 2002); I Light, P Bhachu and S Karageorgis, 'Migration networks and immigrant entrepreneurship' in I Light and P Bhachu (eds), *Immigration and Entrepreneurship: culture, capital and ethnic networks* (London, Routledge, 1993) 25; A Portes, *The Economic Sociology of Immigration: Essays on Networks, Ethnicity and Entrepreneurship* (New York, Russell Sage Foundation, 1995).

immigration matters. As hinted at earlier, the idea of affinity also links back to the concept of distributive justice, since, as mentioned above, 'each person does not count for one and only one'[39] but is the fruit of their personal links and relationships with the world.[40] Taking these aspects into account, I would suggest that once vulnerability has been established and taken into account to determine the initial pool of beneficiaries, then the liberty of the sponsors in choosing from those vulnerable whose situations they take more to heart, whether due to religious, cultural or ethnic factors, could be preserved. The reason why this approach should not be considered discriminatory is addressed in the concluding section of this chapter.

To conclude, when thinking about expanding and reinforcing private sponsorship schemes, or introducing new ones, states should seriously consider naming as one of their features, provided that vulnerability statuses are properly considered. Once that has been accomplished then sponsors should not be restrained from relying on affinity criteria. States could also choose to promote private sponsorship schemes linked to family reunification. In this case vulnerability would be trumped for the sake of the fundamental right to protect one's family unity. This approach promotes the fundamental right to protect one's family life, while not necessarily excluding the endorsement of humanitarian concerns.

B. Additionality

Additionality is an element that characterises some sponsorship programmes that work as tools for resettlement in Europe. However, it could be argued that some private sponsorships that are seen as tools for various forms of entry – in particular, the now expired German family reunification schemes and the Homes for Ukraine programme – could be considered additional, as they target vulnerable people while not counting towards any state quotas.

The core claim for additionality is that additional schemes allow more people to benefit from protection in a safe state. While the debate below will mostly focus on resettlement, the final considerations on how Europe could potentially address additionality should be taken also to include other sponsorships.

As discussed in Chapter one, additionality was first introduced by Canada in its PSR programme. Within the Canadian experience, the favouring of additionality was curtailed over time. Before they were crystallised into law, private

[39] Finnis, above n 32, 177.

[40] The fact that preferences are important to sponsors, and should be taken into account, is implicitly confirmed by Zanzuchi, Dumann, Tissot and Skodo, above n 4, 30. The authors argue that matching procedures should be reconsidered. For example, sponsors' language skills and cultural or religious background should be taken into account to allow sponsors to suggest potential matches themselves (from a pool of already chosen beneficiaries) or even allow the sponsors' preferences to be incorporated in the matching criteria.

sponsorship schemes were 'conceived as being limited only by the generosity and willingness of private Canadians'.[41] This changed with the introduction of the 1976 Immigration Act. It is now up to the immigration minister to decide the annual targets, after having consulted provincial governments, NGOs and the UNHCR,[42] both for government-led resettlement and privately sponsored refugees.[43] Lehr and Dick noted that it was precisely in the early years, before the 1976 immigration Act was introduced, that

> private sponsorship operated as true complements or additions; that is, they were not part of the government's annual resettlement plan, which meant that the only limitations on them related to the availability of the sponsors and visa officers' processing capacity.[44]

As far as Europe is concerned, additionality, subject to predetermined quotas, is allowed in some schemes. No quotas were envisaged in the expired family reunification schemes, although for some of those, for example in Ireland and Switzerland, a temporal window was imposed. Quotas are currently not imposed in the Homes for Ukraine scheme.

Bradley and Duin, when specifically assessing the risks and opportunities of exporting the Canadian model to other countries, highlight how the key issue is that the state is likely to undermine the additionality feature that characterises many sponsorship programmes, by eventually relying on private sponsorship just to fulfil its own resettlement quotas. This, in their view, would become a way to 'privatise' resettlement. In the long run, they continue, the increasing reliance on private sponsorship could effectively lead to a 'burn out' of time and resources publicly spent on resettlement.[45] Their reasoning is based on what has effectively occurred in Canada, where it is the government that now decides how many people can be resettled, both privately and by the state, and since 2017 the PSR programme has outnumbered the state-led resettlement scheme at a ratio of 2:1, effectively cementing the approach of a privatisation of resettlement.[46] As Catherine Dauvergne notes when commenting on the migration laws of Australia and Canada, 'private sponsorship both allows the government an easy response to domestic pressure to act more humanely and allows it to withdraw from direct responsibility for admission totals'.[47]

[41] S Labman, *Crossing Law's Border: Canada's Refugee Resettlement Programme* (Vancouver/ Toronto, UBC Press, 2020) 92.

[42] ibid, 56.

[43] UNCHR Resettlement Handbook, 'Country chapter: Canada', available at: www.unhcr.org/protection/resettlement/3c5e55594/unhcr-resettlement-handbook-country-chapter-canada.html, 6, section 4.3.

[44] S Lerh and B Dick, above n 7, 45.

[45] M Bradley and C Duin, 'A Port in the Storm: Resettlement and Private Sponsorship in the Broader Context of Refugee Regime' in S Labman and G Cameron, *Strangers to Neighbours: Refugee Sponsorship in Context* (Montreal, McGill-Queens University Press, 2000) 74, 79.

[46] Labman, above 41, 56.

[47] Labman, above 41, 107, quoting C Dauvergne, *Humanitarianism, Identity and Nation: Migration Laws of Australia and Canada* (Vancouver, UBC Press, 2005) 93.

In the light of this concrete burden-sharing issue, one might wonder if additionality should continue to be promoted in the European private sponsorship schemes. To answer this question it is worth noting that, for quite a few of the European states that have been analysed in this book, a state-led resettlement programme was already in place before having recourse to private sponsorship of refugees was even contemplated. This is not the case for Canada, where private sponsorships informally operated before state resettlement was introduced, and it was the government that, to some extent, took advantage of the work already done by private sponsors. Private sponsorships in Europe have often joined a plethora of already well-established state schemes. In many examples that have been raised (see, for instance, the UK and Ireland community sponsorship programmes and the new Portuguese pilot) states seem to want to slowly carve out private sponsors' responsibility, piloting and experimenting initially within state quotas and then moving towards capped additionality (this is what happened in the UK and seems to be the aim for the Irish and Portuguese schemes). This, of course, does not rule out the possibility that inappropriate shifts of responsibility from the state to private parties are ever going to occur. However, the slow and reverse approach applied by many European states is hopefully a sign that attention to additionality has been properly granted. In any case, numbers of refugees resettled via government programmes should always be monitored, to make sure that the state fulfils its duties and, to this aim, measures that act as checks and balances should be put in place.

Another reason why additionality should continue to be promoted relates to numbers. As mentioned in the introduction to this chapter, considering only the numbers of the biggest and most established schemes in Europe (St Egidio humanitarian corridors in Italy, France, and Belgium, UK Community Sponsorship and the NesT programme in Germany), roughly 5,681 people have been sponsored and allowed a second chance in Europe. While this is still a small drop in the ocean, behind this figure there are 5,681 extra human beings that have found a new home in a safe place. To these figures, one should also add the 179,000 visas issued through the Homes for Ukraine scheme as at January 2024.[48] Without additionality, the people that benefitted from these programmes could still be in a UNHCR camp, waiting for their turn, or in their countries destroyed by the war.

Finally, it is worth mentioning the important motivational role that additionality plays for the sponsor. As a matter of fact, while some additional sponsorship programmes have managed to use additionality as a very important selling point to the sponsors, programmes that only count towards state quotas have not been so successful in finding supporting sponsors.[49]

[48] Gov.UK, 'UK Family Scheme, UK Sponsorship Scheme (Homes for Ukraine) and Ukraine Extension Scheme visa data, available at: www.gov.uk/government/publications/ukraine-family-scheme-application-data/ukraine-family-scheme-and-ukraine-sponsorship-scheme-homes-for-ukraine-visa-data--2#:~:text=Sponsorship%20Scheme%3A%20220%2C700-,Total%20Ukraine%20Scheme%20visas%20issued%20to%20people%3A%20251%2C000,Ukraine%20Family%20Scheme%20visas%3A%2071%2C700.

[49] Zanzuchi, Dumann, Tissot and Skodo, above n 4, 17.

In the light of the above, I suggest that additionality should be promoted in the current schemes and in any new ones that will be adopted.

III. Framing a New Public–Private Relationship to Promote Naming and Additionality

Section II suggested that naming and additionality should be preserved as important characteristics of private sponsorship schemes in Europe. They should both be promoted in new pilot schemes and enhanced or introduced in the already available schemes.

Quite a few sponsorship programmes in Europe already embrace these features, either together or alone. For instance, the experiences of humanitarian corridors, in Italy, France and Belgium, are characterised by additionality and a diluted – in comparison to the Canadian PSR scheme – form of naming. The UK and Germany have adopted community sponsorship schemes that, while not embracing naming, are characterised by additionality. The Portuguese pilot is currently experimenting with naming. Moreover, all the private sponsorship family reunification schemes, most of which are now expired, where characterised by sponsors' freedom to select the beneficiaries – albeit within family members categories which, in any case, could be quite loose – and were not subject to state quotas. Likewise, the Homes for Ukraine scheme allows the selection of the beneficiaries and is not limited by state quotas.

Despite these various examples, there are still some cases in which neither naming nor additionality are applied. For example, the Irish Community Sponsorship scheme and the Basque country scheme do not feature naming or additionality. Moreover, as already mentioned, while Portugal is experimenting with naming within its pilot and contemplating additionality, it is not certain whether the government will finally approve the scheme in this format. Furthermore, some states that are considering implementing private sponsorship of refugees, such as Sweden, do not seem to see value in naming due to non-discrimination and equality concerns.[50] Likewise, Denmark sees as a key challenge the financial responsibility that would potentially be borne by the sponsor,[51] and which would only increase if a private sponsorship programme characterised by additionality were to be included. These examples suggest that many European states seem to act fairly prudently when it comes to the choice to

[50] NF Tan, 'A study for the potential of introducing a community sponsorship program for refugees in Sweden', scoping report prepared for UNHCR's Representation for the Nordic and Baltic countries (2020), available at: www.unhcr.org/neu/wp-content/uploads/sites/15/2020/12/UNHCR-Study-on-Community-Sponsorship-Program-in-Sweden.pdf, 18.

[51] NF Tan, 'The feasibility of Community-based Sponsorship of refugees in Denmark' (2019), available at: amnesty.dk/wp-content/uploads/media/6130/feasibility-study-community-based-sponsorships.pdf, 18–19.

introduce private sponsorship of refugees, let alone programmes that would fully embrace these features.

In some cases, as addressed earlier, the reluctance towards including naming and additionality, either individually or together, may be the fruit of concerns over discrimination and equality or the fear that the state would slowly withdraw from its share of resettlement responsibilities, overburdening private sponsors. However, the lack of enthusiasm may also be linked to the modern state-centric vision on immigration issues. This means, when translated to resettlement and admission of refugees, that only the state has the power to decide who can cross its borders and to whom resettlement spaces should be allocated. This idea is based on the common current understanding of state sovereignty, which implies that immigration decisions should rest solely upon the state. Indeed, since it is the state that has the power to control and protect its territory and citizens, it is the state that should decide who and how many can access its borders.[52]

As hinted at in Chapter one, however, when looking at the origins of asylum and how that led to the concept of resettlement and private sponsorship of refugees, one can see that it is only relatively recently that the state has managed to claim sovereignty over immigration.[53] Indeed, before the idea of the nation state was born, other powers legitimised the lawful movement of people, such as the church, corporations or private vessels.[54] All this considered, including the fact that, after Westphalia, the role of the state cannot and should not be erased from the bigger picture, the question then becomes whether it is possible for private sponsorship characterised by naming and additionality to fully flourish in Europe, in coexistence with state sovereignty over immigration. If not, could then the classic view of state sovereignty over immigration be tempered to allow private sponsorships characterised by naming and additionality to attain traction in Europe? While this might sound purely theoretical, the question has great practical implications. Indeed, in the light of the continuing European immigration emergency, the growth of privately sponsored schemes which also include naming and additionality could help more people, reduce the number of unnecessary deaths and respond to the global call of social justice. The second part of this chapter will attempt an answer to this question.

IV. The Historical Development of State Sovereignty Over Immigration

This section will lay the groundwork, by trying to shed light on the concept of state sovereignty and its meaning. The concept of a state, as we currently know it,

[52] See the example of Sweden, where one of the key reasons why private sponsorships have not been yet welcomed is the belief that states are solely responsible for the integration policies of immigrants (Tan, above n 50, 17).

[53] J Torpey, *The invention of passport: surveillance, citizenship and the state* (Cambridge, Cambridge University Press, 2010).

[54] ibid, ch 1.

is relatively new and the understanding of it has changed over time. Consequently, also ideas and views on state sovereignty have changed over time and different approaches have been offered over time, and there is little doubt this will continue to be the case.

Initial discourses about state sovereignty commenced in the sixteenth century with Bodin. In his view, the state is the only and absolute law-maker within its territorial borders and no other law-maker can be tolerated, apart from natural law.[55] Some years after, Hobbes built upon Bodin's work and expanded it even more by stating that state sovereignty cannot be limited even by religion or God.[56] Moreover, despite defining it neither organically nor elegantly, Macchiavelli alluded to the concept of state sovereignty as the type of absolute power that the prince could use over his own territories to deal with his domestic and foreign affairs.[57] Sovereignty has also been debated by other philosophers such as De Vitoria, Suarez, Gentili and Grotius, to name just a few. With different nuances, and within the framework of absolute states, they started to refer to the existence of a world community within which the state has to move and relate.[58]

As already mentioned at the beginning of this book, the peace of Westphalia marked the birth of the classical theory of unlimited state sovereignty. According to this theory, the state has the power to define its own laws and competencies within its boundaries and should not interfere in the internal matters of other states.[59] The key characteristics of Westphalian sovereignty continue today. Indeed, the Montevideo Convention on Rights and Duties of States of 1933, at Article 1, identifies as benchmark criteria for statehood a defined territory and population and the presence of a government, along with the capacity to enter into relations with other states.[60] Moreover, the UN Charter of 1945 enshrines the principle of non-intervention in the affairs of member nation-states,[61] with a view to avoiding inter-state illegitimate invasions and aggression.

The evolution, over the centuries, of different forms of states – from the absolute one, to the liberal state of the nineteenth century, to the totalitarian states of the beginning of the twentieth century, to today's examples of what has been described as the post-modern state[62] – has helped to develop a new understanding of the classic idea of state sovereignty. For instance, the development of the concept of state has led, in the twentieth century, to the addition of new features that characterise the nature of the states' arrangements, such as welfare

[55] MP Ferreira-Snyman, 'The evolution of state sovereignty: a historical overview' (2006) 12 *Fundamina: a Journal of Legal History* 1, 5 (For further literature on Bodin see fn 21 to the article).

[56] ibid, 6.

[57] N Macchiavelli, *The Prince (De Principatibus/ Il Principe)* (Milton Keynes, Penguin Classics, 2014 [1513]). Machiavelli's point was argued within the specific context of the unification of Italy.

[58] Ferreira-Snyman, above n 55, 6–9.

[59] ibid, 10–11.

[60] TJ Biersteker, 'State, Sovereignty and Territory' in W Carlsnaes, T Risse and BA Simmons (eds), *Handbook of International Relations* (London, Sage, 2013) 245, 253.

[61] ibid.

[62] For a brief overview of the different forms of state see ibid, 247.

and national security.[63] These new features of the modern state have become new expressions of state sovereignty.

However, the concept of state sovereignty has also been affected by international law which, for the first time, introduced the idea that, effectively, state sovereignty could be curtailed.[64] At the beginning of the twentieth century, the fulfilment of international obligations became a requirement for the state to be recognised as sovereign.[65] Initially, this implied the fulfilment of international commitments concerning property rights. However, by the end of the twentieth century, international commitments broadened to also include the rule of law, democracy, respect for human rights and the protection of minority rights.[66] With this new understanding of state sovereignty, the focus of sovereignty shifted towards responsibilities, or duties, that states ought to have towards individuals.

The Charter of the United Nations of 1945 not only crystallised the idea that state sovereignty can be limited by international law,[67] but also gave authoritative expression to the specific international law of the protection of human rights in its preamble, by stating the commitment 'to reaffirm faith in fundamental human rights, in the dignity and worth of the human person, in the equal rights of men and women and of nations large and small …'. In this way, the Charter confirms that state sovereignty is limited, in particular, by the need to respect the rights and dignity of people. This confirms that the limitation of state sovereignty by international law, and specifically by human rights law, does not only affect the relationship between states, but also the relationship between the state and individuals, including the citizens residing within its borders.[68] In short, state sovereignty can be seen as the expression of state power over its territory. This power, however, can be limited by international law commitments, and in particular by human rights law.

Moving to immigration matters, it is important to highlight that state sovereignty expresses itself in these matters as described above, by not allowing any sort of limitation to its powers, apart from when immigration engages human rights, such as family life. In other words, states are free to admit who they want, and they are also morally free to reject who they want. Walzer defends this position through communitarian theory. Indeed, as a communitarian, Walzer argues that the citizens of a state are members of a political community. The members of the political community, just as the members of a club or an association, are free to decide who can enter the community. This, in his view, is fundamental to preserve their culture, freedom and welfare. This necessary task is to be performed by the liberal state because if the latter relinquishes it, the task would then be taken up

[63] ibid, 249.

[64] For a broader account of how the limitation of state sovereignty by international law occurs see Ferreira-Snyman, above n 55, 12–23.

[65] This idea is the fruit of the nineteenth century and triggered the birth of international law. On this point and the difference between internal and external sovereignty see Ferreira-Snyman, above n 55, 4.

[66] Biersteker, above n 60, 253.

[67] Art 2.

[68] Ferreira-Snyman, above n 55, 25.

by local neighbourhoods, which would ultimately decide who can or cannot enter, turning into a bunch of 'petty fortresses'.[69]

As far as refugee law is concerned, the Geneva Convention and its Protocol reaffirm this position. The Protocol, in a partly convoluted way, refers to the international community and, in practice, puts the responsibility of protection on each of its individual state parties.[70] This point is clarified by the UNHCR Handbook, which states that 'The assessment as to who is a refugee, i.e. the determination of refugee status under the 1951 Convention and the 1967 Protocol, is incumbent upon the Contracting State in whose territory the refugee applies for recognition of refugee status'.[71] This means, as Goodwin-Gill puts it, 'whether a state takes steps to protect refugees within its jurisdiction and, if so, which steps, are matters very much in the realm of sovereign discretion, in the sense that states commonly enjoy choice of means when deciding how to implement their international obligations'.[72] Garvey confirms this point when he says that 'refugee law reaches a dead-end as human rights law because it collides with the principle of national sovereignty' as the latter is protected by the 'undisputed rule of international law, that every state has exclusive control over the individuals within its territory'.[73] As Krivenko reminds us, quoting Anker, the refugee system is distinct from the classic human rights one: 'The international community created two regimes to address human rights abuses: one, the human rights regime, to monitor and deter abuse, and the other, the refugee regime, to provide surrogate state protection to some of those who are able to cross borders'.[74]

Following from this approach, when it comes to resettlement of refugees, the state is free decide how many to resettle or whether to resettle anyone at all. Although many have argued that refugee law, including its aspects of protection and resettlement, should be more generously reconceived in light of human rights protection and international law,[75] and others argued for the application of open borders arrangements[76] to suggest a total dismissal of state power in immigration

[69] M Walzer, *Spheres of* Justice: A Defence of Pluralism and Equality (New York, Basic Books, 1984) 39. A good summary of his thoughts on the matter is given by S Wilcox, 'The Open Borders Debate on Immigration' (2009) 4/5 *Philosophy Compass* 813, 814.

[70] EY Krivenko, 'Hospitality and Sovereignty: What Can We Learn From the Canadian Private Sponsorship of Refugees Program?' (2012) 24 *International Journal of Refugee Law* 579, 582.

[71] ibid. The author refers to the UNHCR 'Handbook on Procedures and Criteria for Determining Refugee Status under the 1951 Convention and the 1967 Protocol relating to the Status of Refugees'.

[72] See GS Goodwin Gill and J McAdam, *The Refugee in International Law* (Oxford, Oxford University Press, 2021) 601.

[73] JI Garvey, 'Toward a Reformulation of International Refugee Law' (1985) 26 *Harvard International Law Journal* 483, 486.

[74] Krivenko, above n 70, 580, referring to D Anker, 'Refugee Law, Gender, and the Human Rights Paradigm' (2002) 15 *Harvard Human Rights Journal* 133, 135.

[75] See, for example, JC Hathaway, 'Reconceiving Refugee Law as Human Rights Protection' (1991) 4 *Journal of Refugee Studies* 113, 120, who suggested that the definition of refugees should include every form of coercive migration. Garvey, above n 73, 498, suggests that new rules should also envisage a system of compensation that would trigger financial responsibility of the state causing the exodus.

[76] The classic idea of state sovereignty over migration, was firstly challenged by Carens (See JH Carens, 'Aliens and Citizens: The Case for Open Borders' (1987) 49 *The Review of Politics* 251). This

matters, the reality is that the state still has full power and legitimisation to decide who and how many refugees to admit or resettle.

V. Developing an Idea of Competing Sovereignties to Promote Private Sponsorship Featuring Naming and Additionality

From the previous section we can conclude that any discussion on immigration and, more specifically, resettlement, has to engage with the idea of state sovereignty, which cannot be dismissed. If it does not seem possible to prescind state sovereignty when dealing with immigration, it has been argued that there could exist other sources of sovereignty that can legitimately coexist with the former. Derrida tries to elaborate on this matter, although his argument is not fully unpacked. He suggests in his essay 'On Cosmopolitanism and Forgiveness'[77] that in our societies an ethic of hospitality should be promoted.[78] According to him, hospitality can be achieved by cities, and in particular, cities of refuge. In his words

> Whether it be the foreigner in general, the immigrant, the exiled, the deported, the stateless or the displaced person … we would ask these new cities of refuge to reorient the politics of the state. We would ask them to transform and reform the modalities of membership by which the city belongs to the state, as in a developing Europe or in international juridical structure still dominated by the inviolable rule of state sovereignty – an intangible rule which is becoming increasingly precarious and problematic nonetheless.[79]

Derrida suggests tackling the problem of refugees through the work of cities. The way he sees this happening is to re-evaluate the respective roles of states, unions, federations or state confederations, on the one hand, and of cities, on the other.[80] In his view, cities, when dealing with issues of hospitality and refuge, should 'elevate' themselves 'above nation states'[81] or, at least, free themselves from states' omni-comprehensive power.[82]

view was supported by Kochenov (D Kochenov, *Citizenship* (Cambridge, The MIT Press, 2019)) and Singer (P Singer, 'Famine, Affluence, and Morality' (1972) 1 *Philosophy and Public Affairs* 229). The open borders view, however, has been challenged. For a more detailed account see Wilcox, above n 69, 816–18.

[77] J Derrida, *On Cosmopolitanism and Forgiveness* (London, Routledge, 2001). Krivenko, in the paper 'Hospitality and Sovereignty: What Can We Learn From the Canadian Private Sponsorship of Refugees Program' (above n 70), refers to Derrida and his theory.

[78] ibid,16.

[79] ibid, 4.

[80] ibid, 9.

[81] ibid.

[82] ibid.

Derrida's idea is original and evocative but has been labelled as utopian.[83] Indeed, while being very challenging from a theoretical perspective, his argument can also be contested from a practical point of view, as cities cannot stand against state sovereignty in the real world, certainly not within the framework of the modern national state. However, from a purely theoretical point of view, Derrida's explanation of how state and city powers can coexist is logical and convincing. Derrida is of the view that ignoring state sovereignty is not possible, as this would destabilise the bases of liberalism, such as freedom and self-determination.[84] Hence, in order to preserve, but overcome at the same time, the concept of state sovereignty, he suggests that the latter should be indivisible and yet shared.[85] Derrida elaborates on this point by focusing on the sovereignty of the other.[86] Translated to his work on universal hospitality and the creation of a network of cities of refuge, the author's point is that cities should be dissociated from the state, and be granted more autonomy and, crucially, sovereignty.[87] The way in which the author argues this point is by looking at the past, when cities of sanctuary would welcome those who committed crimes and save them from the state. In his view, cosmopolitanism and hospitality have their origins in the cities of refuge. The state did not introduce anything new, but simply took over and contaminated the original work of cities.[88] According to the author, it is now up to the cities to welcome the new arrivals before imposing conditions, and, at the same time, to try to do everything possible to assist them individually.[89]

The theoretical approach of Derrida's view on sovereignty, and in particular his focus on the concept of the other, has been reinterpreted and translated to the problem of refugees and resettlement by Krivenko. In that author's reconstruction, based on Derrida's approach, there is another source of sovereignty that could stand up against the power of the state, and that is the sovereignty of the individual. The author poses two very important questions, based on the reconstruction of Derrida's work: 'Who else could share this sovereignty with nation states? Can sovereignty be displaced elsewhere?'.[90] The author's answer to these questions is based on her interpretation of Derrida's work. She suggests that his argument on sovereignty of the other goes deeper when it comes to tackling the problem of human rights. Indeed, she explains that, according to Derrida, the

[83] SK Kelly, 'Derrida's cities of refuge: toward a non-utopian utopia' (2004) 7 *Contemporary Justice Review* 421. In this paper the author argues how Derrida's approach can be seen as a 'non-utopian guide' for 'utopian politics'.

[84] P Damai, 'Messianic-City: Ruins, Refuge and Hospitality in Derrida' (2005) 27 *Discourse* 68, 71.

[85] ibid, 71. This is in contrast with the most purist takes on sovereignty. For instance, Hobbes maintains that whoever claims sovereign power should have it entirely. Bodin, like Macchiavelli, argues that the sovereign power of the prince should be perpetual and indissoluble, and could be passed to someone else just with an unconditional gift.

[86] ibid.

[87] ibid, 72.

[88] ibid, 87.

[89] ibid, 92.

[90] Krivenko, above n 70, 589.

sovereignty of the other is not only displaced in favour of cities but also towards individuals, through the protection of human rights endorsed by the Universal Declaration.[91] In her words 'An individual who emerges through the development of human rights law brings with him or her this other sovereignty that can counter the nation state and its sovereignty'.[92] The author sees the sovereignty of the individual, empowered by human rights, as something different from the sovereignty of the city. Indeed, as far as cities are concerned, even through the reconstruction of Derrida, sovereignty is still linked to the idea of territoriality. Hence, in this scenario, the best one can think of in practical terms is a redistribution or decentralisation of sovereignty between the state and the city. However, in the case of individuals, the emancipation given to them by human rights makes them become the bearers of sovereignty, together with the state.[93]

Krivenko's approach is audacious and intriguing. In particular, the reaffirmation of the sovereignty of the self against state sovereignty is very challenging. In her reconstruction of Derrida's work, the self, empowered by human rights, can raise itself above the sovereignty of the state. However, even Krivenko's application of Derrida's theory is difficult to envisage in reality. In particular, it is difficult to see the state, as sovereign body, bowing down to the sovereignty of the self when it comes to refugees, because refugees, by definition, are not citizens of the sovereign state where they seek protection. Furthermore, refugee law is omitted from the realm of human rights law.

Thinking about private sponsorship of refugees, neither Derrida's view on cities of refuge, nor Krivenko's view, where the sovereignty of the individual, empowered by human rights, should stand up against the state, ends up being fully convincing. Krivenko directly cites the Canadian experience of private sponsorship of refugees as a feasible example of competing sovereignties. The choice of allowing sponsors to support other individuals is a choice made within the realm of state sovereignty, as it is effectively the legislator, through the work of parliament, that creates the space for private sponsorship schemes and allows them to function.[94] However, once this step is taken and the legislation is adopted, the sponsors are then allowed by legislation to operate freely and the sponsorship can take on more power, effectively gaining sovereignty against the state, as the latter will not be able to have the final say on everything as much as it could before the sponsorship was introduced.[95] The author supports this argument by reminding the readers of the numerous delays in processing applications and refusal rates in Canada, to show that the government is at pains in fully accepting what private sponsorship of refugees has become.[96]

[91] ibid.
[92] ibid, 590.
[93] ibid.
[94] ibid, 596–97.
[95] ibid, 597.
[96] ibid.

However, as a counter argument, it is fair to say that the Canadian state has not looked on passively at how private sponsorships developed but has intervened when it was unhappy with some of their features or effects. For instance, the Canadian sponsorship scheme was altered from its original version in 2012. Indeed, since 2012, the number of refugees that can be sponsored has been capped and those that end up being sponsored by Groups of five have necessarily had to fulfil the definition of refugee set out by the Geneva Convention. This shows that, while certainly private sponsorship of refugees has managed to shape the way in which the Canadian government looks at and deals with resettlement, in reality the state still preserves its power to limit and curtail the programmes as it wishes. For this reason, private sponsorship of refugees is not really the fruit of an alternative source of sovereignty that is capable of standing against the state, but simply a concession, more or less generous, that the state is willing to grant to private stakeholders.

To conclude, relying on the idea of competing sovereignties to support the introduction or enhancement of naming and additionality does not seem to be feasible. The Canadian experience teaches us that even when private sponsorship of refugees schemes are generously drafted, as far as naming and additionality are concerned, and fully functioning, the state can always decide to tighten the law to curtail the individual's sponsoring power and the number and categories of beneficiaries.

VI. An Alternative Way to Promote Naming and Additionality: Satisfying State Sovereignty

The battle between state sovereignty and city or individual authorities is a captivating idea. However, unfortunately, it seems to be of little practical application, particularly when it comes to deciding who and how many can enter a certain territory and, consequently, who and how many a private sponsor should be able to support. As seen, the reason is that these theories fail to fully acknowledge the reality that, as things stand now, the state is the body primarily responsible for deciding on immigration matters. As well as the power to make international treaties, and to determine national defence and taxation law, immigration can rightly be considered one of the last bastions of sovereignty. Things could certainly change in the future. States could legitimately end up embracing Derrida's views of the sovereignty of the other. However, this option seems to be a long way away from how the current situation could develop in the short or even medium term, particularly considering the current waves of populism and animosity against foreigners.

Krasner reminds us that the Westphalian sovereign model, characterised by territoriality, mutual recognition, autonomy and control, has never been an accurate definition of the state. The reason rests in the fact that, although its basic rules are shared and known by many, they are also often easily breached and they have always been so.[97] However, despite the frequent violations of state sovereignty – for example the fact that globalisation has made it difficult for states to regulate trans-border movement of assets – a state's authority over its territory is not contested: 'The issue here is not one of authority but rather of control. The right of states to manage their borders is not challenged, but globalization, it is asserted, has eroded their ability to actually do so'.[98]

Prescinding from state sovereignty, effectively building on open border theories or battles between states' authority and other forms of individual sovereignty does not seem to be a viable option, as the state still has full authority regarding its borders. The reasons behind the state's claims of authority and supremacy over its borders, to some extent, are intuitive and 'commonsensical'.[99] Among the various issues there seems to be a problem of social welfare, since if the country provides immigrants 'with the same benefits it offers its own citizens (education for children, healthcare, unemployment benefits, etc.), its social services and welfare services may be stretched to the limit'.[100] Moreover, there appears to be also a problem of integration (and political stability) because, if immigration numbers are large 'the local population may find itself outnumbered by people who speak another language, belong to another culture, and perhaps seek to change the political system'.[101] Finally, states also rely on state sovereignty to control their borders in order to protect themselves against people whom they regard as 'threats to their security'.[102] In other words, it looks legitimate for the state to claim full sovereign powers over border management because, in this way, the state can try to deal (i) with welfare issues for its own citizens, avoiding further expenses for the welcoming of foreigners; (ii) with integration problems, by making sure that limited numbers of immigrants cross the borders and that those that will get access to its territory will become fully part of the society; and (iii) with security matters, by fully scrutinising applicants and allowing entry and residence only to those who are not considered threats.

These reasons, based upon which states seem to claim authority and full sovereignty on decisions over their borders, do not appear negotiable in our modern societies. Indeed welfare, integration and security, and how immigration could negatively impact on them, are important points debated in every political campaign and displayed on every political manifesto. These are issues that can make the difference at elections and, consequently, are very much at stake in political arenas.

[97] SD Krasner, 'Rethinking the sovereign state model' (2001) 27 *Review of International Studies* 17, 17.

[98] ibid, 20.

[99] M Weyner, 'Ethics, National Sovereignty and the Control of Immigration' (1996) 30 *The International Migration Review (Special Issue: Ethics, Migration, and Global Stewardship)* 171, 172.

[100] ibid, 173.

[101] ibid.

[102] ibid, 172.

Going back now to the questions that triggered this discussion on sovereignty – whether it is possible for private sponsorships characterised by naming and additionality to fully flourish and be readily embraced, while coexisting with state sovereignty over immigration, and (ii) if not, whether the classic view of state sovereignty over immigration could be tempered to allow private sponsorships characterised by naming and additionality to get a proper hold in Europe – in light of the above considerations, we are now probably in a position to be able to offer an answer.

To answer to these questions, one could think about approaching the idea of sovereignty over immigration not as a battle between the state and other sources of sovereignty, but from the viewpoint of a collaborative relationship between the state and private sponsors. In concrete terms, the aim of the private sponsorship of refugees schemes is to improve the lives of the beneficiaries of the scheme, but that should, contextually, take into account the need of the state to protect and guarantee the welfare, proper integration and security of its own citizens.

How could this be achieved and applied in practice? It is not undisputable that decisions made by the central state are the best ones. Elinor Ostrom shows this well in relation to market efficiency and the role of the state.[103] She points out that the mid-twentieth-century academic approach was characterised by the view that a central governmental unit was the best solution to deal with the provision of non-private goods, which would 'reduce the "chaotic" structure of metropolitan governance, increase efficiency, limit conflict among governmental units, and best serve a homogeneous view of the public'.[104] However, this approach eventually changed with the development and application of empirical studies. Works on how to organise the provision of water or manage public safety showed that resources can be efficiently organised on multiple scales, defeating the view that a centralised approach would be better,[105] and that 'metropolitan areas with large numbers of autonomous direct service producers achieved higher levels of technical efficiency'.[106] When it comes to immigration issues, nevertheless, the matter becomes more problematic. This is explained by Blank who, while engaging with the principle of subsidiarity and immigration and environmental policies, highlights that

> to be able to scientifically balance the advantages of smallness with the requirements of economic integration, there needs to be a scientific answer determining which externalities need to be internalized (and which should be ignored), the costs of each activity, and other political questions. In other words, in the most important cases, subsidiarity does not provide the answer to the basic political dilemma: who should decide what?.[107]

[103] E Ostrom, 'Beyond Markets and States: Polycentric Governance and Complex Economic Systems' (2010) 100 *American Economic Review* 641.
[104] ibid, 642.
[105] ibid, 643.
[106] ibid, 644.
[107] Y Blank, 'Federalism, Subsidiarity, and the Role of Local Governments in an Age of Global Multilevel Governance' (2010) 37 *Fordham Urban Law Journal* 510, 537.

Translating these insights to private sponsorship of refugees means that the authority to decide who can enter and how many can enter the territory of a country cannot switch from the state to the sponsor – by allowing sponsorships characterised by naming and additionality – based on efficiency considerations, because efficiency would be extremely difficult to assess and calculate. All this considered, perhaps the assessment, rather than being based on efficiency considerations, could alternatively rely on a balance between fairness and states' concerns. It has already been seen how sponsorships characterised by naming and additionality should be promoted, as they open the door to more beneficiaries and, crucially, to more vulnerable people, and this should count towards the claim to global fairness. However, fairness should be balanced against a state's concerns relating to sovereignty. In practical terms, what this suggestion implies is that a state's concerns in preserving its sovereignty in relation to its borders – which are related to protecting welfare, promoting successful integration and security issues – have to be taken into account by the sponsors. Hence, the state should allow sponsors to make final decisions on who (naming) should benefit from sponsorship and that these people are additional, eg not subject to state quotas, when the latter is able to guarantee that the former's concerns have been taken into account and adequately addressed. In other words, the state should allow more freedom of choice to the sponsor when the sponsor's efforts and actions are aimed at addressing and satisfying the state's concerns on welfare, integration and security. Effectively, this means that the state is still the holder of sovereignty over its borders but 'gives in' to the sponsor's decisional freedom when it is satisfied that doing so does not cause any harm.

The decision to grant the sponsor such power should not be left to the whim of the state. Indeed, the state, if fully satisfied with the way the sponsor is planning to tackle its concerns, should allow the latter's determination because, effectively, there would be no reason to refuse it. This suggestion envisages a deep form of collaboration and trust between the state and sponsors, as, effectively, the former is willing to grant decisional power to private individuals as to who should be welcomed in addition to those already welcomed under other programmes. This approach to private sponsorship of refugees also has the potential to turn private schemes from best practice to effective policy, as the state should not use the full force of its power as long as the sponsor has continued to act wisely and effectively. Moreover, it is important to point out that this proposal does not seek to suggest that the state needs to stop acting altruistically if it wants to. For example, remaining within the realm of private sponsorship of refugees, the state could and should still be involved and promote schemes that require its support – financial and non-financial – alongside the support offered by sponsors, if it wants to. At the same time though, the state should not place limits on the possibility of upgrading these programmes or developing others in parallel where its support is not needed because it is the sponsor that can and will satisfy its sovereignty concerns. This consideration will be better elaborated in practice in section VIII of this chapter.

Having reached this point, this proposal now requires a deeper explanation in terms of how it could be implemented in practice. The next section will focus on welfare, integration and security and will look at when, and at to what extent, the decisional power should be delegated to the sponsor.

VII. Welfare, Integration and Security: When Should the Sponsor Be Allowed To Decide?

In the previous section we concluded that the state claims sovereignty over borders for three main reasons: protection of the welfare state, integration, and political stability and state security. It has been suggested that the sponsor involved in a private refugee programme could satisfy the state in relation to these objectives in order to gain, in exchange from the state, decisional freedom as to whom can be sponsored, not subject to state quotas. This has been described as a deeper level of collaboration between private individuals and the state, where the latter concedes its power to the former, but only if satisfied that its concerns over the three listed domains have been properly addressed.

This section will focus on the three key areas of concern over state sovereignty in relation of immigration management, in order to assess if and to what extent the sponsor could take on decisional power, for the sake of promoting sponsorships characterised by naming and additionality, and how state concerns would be acknowledged and tackled by the latter.

A. Welfare

The concept of the welfare state was used to describe Britain under the Labour government after the Second World War. The concept was initially used loosely to refer to equality, meritocracy, social rights, and social services.[108] It is now understood to be a form of governance that sees the state play a proactive role in the protection and enhancement of the well-being of its citizens.

The idea of the welfare state has slowly emerged in Europe. It 'has rarely arisen as a result of grandiose plans or major battles, but mainly as a result of complex processes and the gradual development of social and political engineering in Europe'.[109] European societies have indeed managed to create different forms of welfare state, which vary considerably in terms of spending and choice on how to

[108] A Briggs, 'The Welfare State in Historical Perspective' (1961) 2 *European Journal of Sociology/Archives Européennes de Sociologie* 221, 221–23.

[109] A Hajighasemi, *European Welfare States and Globalization: Strategies in an Era of Economic Restructuring* (Cheltenham, Edward Elgar Publishing, 2019) 68.

protect its citizens against risks.[110] European welfare models can be broadly classified into five categories.[111]

The first category is known as the Anglo-Saxon model or, more commonly, the liberal welfare state. This model is characterised by putting the responsibility on the individual for earning their livelihood. For this reason, benefits are granted only to those that do not earn or do not earn enough, for whatever reason. Benefits are normally considered residual and complementary, rather than comprehensive. This model also offers a basic level of security for pensioners. The model is characterised by weak family policies. In a nutshell, this version of welfare implies that the state has responsibility only for basic welfare, while the individual has to pay the cost of insurance, etc themselves.[112] This welfare model is mostly typical of the UK and Ireland.

The second category of welfare state is the Continental model, also known as the corporativist model, mostly applied in central continental Europe (Germany, France, Austria, Belgium, Luxembourg and Netherlands being key examples). It is possible to see the clear influence of the Church in shaping its features, as it is the family, and not the single individual, which is at the centre of the welfare discourse: indeed 'the family is given responsibility for its members' livelihoods and it is through the family that different social benefits are channelled'.[113] Moreover, unlike the liberal model, the level of benefits to which one is entitled varies in accordance with the recipient's profession and class, and the level of insurance granted is based on payments by the employee. Indeed, the aim of the system is not to reduce social gaps and differences, but to stabilise them.[114]

The third model of welfare state is the Nordic model, also known as the social democratic welfare state, mostly used in Sweden, Denmark, Finland and Norway. This model, unlike the continental one, is characterised by universalism, which means that the system does not target certain categories of citizen, but all citizens equally.[115] As a consequence, everyone can claim the same rights in relation to almost every social service offered by the state.[116] Also, unlike the Continental model and more similarly to the Anglo-Saxon one, the benefits are given to each individual and are not channelled through their household.[117]

The fourth model is known as the Mediterranean model or southern European welfare system, adopted mainly in Spain, Italy, Portugal and Greece. It was included for a long time within the continental model group but it has now evolved

[110] ibid. These differences could have been triggered by political culture, social and class conditions and the balance of power.
[111] ibid, 73. The author specifies that this classification is based on the work of Esping-Andersen, Leibfried, Ferrera, Deacon, Aidukaite and Abrahamsson.
[112] This brief account of the Anglo- Saxon model is based on the description given by Hajighasemi, ibid, 73.
[113] ibid, 74.
[114] This brief account of the Continental model is based on the description given by Hajighasemi, ibid.
[115] ibid, 75.
[116] ibid.
[117] This brief account of the Nordic model is based on the description given by Hajighasemi, ibid.

distinctively to deserve its own cluster.[118] This system is characterised by the idea that the social security system finds its safety net in families, relatives and other social networks, like the Church or other associations.[119] Hence, the state has a weaker position, and fewer responsibilities in terms of providing benefits, than the family.[120] Like the continental model, the level of insurance provided is based on payments by the employee.

Finally, the last welfare model is known as the Post-socialist model, which developed in some countries of Eastern Europe since the fall of the Berlin Wall and is characterised by a socialist welfare approach which resembles universalism, as it covers all the citizens equally, regardless of their position within the market.[121]

The welfare system, in each of these categories, generally thrived after the Second World War. However, it has encountered more and more problems and difficulties in sustaining itself as time has gone by. Many European countries have been facing problems in maintaining a healthy degree of welfare provision due to weakened public finances. It has been argued that this has been caused by ageing populations.[122] This issue has often been tackled by increasing the rewards of labour, by reducing unemployment benefits and allowing more importation of labour. This, however, helped the rise of political parties that argue adamantly against these policies,[123] particularly in relation to more generous immigration policies.

Since the early nineteen nineties, a substantive body of research, particularly in economics, has been dedicated to the relationship between the welfare state and immigration. Friedman is famous for having stated that immigration is incompatible with the welfare state.[124] Further studies developed the welfare-magnet theory. According to this theory, immigrants seem to cluster in states (this was a study in the US) with higher welfare benefits.[125] Research has also shown that immigration has both positive and negative economic impacts in the host country. In relation to positive economic impacts, immigration can trigger the so-called 'immigration surplus', which means that immigration can make the society richer. Immigration can also rebalance the age distribution of the host society, so that the labour market can function more smoothly, and help in creating jobs and income for society as a whole, also increasing the demand for goods and services.[126] However,

[118] ibid, 76.

[119] ibid.

[120] This brief account of the Mediterranean model is based on the description given by Hajighasemi, ibid.

[121] This brief account of the Post-socialist model is based on the description given by Hajighasemi, ibid.

[122] See J Vartiainen, 'The future of the European welfare states: the intriguing role of demography?'(2017) 16 *European View* 131.

[123] ibid.

[124] P Nannestad, 'Immigration and welfare states: a survey of 15 years of research' (2007) 23 *European Journal of Political Economy* 512, 514.

[125] ibid, 515–16. The author quotes JG Borjas' works. The author also notes that the Borjas' theory is not entirely validated (516–17).

[126] ibid, 523–25.

as far as concerns the negative implications connected to immigration, it has been argued that an excessive number of immigrants can reduce the employment rates of the existing population, while also putting pressure on government finances and social security programmes.[127] Based on these considerations, some have argued that immigration is not advantageous for Western welfare states.[128]

Starting from the less optimal case scenario, that immigration has a negative impact on the welfare of people within a given state, one might argue that no one could blame the state for wanting to keep full check on its borders, in relation to whom and how many to welcome, because of its determination not to harm its own (current) citizens' position. However, in relation to the private sponsorship of refugees, it was argued that sponsors could have a say in selecting the beneficiaries (naming) in addition to state quotas (additionality), as long as the state is satisfied that its concerns over its borders' authority have been taken into account in a workable solution. This is because it was argued that one should look at balancing out the global call to fairness with the state's priorities.

Translating this suggestion to the issue of welfare, it can be argued that the state could and should allow far-reaching private sponsorship schemes characterised by naming and additionality, when the sponsors are willing and able to take upon themselves the full welfare responsibility of the beneficiaries. In simple terms, if the sponsors could guarantee their ability to pay and provide for every benefit that would otherwise be bestowed upon the newcomers by the state, the latter should not have justifiable objection, apart from integration or security considerations, to raise against the will of sponsors.

However, this suggestion is subject to a series of limitations, due to the intrinsic nature of private sponsorship, the type of welfare model embraced, and the fact that the state also has concerns and responsibilities around integration and security. The next sub-sections will analyse first integration and then security. Finally, the last section will look at the concrete application of this suggestion and its limitations.

B. Integration

Integration is the other rationale upon which the state claims full authority over its borders. Newcomers arriving in a state need to acquire their 'place in the new society'.[129] However, migrating to a new society, acquiring a place therein, means costs. The costs of immigration can be direct, ranging from business transaction costs, such as translation of documents, knowledge of local business, etc, to

[127] ibid, 526–28.

[128] ibid, 528–29.

[129] R Penninx, 'Integration of Migrants: Economic, Social, Cultural and Political Dimensions' in M Macura, AL MacDonald and W Haug (eds), *The New Demographic Regime: Population Challenges and Policy Responses* (Geneva, United Nations, 2005) 141.

conflicts in society triggering political instability, or indirect, normally associated with higher unemployment rates among immigrants and lower educational outcomes for immigrants' children.[130] Immigration costs have been of concern for governments. Given that the reasonable way forward would seem to be positive steps toward integrating immigrants, the entire process means costs for the state. Given this, it is quite understandable, then, why the state claims full sovereignty over its borders as far as integration is concerned. Indeed, it is often the case that when the state refuses to develop more generous immigration or refugee policies, this is because it fears that admitting too many 'others' will jeopardise peaceful convivence among its citizens, and it would be too costly to ensure that this will not happen.

It has been argued that integration is relevant only for those who intend to stay for longer periods. In these cases, integration is characterised by four dimensions: labour and market; education; language and culture; and legal status, including citizenship.[131] Being able to find a job and being fully part of the economic life of a country is a fundamental aspect of the integration process. In a study on migrants' integration within the European Union, it has been found that asylum seekers can take between 7 and 10 years to gain an employment rate of 50 per cent,[132] in contrast to those admitted as skilled or unskilled workers, who immediately reach higher employment rates within a shorter period of time.[133] Over time, the differences converge, although the employment rate becomes equal only for those with 20 or more years of stay, which is the point in time when the reason why the original entry permit was issued usually does not matter anymore.[134] The key reasons have been identified as the considerable time needed for immigrants to adapt, to learn the language and to get their skills recognised.[135] Naturally, the more the labour market (including the world of professions) is regulated, the more difficult it is for refugees to become integrated.[136]

As far as education is concerned, on one hand, it has been found that the educational attainment of third-country national children, including children of refugees, is on average lower compared to the existing citizens. This exacerbates the disadvantages in terms of entering the labour market, which can be intergenerational.[137] Furthermore, on top of the costs linked to the difficulty of integrating

[130] AM Danzer, 'Economic Benefits of Facilitating the Integration of Immigrants' (2011) 9(4) CESifo DICE Report, pp 14–19. ISSN 1613-6373, München, ifo Institut–Leibniz-Institut für Wirtschaftsforschung an der Universität München, available at: www.econstor.eu/bitstream/10419/167054/1/ifo-dice-report-v09-y2011-i4-p14-19.pdf, 14.

[131] R Münz, 'The Integration of Migrants and Refugees – A European Synopsis' in R Bauböck and M Tripkovic, *The integration of migrants and refugees: An EUI Forum on Migration, Citizenship and Demography* (Florence, EUI, 2017), available at: cadmus.eui.eu/handle/1814/45187 7, 9.

[132] ibid, 10.

[133] ibid.

[134] ibid.

[135] ibid.

[136] ibid.

[137] ibid, 13.

children of refugees into the labour market, one has to consider also the costs related to actively supporting children in education. In a paper on the public costs spent on refugees by Sweden in 2007, the researchers considered also the allocation of public funds in schooling and childcare for refugee children, and concluded that the cost estimates might suffer from underestimation, as refugee children often suffer previous traumatic experiences and are likely to be in need of extra support.[138] Speaking, not only having in mind the children of refugees but also the children of immigrants more generally, Heckmann has suggested increasing financial support for schools with large proportions of migrant students, implicitly confirming the extra costs that have to be faced for immigrant children who are in education.[139]

In relation to language and culture, it is important to note that the two factors are connected in research. Indeed, as cultural integration is difficult to measure, researchers often rely on language as a proxy.[140] Proper command of the language of the host country is difficult to attain for refugees in the short term. In 2014 around 45 per cent of refugees had advanced knowledge of the language of their host country, and only one in two (49 per cent) had acquired advanced knowledge of the language after 10 years of residence in the host country.[141] This, naturally, has an effect on literacy and, consequently, on the level of cultural integration that is achieved. Since the latter is strictly connected to the former, it looks like the process is not particularly fast. Of course, this reality implies costs, in terms of lack of integration, as the individual will likely not be able to make a substantial contribution to the life of the host community, and is connected to the funds that the government might expend to try to bridge the gap.

Finally, a note on legal status and citizenship. There is a substantial literature that argues that obtaining the citizenship status of the host country helps integration because it reinforces the sense of belonging between the individual and the new society.[142] Moreover, it looks like citizenship status can also help the holder in the job market.[143] In order to become a naturalised citizen, the individual has to go through an application process and pay fees, which are

[138] J Ruist, 'The Fiscal Cost of Refugee Immigration: the Example of Sweden' (2015) 41 *Population and Development Review* 567, 576.

[139] F Heckmann, 'Education and the integration of migrants: challenges for European education systems arising from immigration and strategies for the successful integration of migrant children in European schools and societies' (2008) (NESSE Analytical Report, 1) Bamberg, Europäisches forum für migrationsstudien (efms) Institut an der Universität Bamberg, available at: www.ssoar.info/ssoar/handle/document/19250, 61. In recommendation 8 the author states that 'Schools with large proportions of migrant students should be allotted additional financial resources. These finances should not be perceived as costs, but as an investment'.

[140] Münz, above n 131, 15.

[141] ibid.

[142] Among all see R Cohen, 'Citizenship: from three to seven principles of belonging' (2022) 28 *Social Identities* 139.

[143] Münz, above n 131, 17.

normally considerable. This is technically not a cost, but a neutral outcome for state finances if full cost recovery is in place. Moreover, unlike other groups of immigrants, when it comes to refugees it is important to highlight that they are more likely to naturalise and take up the nationality of the host country.[144] This fact should make this element of integration perceived not as a cost but as a gain by the state. However, in most European countries, the time that is required for an immigrant, including refugees, to naturalise varies between five and 10 years. In this way, the state ends up creating a long time window in which individuals, refugees included, cannot yet take advantage of the benefits triggered by being a citizen – for example, relying on the 'citizenship premium' to boost the likelihood of getting a job – and, effectively, might still continue to linger in situations in which state financial support is needed.

The above considerations on the different key aspects of integration have shown that they all trigger a certain increase in state costs. Although integration is associated with overall economic benefits at country level in the long run, the state may try to avoid the risk of facing immediate extra costs by exercising sovereignty over its borders and closing them to foreigners, as much as possible, in the first place.

Returning to the theme of the private sponsorship of refugees, can the state step back from the exercise of state sovereignty over its borders when it comes to integration concerns, by allowing sponsorships characterised by naming and additionality, when integration seems to trigger such high costs? In the previous section dedicated to welfare I suggested that states should indeed step back from their sovereignty and give space to private sponsorship of refugees characterised by naming and additionality when the sponsor is capable and willing to take on the full financial responsibility for the programme's beneficiaries, to avoid those beneficiaries becoming a burden on the welfare system. The same conclusion would apply in relation to integration. As a matter of fact, if the sponsor is capable and willing, based on the classification provided above, to cover the costs connected with the period of unemployment before the beneficiary of the scheme manages to enter the job market, the costs of education, also when children are involved, and the costs related to cultural integration, there is no reason why the state should not step back.

To conclude and in addition to what has already said about welfare, states should be willing to step back from asserting their sovereignty to allow private sponsorship of refugees with the option of naming and additionality, when the sponsor is capable and willing to take on full financial responsibility as far as integration is concerned. As before when welfare was discussed, this proposal has limitations and practical implications, which will soon be looked at, after the discussion on security.

[144] ibid, 17.

C. Security

As discussed above, border control is one of the key elements of state sovereignty. The securitisation of borders is one of the key expressions of a state's authority, and its aims to preserve peace within its borders, by not allowing the entry of foreigners that could cause a threat to security. For a while now, scholars have been discussing the idea of privatisation of borders. By this phraseology we mean a system in which private actors, and not government officials, collaborate with the state towards the activity of border control and application of immigration rules. Vasanthakumar stresses the fact that this is quite a common phenomenon and points out, by way of example, that

> commercial airlines turn away passengers whose travel documents are suspect; a host of private individuals, including doctors, landlords and bank managers, are charged with verifying and monitoring immigration status; and private security companies detain and remove unauthorised migrants, and provide housing and food for those seeking asylum.[145]

Quite recently, the world has been witnessing the increase of automation of immigration decisions through the reliance on artificial intelligence decision-making, provided by giant, private sector businesses. For example, individual automated decision-making in immigration and refugee decisions has been used in Canada since 2014. Moreover, in the United States under the Trump administration, an extreme vetting initiative was piloted, using an algorithm that would make decisions on the basis of whether or not an applicant would be able to positively contribute to the life of the new society.[146]

Some of these expressions of private involvement in the security procedures of the state are characterised by the fact that they are related to the idea of enforcement. This means that, while it is still the state that makes the decision on who can enter or leave, the private actors have been delegated the task to implement it. Also, having recourse to the use of artificial intelligence can be considered a form of privatisation of border control because, while it is still the government that decides to adopt these technologies, it is a private company that develops them and ultimately holds the responsibility for delivering decisions that are in line with the state legislation.

As far as private sponsorship of refugees is concerned, would the state be likely to step back from its sovereignty over border security in favour of the sponsor? When talking about welfare and integration, we envisaged situations where the state could, potentially, relinquish its sovereignty claims, provided that the sponsor is willing to take on the costs. This is because the shift of responsibility would,

[145] A Vasanthakumar, 'Privatising Border Control' (2018) 38 *Oxford Journal of Legal Studies* 411, 411.

[146] On artificial intelligence and immigration see P Molnar, 'AI and Migration Management' in MD Dubber, F Pasquale and S Das (eds), *The Oxford Handbook of Ethics of AI* (Oxford, Oxford Academic, 2020).

ideally, satisfy the state's concerns over welfare and integration, therefore allowing the sponsor to choose who to sponsor in addition to state quotas.

When it comes to security and vetting however, further considerations need to be made. Practice shows that when privatisation is applied to immigration in relation to security and vetting (see examples above), the ultimate liability is still borne by the state. Indeed, it is the latter that that employs or engages the private stakeholders for enforcing its rules.

Dorfman and Harel[147] help us to understand the roots of this approach when they argue that certain goods are inherently public and can only be delivered by the state, since it is only the state that can truly act in the public interest. Translated into immigration matters, the vetting process can only be left in the hands of the state, because it is only the state that has the broader public interest at heart.

However, leaving the vetting within the state's realm does not mean that there are no incentives to naming and additionality when it comes to promoting private sponsorship of refugees. Vasanthakumar, going beyond Dorfam and Harel's position, argues that the state is not always capable of acting as the public agent, particularly in relation to the rights of outsiders, and that, in any case, private agents, relying on their discretion, can help in the protection of the public interest.[148] This is because the state could be blind in the face of the needs of certain groups, while private frontline agents may not be.[149] While it is undeniable that, because of the nature of the public good at stake, the state is best placed to proceed with security checks, sponsors can still inform the screening process by sharing information about the potential beneficiaries of the schemes – gathered perhaps through the process of initial interviews – with the state authorities. In simple terms, this means that the sponsor should still be allowed to engage with naming, while checks and final decisions on those that have been selected by private sponsors have to be left in the hands of the state. It should also be noted that if private sponsors were to bear the full welfare and integration costs of recipients, as proposed here, this would incentivise them to choose potential recipients carefully, and go some way toward aligning the interests of the sponsors with the broader interests of the state.

Furthermore, even additionality should not be an objection because while it is the state that processes the cases and ultimately permits or refuses entry to the named beneficiaries, the costs of this process (screening, interviews, issuing visas etc) will be borne by the sponsor. If this is the case, it could even be argued that the only limit to additionality should be the number of applications that the state case workers are able to process in a year.

[147] See A Dorfman and A Harel, 'The Case against Privatisation' (2013) 41 *Philosophy & Public Affairs* 67, 68. These theories in relation to privatising immigration are well explained in Vasanthakumar, above n 145.

[148] Vasanthakumar, above n 145, 423.

[149] ibid, 422.

To conclude, this section has shown how the state remains the ultimate bastion of sovereignty over border control. However, sponsors can bring insights to the process by proposing a selection of beneficiaries (naming) and by bearing the state's costs of processing the cases, which should allow for additional beneficiaries, as many as the sponsors can afford.

VIII. Concluding Remarks: Practical Implications and Limitations of Sponsorship Featuring Naming and Additionality

This chapter has argued that private sponsorship of refugees in Europe could be enhanced by introducing the elements of naming, subject to the fulfilment of vulnerability criteria, and additionality. In order to create incentives for the state not to shy away from this approach, it has been suggested that the state could step back and allow private sponsorship of refugees characterised by these features to flourish, as long as the sponsor is willing address state concerns over welfare, integration and security. The discussion has highlighted that sponsors could legitimately satisfy the state's concerns over welfare and integration, as long as they are willing to bear the costs. As far as security checks are concerned, the role of the state cannot be replaced by the sponsor, due to the nature of the public good at stake, however the sponsor can still have a say in the selection phase and in taking on the costs of vetting for each beneficiary they are willing to support.

In practice, then, private sponsorship programmes could allow sponsors to select beneficiaries, and in addition to state quotas, provided that the costs of their welfare, integration and security screening are covered by the sponsor. Nevertheless, the final say on whether the selected beneficiaries will be allowed access to the host state should be determined by the state's own application of its security rules. Indeed, it is the state, due to its informational advantages and international networks, that can better assess whether the beneficiary-to-be poses a threat to its borders.

In sum, the way to increase private sponsorship of refugees characterised by the elements of naming and additionality is for sponsors to cover the costs of welfare, integration and the state's costs of screening. As analysed earlier in this chapter, naming should be allowed while making sure that the pool of candidates draws on vulnerability criteria (unless these are trumped by family reasons). Moreover, since the state's costs of screening would be covered by the sponsor, additionality should only be subject to state processing capacity. Finally, once the potential beneficiaries have been selected by the sponsor, it should be the state who gives the final say on whether they can enter or not, although this should only be based on a security assessment.

This theoretical solution has some several practical implications and limitations, which are briefly addressed below.

First, as mentioned at the beginning of this chapter and in the Introduction to this book, it is worth reminding the reader that this proposal is still theoretical. Indeed, although based on available literature on private sponsorship and a theoretical legal framework on sovereignty, this proposal still needs to be tested in reality. For this reason, this proposal is not to replace the already valuable European initiatives, but only raise a debate on whether what is already there could be enhanced or complemented, or perhaps, where nothing is in place, how this proposal (or parts of it) could become a source of inspiration for new pilot private sponsorship schemes.

One should also remember that this proposal is not to be taken as a one-size-fits-all solution. Different state arrangements are vitally important and cannot be stretched or pushed beyond reason. In relation to welfare, for example, while this proposal might work well in theory, in practice it will likely be more achievable, or at least easier to test in pilots, by states where welfare arrangements are less generous and less structured. In fact, this proposal might not be suitable for the schemes implemented by states that have embraced a strong universalist or liberal welfare approach. For instance, in states embracing the Nordic welfare system or Anglo-Saxon system, private sponsors could find it much more costly to pay the welfare and integration costs, in order to secure the naming element within the sponsorships in return, as it would be expensive to match the generous welfare provisions that are normally available to refugees that have entered the country via other schemes. In contrast, in states that embrace the Mediterranean welfare model, sponsors would be more easily be able to meet the costs of the implementation of such a suggestion, as the welfare costs that would be incurred by the sponsor would be lower.

Thinking more broadly, in many of the European programmes that have been analysed, private stakeholders often expect the state to pull more weight in the sponsorship arrangement, especially from a financial perspective, and this perception might be difficult to change. Indeed, in Chapter three and Chapter four it was highlighted that the role and involvement of the sponsor are key for the success of these programmes, but there was criticism on how the large financial responsibilities can hinder their action. A recent report points out how, to increase involvement and retention, programmes may want to limit sponsors' financial responsibilities and length of commitment.[150] Where sponsors already feel too financially burdened, see for instance in the German and Irish expired schemes,[151] it is unlikely that they will agree to take on all the welfare and integration costs of the beneficiaries and this will likely make embracing sponsorship characterised

[150] Zanzuchi, Dumann, Tissot and Skodo, above n 4, 3.

[151] ibid, 12. The Irish family reunification experiment, which was characterised by unlimited financial responsibility, was a short-lived experience. Equally, the German federal programme envisaged the sponsor's responsibility for five years. In the UK a backstop fund was introduced for some time, in order to avoid situations in which the sponsors could find themselves unable to cope with the financial commitments.

by naming and additionality, as a streamline rule, very difficult. This is because sponsors expect the state to put more financial resources into the sponsorship scheme and, in that case, the state will probably want to retain its power on selecting who can benefit from the programme and, potentially, put a stop on additional numbers. However, in these circumstances, countries might consider leaving an option open, in parallel to the private programmes already in place, in the exceptional circumstance that the sponsor can prove that it is effectively in the strong economic position of being able to meet welfare and integration costs for an indefinite period of time. Having this option in place may be particularly important for future, unforeseen, humanitarian emergencies that may unfold.

In Chapters three and four, it was pointed out how a key aspect characterising private sponsorship schemes is the vital role played by the sponsor. As briefly discussed above, the sponsor plays a crucial role in the success of sponsorship but, at the same time, there has also been criticism that sponsors can struggle to perform adequately, especially when challenged by finances. Critiques have also pointed out that other factors can trigger underperformance by the sponsors, such as lack of proper training and knowledge, paternalistic stances, unbalanced interactions, and a possible breakdown of the relationship with the beneficiaries of the programme or with other sponsors. These factors and several others have been recognised as being the cause for lack of retention and recruitment of sponsors.[152] In order to satisfy state sovereignty and encourage private sponsorships characterised by naming and additionality, it is then important to think about the sponsor and to work on proper conditions that can allow sponsors to operate at their best.

In the first instance, it would be beneficial to broaden the pool of sponsors. In most of the sponsorship schemes that are tools for resettlement one can see the involvement of an intermediary organisation, which either takes all or most of the responsibility of the sponsorship, through its finances, and directs members and volunteers (see, for instance, the case of humanitarian corridors) or carries out the task of raising awareness, providing training and recruiting sponsors (see, for example, the NesT programme in Germany). In both instances however, it is evident that sponsors often end up being 'existing volunteers or followers who live within the geographies they serve, and this has limited the scale and diversity of programme recruitment'.[153] In order to reach out to more diverse sponsors, the intermediary organisations could run broader outreach campaigns. Moreover, broadening the pool of sponsors could also mean that the sponsorship model could be designed to include the involvement of not just individuals but also legal persons, such as financially strong organisations or even companies. In the case of the already mentioned humanitarian corridors,

[152] ibid, 2–3.
[153] ibid, 10.

the religious organisations themselves, owing to their strong finances and network, can act as sponsors or guarantors, when something goes wrong in the sponsorship, effectively creating no burden on the state. Other organisations, and not necessarily religious ones, could be involved. Furthermore, in states where the organisation acts just as an intermediary for outreach and recruiting, one could even consider the Group-of-five rule to include, among the five, business people or companies. Indeed, the Canadian experience shows how the sponsor can also be the one that offers job opportunities in the first instance, effectively contributing to a substantive reduction of unemployment costs, for example.[154] Sponsorship of refugees programmes could also take inspiration from the current Displaced Talent Mobility Pilot, a programme currently running in the UK where employers hire people through a competitive, remote recruitment process that can sponsor Talent Beyond Boundaries candidates via the new Skilled Worker Route.[155] The German NesT programme is also considering the involvement of organisations such as companies, housing associations and sports clubs as supporters of the sponsors.[156] These potential arrangements have necessarily to be paired up with strong monitoring checks, to make sure of avoiding any exploitative behaviour. Monitoring groups and help desks, such as those already run in Belgium by Caritas,[157] could not only detect tensions arising within groups and between groups and sponsored individuals, but also identify and raise a red flag in case of exploitative dynamics. Finally, another factor that could work in the sponsors' favour, without imposing any cost on the state, and hence increasing the likelihood of introducing schemes characterised by naming and additionality, is to think more about the role of the intermediate organisation. As mentioned above, intermediate organisations can effectively work as sponsors themselves and /or guarantors (as in the case of the humanitarian corridors), effectively being a safeguard for when an individual sponsor can no longer cope with the demands of the sponsorship. However, in the majority of cases intermediate organisations work simply as the recruiter of sponsors and

[154] See for example the story of Jon Estill, who sponsored 89 Syrian families (over 300 people) and gave work to 28 people in his business ('Businessman Sponsors 300 Refugees for Relocation to Canada', 23 November 2019, available at: www.becomeacanadian.net/en/businessman-sponsors-300-refugees-for-relocation-to-canada/).

[155] For more information see Talent beyond boundaries, 19 July 2021, available at: www.talentbeyondboundaries.org/blog/introducing-the-uks-displaced-talent-mobility-pilot. In March 2024 the STEP (Skills, Talent and Empowerment through Pathways) project begun. The project, funded by the European Union, aims at resettling displaced workers by applying the sponsorship model through the involvement of companies and the civil society. The project will be implemented between 2024 and 2026, in Italy, Ireland and Spain.

[156] F Tissot, N Dumann and M Bitterwolf, 'Das Aufnahmeprogramm "Neustart im Team": Studie zur Programmumsetzung' (2003) Forschungsbericht Bundesamt für Migration und Flüchtlinge, no 44, available at: www.bamf.de/SharedDocs/Anlagen/DE/Forschung/Forschungsberichte/fb44-evaluation-nest.pdf?__blob=publicationFile&v=8, 77.

[157] Zanzuchi, Dumann, Tissot and Skodo, above n 4, 34.

provide them with training. If the sponsorship breaks down due to financial or other struggles of the sponsor, the responsibility moves to the state (see NesT in Germany or the UK Community Sponsorship, for example). All the above considered, one could seriously consider private sponsorship schemes where the individual sponsor is either an organisation with strong financial capacity, or an individual supported by an organisation with strong financial capacity that is willing to step in as guarantor when things run into trouble.

The involvement of intermediary organisations could also be considered for sponsorships such as family reunifications, humanitarian admissions and relocations. Indeed, an intermediary organisation could ease the financial responsibility of the sponsor. Furthermore, if the intermediary organisation and/or the sponsor were to bear the full welfare and integration costs, the temporary nature of the scheme, which characterises most of these sponsorship programmes, would be challenged, as there would be no reason to refuse a more stable solution if it came at no cost for the state. Even with the participation of an organisation that acts as a sponsor or as guarantor, safety nets need to be put in place.[158] Providing financial cover with the aim of achieving complete independence of the beneficiaries from the programmes, entails a considerable risk exposure, even for those for whom money is not a problem. Safety nets could be introduced to help mitigate the risk placed upon sponsors. In Canada, for example, the province of Manitoba established an assurance scheme for sponsors that face financial difficulties.[159] Similarly, Australia provides risk management and insurance schemes for the sponsoring groups.[160] These forms of protection could be easily applied, for the sake of enhancing naming and additionality in exchange for privately covering the costs of the sponsorship.

As far as the role of the sponsor is concerned, some might also see as limitation to the proposed approach the fact that this analysis only focuses on what the sponsor could do economically. While it is true that the sections of this chapter have looked at welfare, integration and security in terms of costs and financial responsibility to be borne by the sponsor, one should rest assured that this is not done to deny what sponsors do beyond the dimension of mere money. Indeed, the current examples of sponsorship bear witness to stories of pure altruism and generosity, which go far beyond providing a roof, maintenance and language tuition fees. However, for the purpose of the proposed approach, it was important to 'reduce' the work of the sponsor into something monetarily quantifiable, in

[158] ibid, 29.

[159] See J Kumin, 'Welcoming Engagement: How Private Sponsorship Can Strengthen Refugee Resettlement in the European Union' (2015) Brussels: Migration Policy Institute Europe, available at: www.migrationpolicy.org/research/welcoming-engagement-how-private-sponsorship-can-strengthen-refugee-resettlement-european, 10.

[160] Community Refugee Sponsorship Australia, Risk Management and Insurance Information for CRSA Program Groups, 28 July 2022, available at: https://refugeesponsorship.org.au/risk-management-and-insurance-information-for-crsa-program-groups/.

order to suggest a possible 'bargaining' negotiation with the state and address its concerns. This concretely means covering the state's costs in return for the freedom for the sponsor.

A final word on the issue of discrimination. A discussion on discrimination and fairness, deriving from naming, has already been undertaken in this chapter. In particular. the role of affinity in the choice of naming has been highlighted and it has been argued that, provided that vulnerability criteria have been fulfilled (outside family reunification schemes), sponsors should be allowed to name anyone, based on their preferences. To avoid discriminatory instances, this suggestion should be coupled with the requirement that any person, regardless of nationality, religion, gender etc, should be allowed to become a sponsor. This is the only way to allow a fair, equal starting point for everyone involved – sponsors and sponsored individuals – and to promote the development of these schemes in an increasingly diverse and multicultural Europe.

One could argue, however, that certain people or certain groups are more likely to become sponsors than others for several reasons, such as knowledge, network and money. If this is the case some might argue that discrimination could still occur, since these groups would be likely to sponsor those among the vulnerable ones, that they feel are closer to their culture, beliefs etc. While earlier this book argued that this is an inevitable factor that plays a role in immigration choices, this does not deny the fact that private sponsorship programmes should be made accessible to everyone. For this reason, it is extremely important to make sure that these programmes are not just open but also properly advertised and promoted to all groups within society and not just to the dominant ones. To overcome the problem of richer and poorer sponsors, collaboration between different groups coming from different backgrounds could be very important. The Belgian humanitarian corridor, for example, together with several promoters belonging to different Christian denominations, sees the involvement of the Muslim Executive of Belgium and The Central Israelite Consistory of Belgium too. The pluralist nature of Europe could then allow, over time, the proliferation of schemes promoted by myriads of sponsors, similarly to what happens already in Canada, where Sponsorship Agreement Holders (SAHs) come from variegated backgrounds, religious and otherwise.

However, broader instances of criticism in relation to discrimination have often been addressed to private sponsorship of refugees schemes. It has been noted that these schemes grant preferential treatment to their beneficiaries, compared to the migrants that apply for asylum once in the territory of the state, and they have been accused of creating preferential routes for immigrants. Along the same lines, particularly in relation to the family reunification schemes characterised by private sponsorship components, it was argued that they were discriminatory as they carried fewer rights compared to other admission routes. States have also been criticised for resorting to private sponsorship of refugees in a 'smoke and mirrors' exercise, to move public attention away from their strict and inhumane migration policies. To promote the growth and a broader application of private sponsorship of refugees it is important not to take these claims lightly. Indeed, the proliferation of these alternative and safe solutions can only be achieved by gaining the public's trust and legitimising them in the law. To avoid backlashes from the civil society and potential constitutional challenges to the legislation, these schemes should be introduced against a background of clear and fair immigration laws. This means that the rights granted to privately sponsored beneficiaries should not be dissimilar to those granted by state-led resettlement programmes, in the case of sponsorship schemes as routes to resettlement, or to those granted under classic family reunification schemes or relocation schemes, in the case of sponsorship schemes that are routes to other forms of accession. The broader question of whether private sponsorship and resettlement are becoming the preferential path to immigration, often seen as 'queue jumpers' at the expense of asylum seekers, should also be addressed.

This chapter has argued that the private sponsorship of refugees characterised by naming and additionality has the advantage of opening new doors for vulnerable people who, normally, are not entitled to resettlement. The possibility of relying on naming and additionality can make private sponsorship programmes available also to individuals that are not officially classified as refugees. As seen, the category of private sponsorship schemes as tools for various forms of entry already shows that private sponsorships are adaptable outside the box of resettlement. For example, through private family reunification programmes, sponsors were allowed to name any member of their family, regardless their refugee status. This has also been the case for the relocation schemes involving St Egidio and the Vatican and the UK Homes for Ukraine sponsorship scheme. Moreover, the example of the humanitarian corridors has shown how private sponsorship can even go beyond the categories of vulnerability envisaged by the UNHCR to be classified as a refugee in need of resettlement. These examples can stir the imaginative creativity of our European legislators and inspire the introduction of further schemes that might also be applicable to those vulnerable people that are still in their country of origin, somewhere in Europe, or at the doors of Europe.

This chapter has also shown that, in theory, whether the state will encourage the introduction of schemes characterised by naming and additionality will likely depend on the breadth and depth of responsibility that the sponsors are willing and able to embrace, to prevent the beneficiaries of the schemes becoming a burden on the state. This might be easier to achieve in states with less rigid and less universalist welfare features. Also, the critical role of the sponsor needs to be considered in ways that do not create burdens on the state, to avoid the breakdown of the sponsorship. More broadly, these schemes need to be considered in how they sit within a state's broader immigration scene, to avoid potential rejections of the sponsorship idea as a whole.

All in all, given the circumstances, it is unlikely that this suggestion will be embraced everywhere, as there are precise private–state dynamics, which are different in every country and that cannot be stretched too far. However, some states might find it appealing to experiment with this proposal perhaps as a parallel exceptional option.

Finally, as covered in the Introduction and hinted to at the beginning of this chapter, much work still needs to be done to fully test the empirical viability of this proposal. In particular, it will be crucial to understand whether, effectively, no extra costs would be borne by states and public administrations in the long run. Moreover, more is required on the negotiation process between states and private actors, to better understand the motivations behind states' choices to adopt or refuse to adopt private sponsorship of refugees, and in particular those schemes characterised by naming and additionality. Finally, future research should also focus on legal persons as sponsors and safety nets and the best ways to support sponsors. All this is beyond the scope of this book, but it should be the subject of further study.

Conclusion

This final chapter brings together the findings of this book and aims to open a discussion for future research on the opportunity for European states and civil society to work together to introduce, when possible and feasible, private sponsorships of refugees characterised by naming and additionality.

This book has taken us on a journey to discover what private sponsorship of refugees schemes are, and how they found a home in Europe. This journey started, in Chapter one, by contextualising how private sponsorship fits within the broader asylum protection background and, more closely, within resettlement, which is one of the classic routes to refugee protection. To this end, the approach adopted in Chapter one was chronological. The chapter pointed out how protection of 'asylees' was not born as a privilege of the state but as a protection granted by cities, temples and, later on, by the church in the West for the sake of protection and redemption of souls. This church prerogative, however, became slowly but surely curtailed by the increasing temporal powers of kings and the power of the state. Chapter one highlighted that the Peace of Westphalia marked a watershed moment, as this was when the state was empowered with sovereignty over its people and borders. With the birth of nation states as we know them today, immigration and, naturally, refugee protection, became a matter of interest to central governments. As far as refugee protection is concerned, the chapter highlighted how, during the two world wars and their aftermath, the refugee problem turned from a purely national issue to a matter of global concern. During these times various initiatives, aimed at finding solutions for European refugees and displaced people, were triggered, such as the permanent forms of refugee protection: integration, repatriation and resettlement. With a change of emphasis over the years, resettlement has become the most wished for route, despite numbers of successful resettled refugees still being low compared to the global figures of people who are in acute need. Private sponsorship of refugees programmes, as the chapter pointed out, were originally experimented with by Canada, even before the Canadian state-led resettlement scheme was introduced, as a proposed solution to the overwhelmingly high number of displaced people and refugees from Europe in the aftermath of the world wars. While for some decades the private sponsorship of refugees remained a unique element of the Canadian refugee system, the last decade triggered wider interest in private sponsorship of refugees schemes as a potential alternative safe path to allow passage and entry to large numbers of people in need in of safety in third countries. Having situated private sponsorship of refugees within this context, the chapter concluded with some considerations, which were more deeply examined in Chapter five. These concerned the public versus private nature of refugee protection and the role of private sponsorship of refugees schemes within the concept of state sovereignty, suggesting that despite their intrinsically 'private nature' – since they necessarily require the involvement and participation of private sponsors – they are not able, as they currently stand, to pierce the veil of state sovereignty, as states are very much in control of how far these schemes can go and their remits.

The journey into the discovery of private sponsorship schemes continued in Chapter two. This chapter also adopted a contextualisation approach, with the twofold aim of not only filling a gap but also of providing an inclusive description of private sponsorship of refugees and a workable classification of the existing (and expired) European programmes. With this aim, the first part of the chapter focused on the precursor of and role model for all the private sponsorship schemes, the Canadian PSR programme. Having described its historical origins, the chapter explained how Canada was involved, following the Syrian crisis, in enabling the proliferation of similar schemes globally, with particular focus on Europe. The chapter continued by highlighting the key characteristics of the PSR scheme – naming and additionality – and by explaining how the programme currently works and fits within the broader Canadian resettlement schemes. Having fulfilled the aim of providing further historical context to the phenomenon of private sponsorship of refugees, the second part of the chapter focused then on definitions. Notwithstanding the fact that many academics and practitioners have provided definitions of the phenomenon, the chapter highlighted how, currently, there is no commonly accepted and precise definition of what private sponsorship of refugees is. For the purpose of this book, Chapter two proposed some descriptions of the phenomenon which encompass some features emphasised by different analysts and by the UNHCR. The proposed descriptions were functional to the classification of the European schemes, as private sponsorships as tools for resettlement, and private sponsorships seen as different forms of admission.

Chapter three and Chapter four applied the classification to the actual schemes and detailed them. In particular, Chapter three focused on European private sponsorship schemes as paths to resettlement, while Chapter four focused on the schemes that are paths to different forms of admission (mainly family reunification, humanitarian admissions and relocation). These two chapters aimed to fulfil a need in providing a comprehensive and updated account of the European private sponsorship of refugees situation, as it stood at the time of writing. These chapters aimed to provide information on how the key sponsorship schemes work in Europe. They both also included a final section where the key strengths and limitations of the schemes were outlined. It was found that most of the strengths and criticisms of the schemes revolved around the features of naming and additionality, the role played by the sponsor in the smooth running of the schemes, and discrimination.

The findings of both chapters fed into the analysis of Chapter five. Chapter five aimed to address whether there might be a way to enhance and improve upon the work done to date in the field of private sponsorship of refugees in Europe. This question was first tackled by highlighting the reasons why naming and additionality should be promoted and facilitated within the European context. In a nutshell, the rationale behind advocating the promotion of naming and additionality is grounded on the fact that these features have the potential to allow an increase in the numbers of people entering a safe host European state and broaden the category of people that, despite not being classified as refugees, could benefit from protection due to their conditions of vulnerability. The chapter noted that currently some European states seem to be slightly reluctant to promote schemes that feature these elements, either together or individually, and that one of the key reasons behind this could be the state-centric view permeating the current approach to immigration issues. As a challenge to this state-centric approach, the final part of the chapter focused on delineating an alternative theoretical approach to the relationship between private sponsorship of refugees and state sovereignty, which is one that sees the state taking a step back from its sovereign power, allowing private stakeholders to step forward when they can show that they are capable of satisfying the state's key concerns – welfare, integration and security – over the protection of its territory and borders. The chapter concluded that, notwithstanding some notable limitations, states would likely experiment more with naming and additionality if the private sponsor took on the responsibility for welfare, integration and security costs of the beneficiaries.

Some readers, perhaps the majority, will think that this proposal is not practical or is even utopian. For those who think that this is the case, please bear with me a little longer, while I try to explain why I think this might not be the case.

The very successful book *The Age of Migration* highlights that some development patterns will likely be dominant in migration during the next few decades. Among some of those that are highlighted, there is an argument that suggests the likelihood for demand for high- and low-skilled workers, that will persist in high-income countries and will increase in middle-income countries.[1] Strictly linked to this development, and likely causal to it, is the fact that many countries have experienced, and are still experiencing, a fast decline in fertility, coupled with much longer life expectancy than in the past.[2] 'Ageing in combination with economic growth is likely to sustain the demand for lower- and higher-skilled migrant labour'.[3] Indeed, the authors conclude that many rich countries, including those in Europe, will likely have to rely on newcomers coming from Asia, Latin America and Africa.[4]

Climate change is also a factor to be taken into account. While the same authors argue that it is unlikely that climate change will lead to massive migration waves in the near future because those in the poorest countries lack the resources to move

[1] H de Haas, S Castles and MJ Miller, *The Age of Migration: International Population Movements in the Modern World* (London, Bloomsbury Academic, 2019) 357.

[2] ibid.

[3] ibid.

[4] ibid.

away,[5] we are already witnessing climate change human rights litigation, and the UN Human Rights Committee, in 2020, opened the door to claims of asylum seekers who see their right to life at risk.[6] Moreover, some are increasingly claiming that, due to climate change, parts of the world will become uninhabitable[7] in the longer term. If that is the case, no walls will be able to restrain the sheer number of people looking for new hospitable lands.

However, even without considering the worst-case scenarios of our future (such as the struggles with low fertility rates and climate change), the call for a more humane approach to immigration should come from a sense of decency and a desire to strive for the common good of our fellow humans. In the strive for a globalised world, from which our societies have gained remarkable advantages, we have discovered that it is not desirable, let alone possible, to operate in terms of self-sufficiency because countries have become, like it or not, more interconnected with and interdependent on each other. Nevertheless, although we seem to prefer thinking about globalisation only in terms of commodities, 'it is difficult to open [the] borders for movements of information, commodities and capital and yet close them to people'.[8]

I would add that closing borders to people is not just difficult, but unfair and selfish, for the following reasons. First of all, international migration should not be seen as an extraordinary event, but as a 'constant, not an aberration, in human history'.[9] Indeed, 'migration should be understood as an intrinsic part of broader processes of development and social transformation (instead of a "problem to be solved", or, conversely a solution to fundamental problems such as development failure)'.[10] If migration is then a process that has always presented itself in human history, and one that needs to be managed, it should be based upon the real absorption capacity of a given state and the willingness of its citizens to support it with their resources.

Furthermore, there are compelling arguments that suggest that at the basis of the liberal state lies the idea of open borders,[11] and that global poverty can be mitigated by freedom of movement.[12] It has also been argued that the concept of citizenship is a tool to create borders and that borders, as conceived today, are not so easily ethically justifiable.[13] Although the idea of state sovereignty has been used

[5] ibid, 354. The authors talk about the 'immobilizing' effect of natural disasters on the poorest countries. On this point see also C Zickgraf, 'Where Are All The Climate Migrants? Explaining Immobility Among Environmental Change' 4 October 2023 Migration Policy Institute, available at: www.migrationpolicy.org/article/climate-change-trapped-populations.

[6] UN Human Rights Committee CCPR/C/127/D/2728/2016, available at: tbinternet.ohchr.org/_layouts/15/treatybodyexternal/Download.aspx?symbolno=CCPR/C/127/D/2728/2016&Lang=en.

[7] Among others see D Wallace-Wells, *The Unhabitable Earth: A Story of the Future* (London, Penguin, 2019).

[8] de Haas, Castles and Miller, above n 1, 357.

[9] ibid, 353.

[10] ibid.

[11] JH Carens, 'Aliens and Citizens: The Case for Open Borders' (1987) 49 *The Review of Politics* 251.

[12] P Singer, 'Famine, Affluence, and Morality' (1972) 1 *Philosophy and Public Affairs* 229.

[13] D Kochenov, *Citizenship* (Cambridge, The MIT Press, 2019) 57.

to counter these views, when facing the reality of the cries of people that search for better opportunities for themselves and their families, often risking their lives, can one righteously hide behind the fictitious construction of the supremacy of state power in all circumstances? Because not only the legitimate claims of state sovereignty are important but also, if not more so, the development of every human being, which can be achieved by expanding their freedom,[14] even the freedom to seek better opportunities for themselves and their loved ones.

The idea behind this book then, perhaps, is not so utopian, because this analysis has tried to take into account the real claims of the state, the cry of people that today are seeking another chance in Europe, and the good will of our societies, in an attempt to outline a concrete proposal to address these tensions just described.

The proposed approach has also multiple collateral advantages. First, it is potentially capable of defusing the extreme political polarisation now witnessed in Europe and in many other countries over immigration matters. Indeed, if it is potentially left to anyone within society to decide who can enter and how many, on condition that they are willing to provide for them, while the security screening is done by the state, there would be no reasonable argument that can stand against this approach in terms of damage done to state welfare, integration or security. As a matter of fact, all these contentious aspects, which ignite heated political quarrels, would simply be taken care of by private sponsors, with their own resources, including their financial resources and social capital from their communities.

Secondly, this proposal implicitly takes into account and values the increasingly multicultural composition of Europe. Indeed, by allowing anyone – from any cultural, ethnic, religious, gender etc background – to become a sponsor, anyone then, among the most vulnerable, from any background, can become the preferred beneficiary, as highlighted in Chapter five.

Finally, and very importantly, this solution would broaden the numbers of vulnerable people that can reach Europe safely. Indeed, this book suggests that this proposal should be introduced in parallel with other state-led forms of admission, and even with other forms of private sponsorship already functioning in a given country. This proposal, rather than sweeping away all the other available solutions, would complement them, in circumstances where sponsors are capable of proving that they have enough resources to take care of and support the beneficiaries until they reach their independence.

This book also opens up potential avenues for further empirical and doctrinal research. One of the key claims that this book has made is that states would be more open to experiment with schemes characterised by naming and additionality if sponsors were willing to take on their shoulders the responsibility for welfare, integration and screening costs. Out of the schemes that have been outlined by the book, the one that most closely embodies this proposal, although not fully, is that of

[14] A Sen, *Development as Freedom* (Oxford, Oxford University Press, 1999).

the Italian humanitarian corridors.[15] As already mentioned, these schemes see the capillary involvement of the Community of St Egidio and the other organisations, both centrally and through the work of its volunteers, as private sponsors. The St Egidio community and the affiliated organisations cover the various expenses for the beneficiaries of the schemes for a time that is limited but which can be renewed until the beneficiaries have become independent and integrated. Following this experience, it would be important to understand, concretely, the degree of cost and responsibility sharing between the sponsor and the Italian state.

It would also be interesting to understand better the role played by local councils and administrations, and whether and to what extent, they are financially burdened when beneficiaries of the schemes are placed within their jurisdictions. Considering the specificities of the Italian welfare system – which is particularly focused on pensions, rather than providing benefits to families or individuals in earlier phases of life – it would be also useful to understand whether the financial help provided by the sponsor aims simply to match a minimum level of support that would otherwise be provided by the state to people in similar circumstances, or goes beyond that.

It would also be important to investigate the negotiation aspect of the Italian humanitarian corridor. In particular, a better understanding of whether, behind the different numbers pledged by the various memoranda of understanding, lay detailed considerations of costs – either on the sponsor, the state or both – and the absorption capacity of Italian society. Finally, in relation to the possibility of naming the beneficiaries, it would be important to discover if this feature is viewed, by the sponsors, as a privilege for which they are willing to provide more resources.

Answering these questions will help to develop the debate on private sponsorships not only as far as the concrete and practical understanding of the Italian humanitarian corridors is concerned, but also in relation to other schemes, current or future, in other countries, which could be better understood and tested in comparison.

To conclude, this book has suggested a way to bring individuals and communities together, while still recognising the ultimate power of the state over immigration. This proposal has the potential to grant individual people a bigger say on these matters which, as we have discovered, have not always been within the state's realm. Considering the current pressing immigration issues, which are here to stay, and the difficulty of state-provided solutions, the role and reshaping of power of private stakeholders in this debate should be welcomed and further explored.

[15] Potentially also the Portuguese sponsorship scheme could embody this proposal, although the scheme is still at a pilot phase, and it is not yet sure if and when it will be officially launched nationally in its final stage.

BIBLIOGRAPHY

Books

Adelman, H, *Canada and the Indochinese Refugees* (Saskatchewan, LA Weigl Education Associates, 1982).

Aquinas, T, *Scriptum super sententiis* (Aldershot, Avebury Publishing Company Limited, 1980).

Burgess, G, *The League of Nations and the Refugees from Nazi Germany* (London, Bloomsbury Academic, 2016).

Dauvergne, C, *Humanitarianism, Identity and Nation: Migration Laws of Australia and Canada* (Vancouver, UBC Press, 2005).

de Haas, H, Castles, S and Miller, MJ, *The Age of Migration: International Population Movements in the Modern World* (London, Bloomsbury Academic, 2019).

Derrida, J, *On Cosmopolitanism and Forgiveness* (London, Routledge, 2001).

Fassin, D, *La raison humanitaire: une histoire morale du temps present* (Paris, Éditions de l'EHESS/ Gallimard/ Seuil, 2010).

Goodwin-Gill, GS and McAdam, J, *The Refugee in International Law* (Oxford, Oxford University Press, 2021).

Hajighasemi, A, *European Welfare States and Globalization: Strategies in an Era of Economic Restructuring* (Cheltenham, Edward Elgar Publishing, 2019).

Kelley, N, Trebilcock, M, *The Making of the Mosaic: A History of Canadian Immigration Policy* (Toronto, University of Toronto Press, 2010).

Kochenov, D, *Citizenship* (Cambridge MA, The MIT Press, 2019).

Kushner, T, *Remembering Refugees: Then and Now* (Manchester, Manchester University Press, 2006).

Macchiavelli, N, *The Prince (De Principatibus/ Il Principe)* (Milton Keynes, Penguin Classics, 2014 [1513]).

Manzoni, A, *The Betrothed* (London, Penguin Classics, 1972).

Labman, S, *Crossing Law's Border: Canada's Refugee Resettlement Programme* (Vancouver/Toronto, UBC Press, 2020).

Labman, S and Cameron, G, *Strangers to Neighbours: Refugee Sponsorship in Context* (Montreal, McGill-Queens University Press, 2000).

Porter, B, *The Refugee Question in Mid Victorian Politics* (Cambridge, Cambridge University Press, 1979).

Portes, A, *The Economic Sociology of Immigration: Essays on Networks, Ethnicity and Entrepreneurship* (New York, Russell Sage Foundation, 1995).

Rabben, L, *Sanctuary and Asylum: A Social and Political History* (Seattle/London, University of Washington Press, 2016).

Rose, H and Saltzman Chafetz, J, *Religion across borders: transnational immigrant networks* (Walnut Creek, Altamira Press, 2002).

Sen, A, *Development as Freedom* (Oxford, Oxford University Press, 1999).

Simpson, AWB, *Human Rights at the End of Empire: Britain and the Genesis of the European Convention* (Oxford, Oxford University Press, 2001).

Skran, C, *Refugees in Interwar Europe: the emergence of a regime* (Oxford, Oxford University Press, 1995).

Torpey, JC, *The invention of passport: surveillance, citizenship and the state* (Cambridge, Cambridge University Press, 2010).

Wallace-Wells, D, *The Unhabitable Earth: A Story of the Future* (London, Penguin, 2019).
Walzer, M, *Spheres of* Justice: A Defence of Pluralism and Equality (New York, Basic Books, 1984).
Whisker, JB, and Spiker, KR, *Asylum and Sanctuary in History and Law: A Social and Political Approach to Temporary Protections Around the World* (Irvine CA, Brown Walker Press, 2021).

Book Chapters

Bianchini, K, 'Humanitarian Admission to Italy through Humanitarian Visas and Corridors' in MC Foblets and L Leboeuf (eds), Humanitarian Admission to Europe (Baden-Baden/Oxford, Nomos/Hart Publishing, 2020) 157–99.
Biersteker, TJ, 'State, Sovereignty and Territory' in W Carlsnaes, T Risse and BA Simmons (eds), *Handbook of International Relations* (London, Sage, 2013) 245–72.
Bodart, S, 'Humanitarian Admission to Belgium' in MC Foblets and L Leboeuf (eds), Humanitarian Admission to Europe (Baden-Baden, Nomos-Hart publishing, 2020) 225–38.
Bradley, M and Duin, C, 'A Port in the Storm: Resettlement and Private Sponsorship in the Broader Context of Refugee Regime' in S Labman and G Cameron (eds), *Strangers to Neighbours: Refugee Sponsorship in Context* (Montreal, McGill-Queens University Press, 2020) 74–92.
Cameron, G, 'Reluctant Partnership: A Political History of Private Sponsorship in Canada (1947–1980)' in S Labman and G Cameron (eds), *Strangers to Neighbours: Refugee Sponsorship in Context* (Montreal, McGill-Queens University Press, 2020) 19–41.
Endres de Oliveira, P, 'Humanitarian Admissions in Germany – Access vs Rights?' in MC Foblets and L Leboeuf (eds), *Humanitarian Admission to Europe: the Law between Promises and Constraints* (Baden-Baden, Nomos, 2020) 199–224.
Korntheuer, A, 'Germany Refugee Protection System' in A Korntheuer, F Pritchard and DB Maehler (eds), *Structural Context of Refugee Integration in Canada and Germany* (Köln, GESIS, 2017) 37–42.
Lenard, PT, 'How should we think about private sponsorship of refugees, book on private sponsorship' in S Labman and G Cameron (eds) *Strangers to Neighbours: Refugee- Sponsorship in Context* (Montreal, McGill-Queens University Press, 2020) 61–73.
Lerh, S and Dick, B, '"Naming" refugees in the Canadian Private Sponsorship of Refugees Program: Diverse Intentions and Consequences' in S Labman and G Cameron (eds), *Strangers to Neighbours: Refugee Sponsorship in Context* (Montreal, McGill-Queens University Press, 2000) 42–60.
Light, I, Bhachu, P and Karageorgis, S, 'Migration networks and immigrant entrepreneurship' in I Light and P Bhachu (eds), *Immigration and Entrepreneurship: culture, capital and ethnic networks* (London, Routledge, 1993) 25–50.
McNally, R, 'Blended Visa Office-Referred Program: Perspectives and Experiences from Rural Nova Scotia' in S Labman and G Cameron (eds), *Strangers to Neighbours: Refugee Sponsorship in Context* (Montreal, McGill-Queens University Press, 2020) 134–51.
Molnar, P, 'AI and Migration Management' in MD Dubber, F Pasquale and S Das (eds), *The Oxford Handbook of Ethics of AI* (Oxford, Oxford Academic, 2020) 769–787.
Münz, R, 'The Integration of Migrants and Refugees – A European Synopsis' in R Bauböck and M Tripkovic, *The integration of migrants and refugees: An EUI Forum on Migration, Citizenship and Demography* (Florence, EUI, 2017), available at: cadmus.eui.eu/handle/1814/45187, 7–22.
Penninx, R, 'Integration of Migrants: Economic, Social, Cultural and Political Dimensions' in M Macura, AL MacDonald and W Haug (eds), *The New Demographic Regime: Population Challenges and Policy Responses* (Geneva, United Nations, 2005) 137–50.
Ricciardi Celsi, F, 'Asilo (diritto di)' in *Enciclopedia Giuridica Treccani* (Roma, Istitituto dell'Enciclopedia Italiana, 2010).
Smith, CD, 'A Model for the World? Policy Transfer Theory and the Challenges of "Exporting" Private Sponsorship to Europe' in S Labman and G Cameron (eds), *Strangers to Neighbours: Refugee Sponsorship in Context* (Montreal, McGill-Queens University Press, 2020) 286–302.

Tan, NF, 'Community Sponsorship, The Pact and The Compact: Towards Protection Principles' in S Carrera and A Geddes (eds), *The EU Pact on Migration and Asylum in light of the United Nations Global Compact on Refugees* (European University Institute, Florence, 2021) 71–80, available at: cadmus.eui.eu/handle/1814/70600.

Vacchiano, F, 'On marginal inclusion: refugees at the fringes of citizenship in Portugal' in S Aboim, P Granjo and A Ramos (eds), *Changing Societies: Legacies and Challenges. Ambiguous Inclusions: inside out, outside in, Ambiguous inclusions: inside out, outside in*, vol. 1 (Lisbon, Universidade de Lisboa, 2018) 99, available at: www.ics.ulisboa.pt/books/book1/full.pdf.

Van Selm, J, 'Community based sponsorship of refugees resettling in the UK: British values in action?' in EM Gozdziak, I Main and B Suter (eds), *Europe and the Refugee Response: a Crisis of Values?* (London, Routledge, 2021) 185–200.

Journal Articles

Ambrosini, M and Schnyder von Wartensee, I, 'Actions speak louder than claims: humanitarian corridors, civil society and asylum policies' (2022) 48 *Journal of Ethnic and Migration Studies* 3965–84.

Anker, D, 'Refugee Law, Gender, and the Human Rights Paradigm' (2002) 15 *Harvard Human Rights Journal* 133–54.

Atanasova, R, 'Portugal as a state of relocation under the Provisional EU Relocation Scheme' (2016) 13 *Revista Migrações – Número Temático Planos de Integração para Migrantes* 109–22, available at: www.om.acm.gov.pt/documents/58428/569795/Portugal+as+a+State+of+Relocation+under+the+Provisional+EU+Relocation+Scheme+-+Rositsa+Atanasova.pdf/7178aec3-b14a-48dd-89bb-2517bd714dde.

Barnett, L, 'Global governance and the evolution of the international refugee regime' (2002) 14 *International Journal of Refugee Law* 238–62.

Bashford, A and McAdam, J, 'The Right to Asylum: Britain's 1950 Aliens Act and the Evolution of Refugee Law' (2014) 32 *Law and History Review* 309–50.

Bertram, D, Maleki, A and Karsten, N, 'Factoring in Societal Culture in Policy Transfer Design: the Proliferation of Private Sponsorship of Refugees' (2020) 21 *Journal of International Migration & Integration* 253–71.

Blank, Y, 'Federalism, Subsidiarity, and the Role of Local Governments in an Age of Global Multilevel Governance' (2010) 37 *Fordham Urban Law Journal* 510–558.

Bond, J and Kwadrans, A, 'Resettling Refugees through Community Sponsorship: a Revolutionary Operational Approach Built on Traditional Legal Infrastructure' (2019) 35 *Refuge: Canada's Journal on Refugees* 87–109.

Briggs, A, 'The Welfare State in Historical Perspective' (1961) 2 *European Journal of Sociology/ Archives Européennes de Sociologie* 221–58.

Brljavac, B, 'Refugee Crisis in Europe: The Cases Studies of Sweden and Slovakia' (2017) 3 *Journal of Liberty and International Affairs* 91–107.

Carens, JH, 'Aliens and Citizens: The Case for Open Borders' (1987) 49 *The Review of Politics* 251–73.

Challinor, E, 'Refugee Hospitality Encounters in Northern Portugal: "Cultural Orientations" and "Contextual Protections"' (2018) 96 *Migration and Society* 96–122.

Chetail, V, 'Fridtjof Nansen and the International Protection of Refugees: An Introduction' (2003) 22 *Refugee Survey Quarterly* 1–6.

Chimni, BS, 'From Resettlement to Involuntary Repatriation: Towards a Critical History of Durable Solutions to Refugee Problems' (2004) 23 *Refugee Survey Quarterly* 55–73.

Cohen, R, 'Citizenship: from three to seven principles of belonging' (2022) 28 *Social Identities* 139–46.

Constantino, C, Minas, M, 'My new home? Strategies and challenges of refugee integration programs in Portugal' (2022) 50 *Journal of Community Psychology* 3792–3808.

Dajani, D, 'Refuge under austerity: the UK's refugee settlement schemes and the multiplying practices of bordering' (2020) 44 *Ethnic and Racial Studies* 58–76.

Damai, P, 'Messianic-City: Ruins, Refuge and Hospitality in Derrida' (2005) 27 *Discourse* 68–94.

Denton, T, 'Understanding private refugee sponsorship in Manitoba' (2003) 4 *Journal of International Migration and Integration* 257–72.

Dorfman, A, Harel, A, 'The Case against Privatisation' (2013) 41 *Philosophy & Public Affairs* 67–102.

D'Avino, G, 'Framing Community Sponsorship in the context of the UK's hostile environment' (2022) 42 *Critical Social Policy* 327–49.

Ferreira-Snyman, MP, 'The evolution of state sovereignty: a historical overview' (2006) 12 *Fundamina: a Journal of Legal History* 1–28.

Fihel, A, Kaczmarczyk, P, Stefańska, R, 'Recent Trends in International Migration in Poland' (2012) 1 *Central and Eastern European Migration Review* 69–90.

Garvey, JI, 'Toward a Reformulation of International Refugee Law' (1985) 26 *Harvard International Law Journal* 483–500.

Gerver, M, 'Refugee repatriation and the problem of consent' (2018) 48 *British Journal of Political Science* 855–75.

Goodwin-Gill, GS, 'The International Protection of Refugees: What Future?' (2000) 12 *International Journal of Refugee Law* 1–6.

Guardado, L, 'Sanctuary for Asylum Seekers: Revisiting the Religious Principle and Practice of Refuge in the Church' (2021) 82 *Theological Studies* 285–309.

Hathaway, JC, 'Reconceiving Refugee Law as Human Rights Protection' 4 (1991) *Journal of Refugee Studies* 113–31.

—— 'Selective Concern: An Overview of Refugee Law in Canada' (1987–88) 33 *McGill Law Journal* 676–715.

Hirsh, AL, Hoang, K and Vogl, A, 'Australia's private refugee sponsorship programme: creating complementary pathways or privatising humanitarianism' (2019) 35 *Refuge: Canada's Journal on Refugees* 110–23.

Holborn, LW, 'The League of Nations and the Refugee Problem' (1939) 203 *The ANNALS of the American Academy of Political and Social Science* 124–35.

Hyndman, J, Payne, W and Jimenez, S, 'Private Sponsorship of Refugees in Canada' (2017) 54 *Forced Migration Review* 56–59.

Ineli-Ciger, M, 'Is Resettlement Still a Durable Solution? An Analysis in Light of the Proposal for a Regulation Establishing a Union Resettlement Framework' (2022) 24 *European Journal of Migration and Law* 27–55.

Jaeger, G, 'On the history of the international protection of refugees', (2001) 83 *International Review of the Red Cross* 727–37.

Janzen, W, 'The 1979 MCC Canada Master Agreement for the Sponsorship of Refugees in Historical Perspective' (2006) 24 *Journal of Mennonite Studies* 211–22.

Jelínková, M, 'A Refugee Crisis Without Refugees: Policy and media discourse on refugees in the Czech Republic and its implications' (2019) 13 *Central European Journal of Public Policy* 33–45.

Jennings, RY, 'Some International Law Aspects of the Refugee Question' (1939) 20 *The British Yearbook of International Law* 98–114.

Kelly, SK, 'Derrida's cities of refuge: toward a non-utopian utopia' (2004) 7 *Contemporary Justice Review* 421–439.

Kortsaris, P, 'The Syrian Refugee Crisis: Resettlement and Other Complementary Pathways of Admission to Third Countries as Part of the Response' (2018) 149 *Nação e Defesa* 134–63, available at: core.ac.uk/download/pdf/322889116.pdf.

Krasner, SD, 'Rethinking the sovereign state model' (2001) 27 *Review of International Studies* 17–42.

Krivenko, EY, 'Hospitality and Sovereignty: What Can We Learn From the Canadian Private Sponsorship of Refugees Program?' (2012) 24 *International Journal of Refugee Law* 579–602.

Labman, S, 'Private Sponsorship: Complementary of Conflicting Interests?' (2016) 32 *Refuge: Canada's Journal on Refugees* 67–80.

Labman, S and Pearlman, M, 'Blending, Bargaining and Burden Sharing: Canada's Resettlement Programs' (2018) 19 *Journal of International Migration and Integration* 439–49.
Long, K and Crisp, J, 'Migration, mobility and solutions: an evolving perspective' (2010) 35 *Forced Migration Review* 56–57.
Machin, R, 'The UK – a home for Ukrainians? An analysis of social security and housing policy' 31 (2023) *Journal of Poverty and Social Justice* 298–305.
Macklin, A, Berber, K, Goldring, L, Hyndman, J, Korteweg, A, Labman, S and Zyfi, J, 'A preliminary investigation into Private Refugee Sponsors' (2018) 50 *Canadian Ethnic Studies* 35–58.
Molloy, MJ and Madokoro, L, 'Effecting Change: Civil Servants and Refugee Policy in 1970s Canada' (2017) 33 *Refuge: Canada's Journal on Refugees* 52–61.
Morozzo della Rocca, P, 'I due protocolli d' intesa sui "corridoi umanitari" tra alcuni enti di ispirazione religiosa ed il governo ed il loro possibile impatto sulle politiche di asilo e immigrazione' (2017) 1 *Diritto, Immigrazione e Cittadinanza* 1–31.
Nannestad, P, 'Immigration and welfare states: a survey of 15 years of research' (2007) 23 *European Journal of Political Economy* 512–32.
Ngombe, M, 'Les Couloirs Humanitaires: un régime d'exception pour gérer des réfugiés "désirables"' (2020) 1 *Revue internationale des études du développement* 65–86.
Orchard, P, 'The Dawn of International Refugee Protection: States, Tacit Cooperation and Non-Extradition' (2017) 30 *Journal of Refugee Studies* 282–300.
Ostrand, N, 'The Syrian Refugee crisis: a comparison of responses by Germany, Sweden, the United Kingdom, and the United States' (2015) 3 *Journal of Migration and Human Security* 255–79.
Ostrom, E, 'Beyond Markets and States: Polycentric Governance and Complex Economic Systems' (2010) 100 *American Economic Review* 641–672.
Panagiotidis, J, '"Not the Concern of the Organisation?" The IRO and Overseas Resettlement of Ethnic Germans from Eastern Europe After World War II' (2020) 45 *Historical Social Research* 173–202.
Patton, S, 'The Peace of Westphalia and it Affects on International Relations, Diplomacy and Foreign Policy' (2019) 10 *The Histories* 91–98, available at: digitalcommons.lasalle.edu/the_histories/vol10/iss1/5.
'Paul Fauchille on the Rights of Emigration and Immigration' (2005) 31 *Population and Development Review* 765–73.
Phillimore, J, Reyes-Soto, M, d'Avino, G and Nicholls, N, 'I Have Felt So Much Joy: The Role of Emotions in Community Sponsorship of Refugees' (2022) 33 *International Journal of Voluntary and Nonprofit Organisations* 386–96.
Pope, S, 'Sanctuary: The Legal Institution in England' (1987) 10 *Seattle University Law Review* 677–97.
Reyes-Soto, M, '"It's About the Power of Little People": the UK Community Sponsorship Scheme, a New Space for Solidarity, Civic Engagement and Activism' (2023) 24 *Journal of International Migration and Integration* 1939–55.
Ricci, C, 'The Necessity for Alternative Legal Pathways: The Best Practice of Humanitarian Corridors Opened by Private Sponsors in Italy' (2020) 21 *German Law Journal* 265–83.
Ruist, J, 'The Fiscal Cost of Refugee Immigration: the Example of Sweden' 41 (2015) *Population and Development Review* 567–81.
Shuster, L, 'Asylum and the Lessons of History' (2002) 44 *Race & Class* 40–56.
Siccardi, C, 'Quali Vie Di Ingresso Legale Per I Richiedenti Protezione In Europa? Contesto Europeo E Costituzionale' 2 (2022) *Diritto, Immigrazione e Cittadinanza* 75–132.
Singer, P, 'Famine, Affluence, and Morality' (1972) 1 *Philosophy and Public Affairs* 229–43.
Sivis, S, 'Integrating Bottom-up into Top-down: The Role of Local Actors in Labour Market Integration of Syrian Refugees in Turkey' (2021) 59 *International Migration* 190–206.
Tan, NF, 'Community Sponsorship in Europe: Taking Stock, Policy Transfer and What the Future might Hold' (2021) 3 *Frontiers in Human Dynamics: Refugees and Conflict*, available at: www.frontiersin.org/articles/10.3389/fhumd.2021.564084/full.
Tometten, C, 'Resettlement, Humanitarian Admissions and Family Reunion: the Intricacies of Germany's Legal Entry Regimes for Syrian Refugees' (2018) 37 *Refugees Survey Quarterly* 187–203.

Treviranus, B and Casasola, M, 'Canada's Private Sponsorship of Refugees Program: A practitioner's Perspective of its past and future' (2003) 4 *Journal of International Migration and Integration* 177–202.
Vacchiano, F, 'Camouflaging borders: relocation, neglect and disciplines of emplacement in Portugal' (2019) 5 *International Journal of Migration and Border Studies* 273–91.
Van Selm, J, 'Complementary Pathways to Protection: Promoting the Integration and Inclusion of Refugees in Europe?' (2020) 690 *The ANNALS of the American Academy of Political and Social Science* 136–52.
Vartiainen, J, 'The future of the European welfare states: the intriguing role of demography?' (2017) 16 *European View* 131–39.
Vasanthakumar, A, 'Privatising Border Control' (2018) 38 *Oxford Journal of Legal Studies* 411–29.
Webber, F, 'How voluntary are voluntary returns?' (2011) 52 *Race & Class* 98–107.
Weyner, M, 'Ethics, National Sovereignty and the Control of Immigration' (1996) 30 *The International Migration Review (Special Issue: Ethics, Migration, and Global Stewardship)* 171–97.
Wihtol de Wenden, C, 'La crise de l'asile' (2002) 1238 *Hommes & Migrations* 6–12.
Wilcox, S, 'The Open Borders Debate on Immigration' (2009) 4/5 *Philosophy Compass* 813–21.
Zimmermann, S, 'Understanding repatriation: refugee perspectives on the importance of safety, reintegration and hope' (2012) 18 *Population, Space and Place* 45–57.

Green Papers, Policy Papers, Reports

Alto Commissariado Para Migrações, Relatório de Avaliação da Política Portuguesa de Acolhimento de Pessoas Refugiadas (2017), available at: www.acm.gov.pt/documents/10181/27754/Relatorio_Acolhimento%2BPessoas%2BRefugiadas_Dez.2017.pdf/d21546b3-7588-483d-92a3-fa8185d61b5b.
Arnold, S and Quinn, E, 'Resettlement of Refugees and Private Sponsorships in Ireland' (2016) EMRI Research series no 55, available at: emn.ie/files/p_201612120402502016_Resettlement%20Report.pdf.
Arnold, S, Ryan, C and Quinn, E, 'Ireland's response to recent trends in international protection applications' (2018) ESRI Research Series no 72, available at: www.tara.tcd.ie/bitstream/handle/2262/83795/RS72.pdf?sequence=2.
Benson, M, Sigona, N and Zambelli, E, 'Humanitarian visas in a hostile environment: historical legacies, geopolitical ties and everyday experiences' Migzen Research Brief no 5, available at: zenodo.org/records/10571433.
Betts, A, 'Towards a "soft law" framework for the protection of vulnerable migrants' (2008) Research Paper no 62 *New Issues in Refugee Research*, available at: www.unhcr.org/sites/default/files/legacy-pdf/48b7f9642.pdf.
Canadian Council for Refugees, 'Blended Visa Office-Referred (BVOR) Program CCR Positions' (2018), available at: ccrweb.ca/sites/ccrweb.ca/files/bvor-feb-2018-positions.pdf.
—— 'Important changes in Canada's Private Sponsorship of Refugees Program' (2013), available at: ccrweb.ca/en/changes-private-sponsorship-refugees.
Chapman, A, 'Private Sponsorship and Public Policy: Political Barriers to Church-Connected resettlement in Canada' report prepared for Citizens for Public Justice (2014) available at: https://cpj.ca/wp-content/uploads/PrivateSponsorshipandPublicPolicyReport-1.pdf.
Citizenship and Immigration Canada, Corporate Review, Planning Review and Renewal, 'Study Report on the Review and Development of a Process for Matching Refugees and Sponsors' (Ottawa, CIC, February 1995).
Danzer, AM, 'Economic Benefits of Facilitating the Integration of Immigrants' (2011) 9(4) CESifo DICE Report 14–19, ISSN 1613-6373, Munchen, IFO Institut – Leibniz-Institut für Wirtschaftsforschung an der Universität München, available at: www.econstor.eu/bitstream/10419/167054/1/ifo-dice-report-v09-y2011-i4-p14-19.pdf.

Department of Justice and Equality, 'Community Sponsorship Ireland: Initial Policy Framework', available at: www.redcross.ie/wp-content/uploads/2019/03/CSI-Policy-Framework-WEB.pdf.

ERN feasibility study 'Towards a Private Sponsorship Model in France' (2018), available at: www.iom.int/sites/g/files/tmzbdl486/files/documents/ERN%2Bfeasibility-study-Towards-a-Private-Sponsorship-Model-in-France.pdf.

ERN scoping paper 'Humanitarian Admission Programmes in Europe: expanding complementary pathways of admission for persons in need of international protection' (2018), available at: www.iom.int/sites/g/files/tmzbdl486/files/documents/ERN%2Bscoping-paper-Humanitarian-Admission-Programmes-in-Europe.pdf.

—— 'Private Sponsorship in Europe: expanding complementary pathways for refugee resettlement' (2017), available at: www.iom.int/sites/g/files/tmzbdl486/files/documents/ERN%2Bscoping-paper-Private-Sponsorship-in-Europe.pdf.

—— 'Student Scholarships for Refugees: Expanding complementary pathways of admission to Europe' (2017), available at: www.iom.int/sites/g/files/tmzbdl486/files/documents/ERN%2Bscoping-paper-Student-Scholarships-for-Refugees.pdf.

ERN strategic assessment 'Expanding Solutions for Refugees: Complementary Pathways of Admission to Europe' (2018), available at: www.iom.int/sites/g/files/tmzbdl486/files/documents/ERN%2BFinal-Study-A-strategic-assessment-of-expanding-complementary-pathways-of-admission-to-Europe.pdf.

European Commission, 'Study on the feasibility and added value of sponsorship schemes as possible pathway to safe channels for admission to the EU, including resettlement' final report (2018), available at: op.europa.eu/en/publication-detail/-/publication/1dbb0873-d349-11e8-9424-01aa75ed71a1.

European Migration Network, 'Resettlement and Humanitarian Admission Programmes in Europe – what works?' (2016), available at: home-affairs.ec.europa.eu/system/files/2020-09/emn-studies-00_resettlement_synthesis_report_final_en_0.pdf.

European Parliament, 'Community sponsorship schemes under the new pact on migration and asylum' (2021), available at: www.europarl.europa.eu/RegData/etudes/BRIE/2021/690675/EPRS_BRI(2021)690675_EN.pdf.

Fratzke, S, 'Engaging Communities in Refugee Protection: the Potential of Private Sponsorship in Europe' (2017) Brussels Migration Policy Institute Europe, available at: www.migrationpolicy.org/research/engaging-communities-refugee-protection-potential-private-sponsorship-europe.

Fratzke, S and Salant, B, 'Tracing the Channels Refugees Use to Seek Protection in Europe' (2017), available at: www.migrationpolicy.org/sites/default/files/publications/MPI-EPIM_ChannelsOfEntry_FINALWEB.pdf.

General Secretariat of Human Rights, Coexistence and Cooperation, 'Auzolana II Pilot Community Sponsorship Experience – Evaluation Report', available at: static1.squarespace.com/static/61701919c9cd9200cd8e6ccc/t/61ba033d142a2518f09b6cd2/1639580483721/Basque+Country-+Pilot+Community+Sponsorship+Evaluation+_Full+report_EN.pdf.

Grote, J, Bitterwolf, M and Baraulina, T, 'Resettlement and Humanitarian Admission Programmes in Germany: Focus-Study by the German National Contact Point for the European Migration Network (EMN)' (2016) working paper no 68, available at: www.ssoar.info/ssoar/bitstream/handle/document/67691/ssoar-2016-grote_et_al-Resettlement_and_Humanitarian_Admission_Programmes.pdf?sequence=1&isAllowed=y&lnkname=ssoar-2016-grote_et_al-Resettlement_and_Humanitarian_Admission_Programmes.pdf.

Haren, IV, 'Canada's Private Sponsorship Model Represents and Complementary Pathway for refugee Resettlement'(2021) Migration Policy Institute, available at: www.migrationpolicy.org/article/canada-private-sponsorship-model-refugee-resettlement.

Heckmann, F, 'Education and the integration of migrants: challenges for European education systems arising from immigration and strategies for the successful integration of migrant children in European schools and societies' (2008) (NESSE Analytical Report, 1) Bamberg, europäisches forum für migrationsstudien (EFMS) Institut an der Universität Bamberg, available at: www.ssoar.info/ssoar/handle/document/19250.

Humanitarian Corridors, 'Corridoi umanitari: le procedure di implementazione per la loro estensione su scala europea' (2016), available at: www.humanitariancorridor.org/wp-content/uploads/2019/12/REPORT_ITA_WEB.pdf.

Independent Chief Inspector of Borders and Immigration, 'An Inspection of UK Refugee Resettlement Schemes' (November 2019–May 2020), available at: assets.publishing.service.gov.uk/government/uploads/system/uploads/attachment_data/file/933956/An_inspection_of_UK_Refugee_Resettlement_Schemes.pdf.

—— 'An Inspection of the Vulnerable Persons Resettlement Scheme' (August 2017–January 2018), available at: assets.publishing.service.gov.uk/government/uploads/system/uploads/attachment_data/file/705155/VPRS_Final_Artwork_revised.pdf.

Kreienbrink, A, 'Jahresbericht 2019 des Forschungszentrums Migration, Integration und Asyl' (2020) (Jahresbericht / Bundesamt für Migration und Flüchtlinge (BAMF) Forschungszentrum Migration, Integration und Asyl (FZ)) Nürnberg, BAMF und FZ, available at: www.ssoar.info/ssoar/handle/document/71250.

Kumin, J, 'Welcoming Engagement: How Private Sponsorship Can Strengthen Refugee Resettlement in the European Union' (2015) Brussels: Migration Policy Institute Europe, available at: www.migrationpolicy.org/research/welcoming-engagement-how-private-sponsorship-can-strengthen-refugee-resettlement-european.

Manzanedo, C, 'Community-Based Refugee Sponsorship in Spain: What Are the Experiences?' (2019) *Q&A Trending Issues on Migration*, available at: library.fes.de/pdf-files/bueros/budapest/15599.pdf.

Panchetti, B and Schnyder von Wartensee, I, 'Humanitarian Corridors and Reception: Pre-Arrival Preparation and Challenges' (21 May 2020) HLR 2 report, available at: https://humanlines.org/media/publications/HLR2_ENG.pdf.

—— 'L'esperienza dei corridoi umanitari' (10 March 2020) HLR 1 report, available at: humanlines.org/media/publications/HLR1_ITA_VERSION.pdf.

Paravati, C and Ricci A (eds), 'Sponsoring Integration: Impact assessment of Humanitarian Corridors Program primary achievements in Italy and France' (2020), available at: www.eurodiaconia.org/wordpress/wp-content/uploads/2020/08/AMIF-PPI-Impact-Assessment-Report-FINAL-27072020.pdf.

Phillimore, J and Reyes, M, 'Community Sponsorship in the UK: from application to integration' July 2019 interim report, available at: www.birmingham.ac.uk/documents/college-social-sciences/social-policy/misc/cs-uk-iris-june-2019.pdf.

Pohlmann, V and Schwiertz, H, 'Private sponsorship in refugee admission Standard in Canada, trend in Germany?' (2020–21) research brief no 1, available at: km4s.ca/wp-content/uploads/Private-sponsorship-in-refugee-admission-Standard-in-Canada-trend-in-Germany.pdf.

Policy brief 'Private sponsorship per l'integrazione: verso il modello Europeo' (2021), available at: www.eurodiaconia.org/wordpress/wp-content/uploads/2021/01/Private_sponsorship_integration_verso_modello_europeo_WEB.pdf.

Solf, B and Rehberg, K, 'The Resettlement Gap: a Record Number of Global Refugees, but Few are Resettled' (2021), available at: www.migrationpolicy.org/article/refugee-resettlement-gap.

Tan, NF, 'A study for the potential of introducing a community sponsorship program for refugees in Sweden', scoping report prepared for UNHCR's Representation for the Nordic and Baltic countries (2020), available at: www.unhcr.org/neu/wp-content/uploads/sites/15/2020/12/UNHCR-Study-on-Community-Sponsorship-Program-in-Sweden.pdf.

—— 'The feasibility of Community-based Sponsorship of refugees in Denmark' (2019), available at: amnesty.dk/wp-content/uploads/media/6130/feasibility-study-community-based-sponsorships.pdf.

Tissot, F, Dumann, N and Bitterwolf, M, 'Das Aufnahmeprogramm "Neustart im Team": Studie zur Programmumsetzung' (2003) Forschungsbericht Bundesamt für Migration und Flüchtlinge, no 44, available at: www.bamf.de/SharedDocs/Anlagen/DE/Forschung/Forschungsberichte/fb44-evaluation-nest.pdf?__blob=publicationFile&v=8.

Turk, V, 'UNHCR's Supervisory Responsibility' (2002) working paper no 67 *New Issues in Refugee Research*, available at: www.refworld.org/pdfid/4fe405ef2.pdf.

Turtiainen, K Sapir, H, 'Feasibility study on the potential of community-based sponsorship in Finland' Publications of the Ministry of Economic Affairs and Employment 2021:37, available at julkaisut.valtioneuvosto.fi/bitstream/handle/10024/163177/TEM_2021_37.pdf.

UNHCR, 'Brazil', available at: reporting.unhcr.org/sites/default/files/Brazil%20Factsheet_August%202021.pdf.

—— 'Complementary Pathways for Admission of Refugees to Third Countries: Key Considerations' (2019), available at: https://www.refworld.org/docid/5cebf3fc4.html

—— executive committee meetings, 'Conclusion on Local Integration' No 104 (LVI)–2005 UNHCR, available at: www.unhcr.org/uk/excom/exconc/4357a91b2/conclusion-local-integration.html.

—— 'Global Compact on Refugees', available at: www.unhcr.org/about-unhcr/who-we-are/global-compact-refugees.

—— 'Global Refugee Forum' available at globalcompactrefugees.org/global-refugee-forum.

—— 'New York Declaration for Refugees and Migrants', available at: www.unhcr.org/uk/new-york-declaration-for-refugees-and-migrants.html.

—— 'Refugee Protection and Mixed Migration: A -10 Point Plan of Action' (2007), available at: www.unhcr.org/sites/default/files/legacy-pdf/4742a30b4.pdf.

—— 'The History of Resettlement: Celebrating 25 Years of the ATCR', available at: www.unhcr.org/5d1633657.pdf.

—— 'What is resettlement?', available at: www.unhcr.org/5fe06e8b4.

Urban Justice Center, 'Models of Private Sponsorship: Past and Present Programs, and How the Private Sector Can Create Alternative and Complementary Pathways or Expand Resettlement for Refugees' (2018), available at: refugeerights.org/news-resources/models-of-private-sponsorship.

Zanzuchi, MB, Dumann, N, Tissot, F, Skodo, A, 'Attracting, Retaining, and Diversifying Sponsors for Refugees in Community Sponsorship Programmes' September 2023 Migration Policy Institute, available at: www.migrationpolicy.org/sites/default/files/publications/mpie-caps-eu_sponsor-recruitment-2023_final.pdf.

Zickgraf, C, 'Where Are All The Climate Migrants? Explaining Immobility Among Environmental Change' 4 October 2023 Migration Policy Institute, available at: www.migrationpolicy.org/article/climate-change-trapped-populations.

Conference Papers and Speeches

Ban Ki Moon, 'Secretary-General's remarks at meeting with resettled refugees from Afghanistan, the Democratic Republic of the Congo, Myanmar and Syria [as prepared for delivery]' 25 May 2015, available at: www.un.org/sg/en/content/sg/statement/2015-05-25/secretary-generals-remarks-meeting-resettled-refugees-afghanistan.

Pope Francis, 'Angelus 6 September 2015', available at: www.vatican.va/content/francesco/en/angelus/2015/documents/papa-francesco_angelus_20150906.html.

—— 'Solemnity of the Nativity of the Lord Papal Mass, Homily of His Holiness Pope Francis, 24 December 2017', available at: www.vatican.va/content/francesco/en/homilies/2017/documents/papa-francesco_20171224_omelia-natale.html.

Junker, JC, 'State of the Union 2015: Time for Honesty, Unity and Solidarity' 9 September 2015, available at: ec.europa.eu/commission/presscorner/detail/en/SPEECH_15_5614.

Theresa May, 'Theresa May's speech to the Conservative Party Conference – in full' 6 October 2015 *The Independent*, available at: www.independent.co.uk/news/uk/politics/theresa-may-s-speech-to-the-conservative-party-conference-in-full-a6681901.html.

Other Electronic Sources

Agenzia stampa della federazione delle chiese evangeliche in Italia, 'La buona pratica dei corridoi umanitari. L'annuncio del protocollo per la Libia' 17 June 2021, available at: www.nev.it/nev/2021/06/17/governare-le-migrazioni-la-buona-pratica-dei-corridoi-umanitari-2/.

BBC news, 'Mediterranean migrants: Hundreds feared dead after boat capsizes' 19 April 2015, available at: www.bbc.com/news/world-europe-32371348.

Bernard, L, 'Le couloir humanitaire conduit en Belgique par la communauté de Sant' Egidio, entre alternative face à la gestion migratoire européenne et instrumentalisation au service du politique?' 2018–19 thesis written at Université de Liège, Faculté de Droit, Science Politique et Criminologie under the supervision of Professor Geoffrey Grandjean.

Businessman Sponsors 300 Refugees for Relocation to Canada, 23 November 2019, available at: www.becomeacanadian.net/en/businessman-sponsors-300-refugees-for-relocation-to-canada/.

Bolla Officii Nostri (1749), available at: www.vatican.va/content/benedictus-xiv/it/documents/bolla--i-officii-nostri--i---15-marzo-1749--poiche-sono-sorti-di.html.

Britannica Encyclopaedia, 'United Nations Relief and Rehabilitation Administration' *Encyclopedia*, available at: www.britannica.com/topic/United-Nations-Relief-and-Rehabilitation-Administration.

Cappello, E, 'Corridoi umanitari: accoglienza, integrazione e contagio' 2018/2019 tesi del corso di laurea in scienze internazionali, dello sviluppo e della cooperazione, University of Turin, under the supervision of Professor R Ricucci, available at: inmigration.caritas.it/sites/default/files/docs/2021-09/Emanuele%20Cappello%20Tesi%20triennale%20SISCO%20Corridoi%20umanitari.pdf.

CattCh, 'Profughi, Sant'Egidio; anche Andorra apre i corridoi umanitari' 8 May 2018, available at: www.catt.ch/newsi/profughi-santegidio-anche-andorra-apre-i-corridoi-umanitari/.

Costa, PM and Sousa, L, 'Portugal's Openness to Refugees Makes Demographic and Economic Sense' 10 February 2017, available at: deeply.thenewhumanitarian.org/refugees/community/2017/02/10/portugals-openness-to-refugees-makes-demographic-and-economic-sense.

Church Times, 'At Lambeth Palace, Amber Rudd pledges more help to settle Syrian refugees' 19 July 2017, available at: www.churchtimes.co.uk/articles/2017/14-july/news/uk/rudd-pledges-more-help-to-settle-syrian-refugees.

Community Refugee Sponsorship Australia, Risk Management and Insurance Information for CRSA Program Groups, 28 July 2022, available at: https://refugeesponsorship.org.au/risk-management-and-insurance-information-for-crsa-program-groups/

de Andrés, C, 'EASO and the European Commission:2020 first meeting and of its Resettlement and Humanitarian Admission Network' 28 January 2020, available at: www.europeancommunicationstrategies.com/EASO-and-the-European-Commission-2020-first-meeting-of-its-Resettlement-and-Humanitarian-Admission-Network_a109.html.

Electronic Immigration Network, 'No new routes proposed in the Home Office's Illegal Migration Act report on safe and legal routes to the UK' 11 January 2024, available at: www.ein.org.uk/news/no-new-routes-proposed-home-offices-illegal-migration-act-report-safe-and-legal-routes-uk.

European Commission, 'Relocation: EU solidarity in practice', available at: home-affairs.ec.europa.eu/policies/migration-and-asylum/migration-management/relocation-eu-solidarity-practice_en.

European Parliament, 'At glance: Emergency measures on migration: Article 78(3) TFEU' (2020), available at: www.europarl.europa.eu/RegData/etudes/ATAG/2020/649325/EPRS_ATA(2020)649325_EN.pdf.

European website on integration, 'Spain: Pilot programme for the reception and integration of refugees' available at ec.europa.eu/migrant-integration/news/spain-pilot-programme-reception-and-integration-refugees_en.

Fedasil, 'Community Sponsorship', available at: www.fedasil.be/en/resettlement/community-sponsorship.

Federal Office for Migration and Refugees, 'Humanitäre Flüchtlingsaufnahme im Programm "Neustart im Team" (NesT)' 21 June 2023, available at: www.bamf.de/SharedDocs/ProjekteReportagen/DE/Forschung/Migration/evaluation-resettlement-programm-nest.html?nn=447036.

Financial Times, 'Poland favours Christian refugees from Syria' 21 August 2015, available at: www.ft.com/content/6edfdd30-472a-11e5-b3b2-1672f710807b.

Fraztke, S and Beirens, H, 'Three things the European Union can do to support private sponsorship for refugees' (2018) Migration Policy Institute, available at: www.migrationpolicy.org/news/three-things-european-union-can-do-support-private-sponsorship-refugees.

Free movement, 'Can Ukrainians take refuge in the UK? The Ukraine Family Scheme and other routes', available at: freemovement.org.uk/can-ukrainians-take-refuge-in-the-uk-immigration-concessions-and-asylum-policy/.

Global Compact on Refugees, 'Pledges and contributions', available at: globalcompactrefugees.org/pledges-contributions.

Gov.ie, 'Background to the Irish Refugee Protection Programme', available at: www.gov.ie/ga/foilsiu-chan/fec0a-background-to-the-irish-refugee-protection-programme/.

—— 'Irish Refugee Protection Programme', available at: www.gov.ie/en/publication/ede36-irish-refugee-protection-programme/.

—— 'Minister Stanton launches Refugee Community Sponsorship Ireland, available at: www.gov.ie/ga/preasraitis/3c1fbe-minister-stanton-officially-launches-refugee-community-sponsorship-i/.

Gov.UK, 'Afghan citizens resettlement scheme' 17 October 2023, available at: www.gov.uk/guidance/afghan-citizens-resettlement-scheme.

—— 'Apply for a Ukraine Family Scheme Visa' 19 December 2023, available at: www.gov.uk/guidance/apply-for-a-ukraine-family-scheme-visa.

—— 'Apply for community sponsorship' 16 August 2023, available at: www.gov.uk/government/publications/apply-for-full-community-sponsorship.

—— 'Apply to stay in the UK under the Ukraine extension scheme' 19 December 2023, available at: www.gov.uk/guidance/apply-to-stay-in-the-uk-under-the-ukraine-extension-scheme.

—— 'Community sponsorship: guidance for prospective sponsors' 16 August 2023, available at: www.gov.uk/government/publications/apply-for-full-community-sponsorship/community-sponsorship-guidance-for-prospective-sponsors.

—— 'Funding Instructions for local authorities in support of the United Kingdom's resettlement schemes (accessible)' 1 November 2023. available at: www.gov.uk/government/publications/uk-resettlement-programmes-funding-instruction-2023-to-2024/funding-instruction-for-local-authorities-in-the-support-of-the-united-kingdoms-resettlement-schemes-accessible.

—— 'Homes for Ukraine scheme: frequently asked questions' 29 July 2022, available at: www.gov.uk/guidance/homes-for-ukraine-scheme-frequently-asked-questions.

—— 'Immigration Rules' 31 January 2024, available at: www.gov.uk/guidance/immigration-rules/immigration-rules-appendix-ukraine-scheme.

—— 'Immigration system statistics data tables' 23 November 2023 (see under Ukraine visa schemes summary tables, year ending September 2023) available at www.gov.uk/government/statistical-data-sets/immigration-system-statistics-data-tables#ukraine-visa-schemes.

—— 'Local communities welcome hundreds of refugee families' 16 August 2023, available at: www.gov.uk/government/news/local-communities-welcome-hundreds-of-refugee-families#:~:text=Over%201%2C000%20vulnerable%20refugees%2C%20fleeing,through%20the%20community%20sponsorship%20scheme.

—— 'Setting up a social enterprise', available at: www.gov.uk/set-up-a-social-enterprise.

—— 'UK Family Scheme, UK Sponsorship Scheme (Homes for Ukraine) and Ukraine Extension Scheme visa data', available at: www.gov.uk/government/publications/ukraine-family-scheme-application-data/ukraine-family-scheme-and-ukraine-sponsorship-scheme-homes-for-ukraine-visa-data--2#:~:text=Sponsorship%20Scheme%3A%20220%2C700-,Total%20Ukraine%20Scheme%20visas%20issued%20to%20people%3A%20251%2C000,Ukraine%20Family%20Scheme%20visas%3A%2071%2C700.

Government of Canada, 'Financial support for Government-Assisted Refugees', available at: www.cic.gc.ca/english/helpcentre/results-by-topic.asp?st=11.2.

—— 'Global cap for sponsorship agreement holders' (2021). available at: www.canada.ca/en/immigration-refugees-citizenship/corporate/mandate/policies-operational-instructions-agreements/timely-protection-privately-sponsored-refugees.html.

—— 'Guide to the Private Sponsorship of Refugees program, introduction', available at: www.canada.ca/en/immigration-refugees-citizenship/corporate/publications-manuals/guide-private-sponsorship-refugees-program/section-1.html.

—— '2. Private Sponsorship of Refugees program' (2022), available at: www.canada.ca/en/immigration-refugees-citizenship/corporate/publications-manuals/guide-private-sponsorship-refugees-program/section-2.html.

—— 'Sponsor a refugee', available at: www.canada.ca/en/immigration-refugees-citizenship/services/refugees/help-outside-canada/private-sponsorship-program.html.

Home Office, 'Leave outside the Immigration Rules' August 2023, available at: assets.publishing.service.gov.uk/media/64eef28f13ae1500116e3013/Leave_outside_the_Immigration_Rules.pdf.

—— Public Health England, IOM, 'Health Protocol, Pre-entry health assessments for UK bound refugees' June 2020, available at: assets.publishing.service.gov.uk/government/uploads/system/uploads/attachment_data/file/892799/Badged_HA_protocol_I.

—— 'Ukraine Family Scheme', available at: assets.publishing.service.gov.uk/media/6565bacd1524e60011a101a3/Ukraine+Family+Scheme+Guidance.pdf.

—— 'UK Refugee Resettlement: Policy Guidance' August 2021, available at: assets.publishing.service.gov.uk/government/uploads/system/uploads/attachment_data/file/1011824/Resettlement_Policy_Guidance_2021.pdf.

House of the Oireachtas, 'International Protection' debate 24 March 2022, available at: www.oireachtas.ie/en/debates/question/2022-03-24/341/.

Info Migrants, 'San Marino approves legislation to host unaccompanied minors' (2021), available at: www.infomigrants.net/en/post/31968/san-marino-approves-legislation-to-host-unaccompanied-minors.

Irish Refugee Council 30 Years, 'Community Sponsorship', available at: www.irishrefugeecouncil.ie/listing/category/community-sponsorship.

IriS, 'Expectations and Understanding of Community Sponsorship before Refugee Arrival' (2017), available at: www.birmingham.ac.uk/Documents/college-social-sciences/social-policy/iris/2020/1-expectations-and-understanding-policy.pdf.

ISS of BC, 'Resources for Private Sponsorship of Refugees', available at: issbc.org/our-resources/resources-for-private-sponsorship-of-refugees/.

King's College London, 'University Sponsorship: Providing sanctuary for Ukrainian students and academics' 21 February 2023, available at: www.kcl.ac.uk/university-sponsorship.

Le portail du Gouvernement Suisse, 'Octroi Facilite de visas aux parents de ressortissants syriens vivant en Suisse: levee de la mesure provisoire' (2013), available at: www.admin.ch/gov/fr/start/dokumentation/medienmitteilungen.msg-id-51180.html.

Little, B, 'Claiming Sanctuary in a Medieval Church Could Save Your life – But Lead to Exile' 18 April 2019 (updated on 19 September 2023) in *History*, available at: https://www.history.com/news/church-sanctuary-asylum-middle-ages.

Maiani, F, 'Hotspots and Relocation Schemes: the right therapy for the Common European Asylum System?' 3 February 2016 EU Immigration and Asylum Law and Policy Blog, available at: eumigrationlawblog.eu/hotspots-and-relocation-schemes-the-right-therapy-for-the-common-european-asylum-system/.

McKinlay, C, 'Welcoming the Stranger: the Canadian Church and the Private Sponsorship of Refugees Programme' (2008) Toronto Metropolitan University thesis, available at: rshare.library.torontomu.ca/articles/thesis/Welcoming_the_Stranger_The_Canadian_Church_and_the_Private_Sponsorship_of_Refugees_Program/14647872.

Ministero Interno, '300 richiedenti asilo da Lesbo in Italia grazie a corridoio umanitario' 22 settembre 2020, available at: www.interno.gov.it/it/notizie/300-richiedenti-asilo-lesbo-italia-grazie-corridoio-umanitario.

NesT, 'NesT-New Start in a Team: working together to help refugees', available at: resettlement.de/wp-content/uploads/nest_broschuere_quadratisch_auflage_EN_v03.pdf.

'Note sant'egidio sur le projet "couloirs humanitaires"' (2017–2018) pour l'audition a la commission affaires interieures de la chambre 5 février 2019', available at: www.santegidio.be/wp-content/uploads/2019/02/2019-Note-CH-Audition-Commission-AI-Chambre-5-fe%C4%9Bvrier.pdf.

Onu Italia.com Il giornale italiano della Nazioni Unite, 'Corridoi umanitari: con nuovo protocollo speranza in Italia per 1500 rifugiati dalla Libia' 20 December 2023, available at: www.onuitalia.com/2023/12/20/corridoi-umanitari-con-nuovo-protocollo-speranza-in-italia-per-1500-rifugiati-dalla-libia/.

Pledges and Contributions Digital Platform, available at: globalcompactrefugees.org/pledges-contributions, GRF00888.

Rai news, 'Daniela Pompei, Comunità di Sant'Egidio: l'arrivo del papa a Cipro è una spinta per tutti' 2 December 2021, available at: www.rainews.it/archivio-rainews/articoli/daniela-pompei-corridoi-umanitari-santegidio-6d95acbc-e7d0-47cb-ad9d-050a81640ee9.html.

—— 'Migranti. Strage 3 ottobre 2013, Lampedusa ricorda le 368 vittime' 3 October 2021, available at: https://www.rainews.it/archivio-rainews/articoli/migranti-strage-3-ottobre-lampedusa-ricordo-vittime-0ac90280-80d6-4748-b903-483781d5502e.html.

Refugee Council of Australia, 'Global Refugee Forum pledge on resettlement and complementary pathways' 20 December 2023, available at: www.refugeecouncil.org.au/global-refugee-forum-pledge-on-resettlement-and-complementary-pathways/.

Refugee Sponsorship Training Program, 'Overview of Sponsorship Responsibilities', available at: www.rstp.ca/en/sponsorship-responsibilities/responsibilities/.

—— 'RAP (Resettlement Assistance Program) Rates', available at: www.rstp.ca/en/bvor/rap-rates/.

—— 'The Joint Assistance Sponsorship (JAS) Program' (2023), available at: www.rstp.ca/en/jas/joint-assistance-sponsorships/#:~:text=Joint%20Assistance%20Sponsorship%20(JAS)%20refers,in%20Canada%20than%20other%20refugees.

Reliefweb, 'United States Announces New Pledges At the 2023 Global Refugee Forum' 16 December 2023 available at reliefweb.int/report/world/united-states-announces-new-pledges-2023-global-refugee-forum.

Reset, 'About Reset', available at: resetuk.org/about/about-reset.

—— 'Available sources for funding-key things to do' 17 November 2021, available at: training-resetuk.org/application-process/available-sources-funding-key-things-do/.

Sant' Egidio, 'Al via ai primi corridoi umanitari ad Andorra', 25 October 2018, available at: www.santegidio.org/pageID/30496/langID/it/itemID/496/SantEgidio-al-via-i-primi-corridoi-umanitari-ad-Andorra.html.

—— 'Dossier sui corridoi umanitari in Europa' January 2022, available at: www.santegidio.org/pageID/34176/langID/it/Dossier-sui-corridoi-umanitari-in-Europa.html.

—— 'Corridoi umanitari: firmato un nuovo protocollo per mille arrivi di profughi dal Libano' 5 August 2021, available at: www.santegidio.org/pageID/30284/langID/it/itemID/43657/Corridoi-umanitari-firmato-un-nuovo-protocollo-per-mille-arrivi-di-profughi-dal-Libano.html.

—— 'Humanitarian corridors in figures' 14 January 2022, available at: www.santegidio.org//downloads/EN-Humanitarian-corridors-20220114.pdf.

—— 'Humanitarian Corridors in France: a new agreement for the entry of 300 refugees' 13 April 2021, available at: www.santegidio.org/pageID/30284/langID/en/itemID/41621/Humanitarian-Corridors-in-France-a-new-agreement-for-the-entry-of-300-refugees.html.

—— 'There is a new humanitarian corridor for 250 refugees, who are in their most vulnerable condition, in Belgium' 25 December 2021, available at: www.santegidio.org/pageID/30284/langID/en/itemID/45781/There-is-a-new-humanitarian-corridor-for-250-refugees-who-are-in-their-most-vulnerable-condition-in-Belgium.html.

Share Network, 'Regional governments piloting Community Sponsorship Programmes – Evaluating the Basque Country Programme (2019–21), available at: www.share-network.eu/articles-and-resources/story1.

—— 'Resettlement and Community Sponsorship across Europe', available at: www.share-network.eu/articles-and-resources/sponsorship.

Sir Agenzia d'informazione, 'Corridoi umanitari: Capitani reggenti di San Marino in visita a Sant'Egidio. Firmato memorandum per accogliere minori stranieri non accompagnati' (2021), available at: www.agensir.it/quotidiano/2021/5/26/corridoi-umanitari-capitani-reggenti-di-san-marino-in-visita-a-santegidio-firmato-memorandum-per-accogliere-minori-stranieri-non-accompagnati/.

Smith, H, 'Pope Francis takes refugees to Rome after Lesbos visit' 16 April 2016, *The Guardian*, available at: www.theguardian.com/world/2016/apr/16/pope-francis-flies-to-lesbos-to-highlight-humanitarian-crisis-in-europe.

State Secretariat for Migration SEM, 'Resettlement Programmes since 2013' (2023) available at www.sem.admin.ch/sem/en/home/asyl/resettlement/programme.html.

Talent beyond boundaries, 19 July 2021, available at: www.talentbeyondboundaries.org/blog/introducing-the-uks-displaced-talent-mobility-pilot.

Text of the Council of Trent available at history.hanover.edu/texts/trent/trentall.html.

The Brussels Times, 'Around 3,500 people march under the slogan "Together in Peace, Liberty and Respect"' 16 March 2015, available at: www.brusselstimes.com/news/belgium-all-news/31976/around-3-500-people-march-under-the-slogan-together-in-peace-liberty-and-respect.

Trotta, S, 'Safe and Legal Passages to Europe: A Case Study of Faith-Based Humanitarian Corridors to Italy' (2017) 5 UCL migration research unit, available at: www.ucl.ac.uk/geography/sites/geography_redesign/files/mru_wp_susanna_trotta_2017_5.pdf.

UNHCR, 'Community Sponsorship' available at www.unhcr.org/what-we-do/build-better-futures/long-term-solutions/local-integration/community-sponsorship.

UNHCR, 'Finding solutions for Syrian refugees' 27 November 2014, available at: www.europarl.europa.eu/meetdocs/2014_2019/documents/libe/dv/8_1_syria_refugeees_unhcr_2014_11_27_/8_1_syria_refugeees_unhcr_2014_11_27_en.pdf.

—— 'Portugal: Relocation and Humanitarian Admission', available at: help.unhcr.org/portugal/relocation/.

—— 'UNHCR welcomes establishment of Spain's resettlement programme', available at: unhcr.org/news/briefing-notes/unhcr-welcomes-establishment-spains-resettlement-programme.

—— 'Resettlement Country: New Zealand', available at: www.unhcr.org/resettlement-handbook/wp-content/uploads/sites/153/2023/04/Country-Chapter-New-Zealand-2023.pdf.

—— 'UNHCR: Global refugee resettlement needs grow in 2024' 26 June 2023, available at: www.unhcr.org/news/press-releases/unhcr-global-refugee-resettlement-needs-grow-2024.

—— 'UNHCR factsheet, Poland, available at: www.unhcr.org/ceu/wp-content/uploads/sites/17/2019/09/Poland.pdf.

UNHCR UK, 'Refugees and displaced persons: resolution of 3 October 1946 (document E/236) E/RES/18 (III)', available at: www.unhcr.org/uk/publications/refugees-and-displaced-persons-resolution-3-october-1946-document-e-236.

UNHCR Resettlement Handbook, 'Country chapter: Belgium', available at: www.unhcr.org/uk/media/unhcr-resettlement-handbook-country-chapter-belgium.

—— 'Country chapter: Canada', available at: www.unhcr.org/protection/resettlement/3c5e55594/unhcr-resettlement-handbook-country-chapter-canada.html.

—— 'Country chapter: Czech Republic', available at: www.unhcr.org/4e2d65a79.pdf.

—— 'Country chapter: France', available at: www.unhcr.org/media/unhcr-resettlement-handbook-country-chapter-france.

—— 'Country chapter: Germany', available at: www.unhcr.org/media/unhcr-resettlement-handbook-country-chapter-germany.

—— 'Country chapter: Ireland', available at: www.unhcr.org/protection/resettlement/3cac29da4/unhcr-resettlement-handbook-country-chapter-ireland.html.

—— 'Country chapter: Italy', available at: www.unhcr.org/uk/media/unhcr-resettlement-handbook-country-chapter-italy.

UNHCR, Voluntary Repatriation No. 40 (XXXVI) – 1985 available at www.unhcr.org/publications/voluntary-repatriation.

Vatican news, 'Afghanistan, al via per 1200 profughi un corridoio umanitario verso l'Italia' 4 November 2021, available at: www.vaticannews.va/it/mondo/news/2021-11/afghanistan-profughi-italia-protocollo-corridoi-umanitari-egidio.html.

—— 'Un primo gruppo di rifugiati da Cipro in Italia con il sostegno della Santa Sede' 3 December 2021, available at: www.vaticannews.va/it/papa/news/2021-12/papa-francesco-cipro-accoglienza-migranti-vaticano.html.

Welcome to Ontario, 'What Happens When a Sponsorship Breaks Down?', available at: welcomeontario.ca/en/articles/what-happens-when-a-sponsorship-breaks-down#:~:text=Breakdown%20process&text=They%20should%20contact%20the%20Resettlement,to%20fix%20the%20issue%20independently.

Wonkhe, 'Ukraine one year on: how the HE sector can support those displaced by conflict' 24 February 2023, available at: wonkhe.com/blogs/ukraine-one-year-on-how-the-he-sector-can-support-those-displaced-by-conflict/

Videos

M Siegel 'Community (Private) Refugee Sponsorship Programs Around the World', available at: www.youtube.com/watch?v=VAy2tUI7hMU&t=809s.

INDEX

S

www.ingramcontent.com/pod-product-compliance
Ingram Content Group UK Ltd.
Pitfield, Milton Keynes, MK11 3LW, UK
UKHW020814290926
15470UKWH00003B/1143

9 781509 922185